CHRIST AND CULTURE
and
"WHO IS MY NEIGHBOR?'
CHRISTIAN CONDUCT IN A DANGEROUS WORLD

Proceedings of the 2001 and 2002 Christianity in the Academy Conferences

William R. Marty and Bruce W. Speck, Editors

CAROLINAS PRESS

Copyright (©) 2004 by William R. Marty and Bruce W. Speck

Carolinas Press
755 E. Hedgelawn Way
Southern Pines, NC 28387

Karo1942@mindspring.com

All rights reserved.

No part of this book may be reproduced, stored in a retrieval system, or transmitted in any form or by any means, electronic, mechanical, photocopying, microfilming, recording or otherwise, without written permission of the publisher.

Printed in the United States of America.

ISBN 1-891026-24-0

The cover painting, "Adam," is used by permission of the artist, David Douglas. "Adam" is one of a series David painted on prefigurations of Christ (types) in the Old Testament.

Christ and Culture

Proceedings of the 2001 Christianity in the Academy Conference

Edited by

William R. Marty

Bruce W. Speck

Carolinas Press
Southern Pines, North Carolina

The cover painting, "Adam," is used by permission of the artist, David Douglas "Adam" is one of a series David painted on prefigurations of Christ ("types") in the Old Testament.

Contents

Introduction   v
William R. Marty and Bruce W. Speck, Editors

Calvinism and the Cultural Mandate: A Reformed Critique of the Christian's Covenantal Role in Culture   1
Keynote Address by Bruce W. Speck

Nicene/Chalcedonian Theological Reflection and Inclusive Language for God in Post-Modern Western Culture   13
W. E. Knickerbocker, Jr.

Is Naturalism Self-Defeating?: Plantinga's Critique of Naturalism   17
Larry Lacy

A Consistent Ethic of Life Critique of Christian Complicity in a Culture of Death   23
Peter R. Gathje

On the Purpose of Christian Art   35
Scot Lahaie

Pope John Paul II, *Fides et Ratio*: A Challenge and a Declaration of Hope   41
Pamela Werrbach Proietti

Christ, Creed, and Culture   49
Bill Jenkins

Gabriel Marcel and The Spirit of Teaching: Reflections on Presence and Transcendence   57
Gray Matthews

Hermeneutical Adequacy: A Brief Case for Reading Scripture as *Scripture*   69
Dan Wilson

Alexander Hamilton, Montesquieu and the Humanity of the Modern Commerical Republic   77
John Stack

Immersed in a Culture of Science: Cautionary Tales and Reflections   91
William R. Marty

Introduction

William R. Marty, The University of Memphis
Bruce W. Speck, Austin Peay State University
Editors

The Christianity in the Academy (CA) Conference was born out of theological dispute. Two professors, both avowed Christians, disagreed about the role the Christian professor should play in expressing his or her faith in the secular classroom. One professor espoused the position that a professor should openly tell students about his or her faith. This open expression of faith included a "testimony" of sorts on the first day of class and the invitation for the students to ask the professor further questions about his or her religious ideals. The other professor objected to this approach, noting that (1) because professors have a position of privilege and power students could misinterpret explicit statements about professors' religious faith, believing that acquiescence to a professor's religious preference would be academically advantageous and (2) if Christian professors could openly proselytize, why couldn't Buddhist or Islamic or Hindu professors also openly proselytize? And if they could openly proselytize in, say, an engineering class, what would be the justification? Because the two professors were members of a group of Christian academics, their dispute aroused some interest among their colleagues, and, being academics at heart, the group of Christian colleagues decided to air the dispute by starting a conference. Thus was born the first conference, "The Role and Responsibilities of the Christian Professor in the Academy," which was held April 5, 1996 at The University of Memphis in Tennessee.

The first conference generated sufficient enthusiasm that a board of colleagues was gathered to discuss plans for another conference. A second conference, with the same title as the first, was held on April 4, 1997, again at The University of Memphis. After the second conference, the board decided that the title for the conference should be changed to Christianity in the Academy (CA) Conference and that each Conference would have a unique theme. The theme for the Third Annual CA Conference (1998) was "C.S. Lewis as Christian Professor"; for the Fourth Annual CA Conference (1999) the theme was "Bridges to the Culture: C.S. Lewis and Others"; for the Fifth Annual CA Conference (2000) the theme was "Christianity and the New Millennium"; and for the Sixth Annual CA Conference (2001) the theme was "Christ and Culture."

Comprised of selected papers presented at the Sixth Annual Christianity in the Academy (CA) Conference on March 30, 2001, this volume is the first to issue from the CA Conference and marks a milestone in the development of the Conference. The papers in this volume represent a wide range of theological views over a splendid array of topics, a feature that has been common to previous conferences. As editors, we are delighted to present the thoughtful analysis of Christian academics embodied in the papers, partly because we think it important to show that Christianity, particularly a Christianity grounded in conservative theological traditions that do not simply mirror the spirit of the age, can engage the mind, and partly because the papers, joined together, provide perspectives that both complement and challenge each other. We believe that Christianity has a natural inclination for inclusion within an exclusive perspective, allowing for diversity and unity, so we are pleased that the authors whose papers are included in this volume have consented to link their works with the works of other professing Christians who may hold very different views about theological issues that are of great moment. After all, the CA Conference was born out of amicable theological controversy, and we hope that the amicability and the controversy, both so essential for Christian tolerance, will last as long as the CA Conference lasts.

Calvinism and the Cultural Mandate: A Reformed Critique of the Christian's Covenantal Role in Culture

Bruce W. Speck[*]

Christians have a Biblical duty to do good works to promote a Godly social order, but they are unable to do good in and of themselves. This paradox of obligation and inability must be resolved by appealing to Christ's work in fulfilling the covenant of grace and the Christian's union with Christ. If, however, the paradox is resolved otherwise, Christian works become idolatrous. The explanation of this paradox is found in the Biblical teaching about the covenant and the cultural mandate. My theological point of reference in explaining the paradox is Calvinism, the clearest, most cogent interpretation of Biblical teaching. But Calvinism is often discounted theologically because it is misunderstood, so I will begin by offering a defense of Calvinism before explicating the Biblical concepts of the covenant and the cultural mandate.

Calvinism

Calvinism is a misunderstood term, and in many quarters, even Christian quarters, the term Calvinism is hated, mocked, and feared. For instance, several years ago, I heard a prominent member of the protestant religious community in Memphis articulate his understanding of the Five Points of Calvinism, which is organized under the acronym TULIP (Total Depravity, Unconditional Election, Limited Atonement, Irresistible Grace, and Perseverance of the Saints).[1] Frankly, I was astounded at this minister's depth of misunderstanding. No Calvinist I know would have endorsed his faulty and misleading definitions, his slight-of-hand treatment of the TULIP. He was, to be generous, theologically ignorant of the topic he addressed. And, as you might guess, he concluded by noting that he really couldn't endorse the TULIP the way a "hyper-Calvinist" would.

Let me insert a word about rhetoric here. I advise you to use the word *hyper* as a pejorative term anytime you disagree with someone. For instance, if you are opposed to immersion, call all Baptists who hold to immersion "Hyper-Baptists." But if you are an immersionist, call all those who hold to infant baptism "Hyper-Methodists" or "Hyper-Catholics" or "Hyper-Presbyterians." Never use *hyper* in a true technical sense because that will confuse people. Most folks have come to see *hyper* as a term of derision, so I don't see why we should try to change their views, no matter how incorrect they are.

---

[*] Bruce W. Speck is Vice President for Academic Affairs and Professor of English at Austin Peay State University in Clarksville, Tennessee.

[1] The TULIP is useful in providing a memorable acronym, but it can be misleading, particularly concerning Total Depravity, which does not mean that people are as bad as they could be. Rather, Total Depravity means that people are unable to do good because they are born in sin, and sin has a negative influence on every part of their being. At root, people are depraved. They do not have the ability or inclination to obey God, but they do have the capacity to be more rebellious than they are.

And when a Christian leader of national prominence labels something as *hyper,* as in Hyper-Calvinism, all you really need to know is that the already tainted Calvinism is even more shockingly decadent than you had imagined. Thus ends a sophist's rhetoric lesson.

The ignorance about Calvinism is so vast, based on so little understanding of what Calvin and those who follow in his train taught, that I could spend my time, and more, to refute some of the major misconceptions that cling like leeches to Calvinism, continually attempting to drain the life from a body of theology that has produced major positive social changes throughout the world. But I don't cherish the hope of converting anyone to Calvinism in 30 minutes. I feel a bit like Paul when he presented the case for Christ before King Agrippa in Acts 26. King Agrippa, astonished at Paul's theology and accusing Paul of being mad, said, "In a short time you will persuade me to become a Calvinist?" I am paraphrasing. Were I Paul, my response would be, "I would to God, that whether in a short or long time, not only you, but also all who hear me this day, might become such as I am—a Calvinist—except for these time limitations on my talk." I hold no illusion that in a brief time I can convince anyone to become a Calvinist. However, I will begin an apologia of Calvin and Calvinism to show that Calvinism is worthy of our study when we approach the issue of the Christian's relationship to culture.

I begin by appealing to Alister McGrath's *A Life of John Calvin.* First published in 1990, McGrath's biography greatly aids us in our understanding of Calvinism. McGrath, a meticulous scholar, provides excellent evidence to disprove many of the myths of Calvinism. One of the myths is that Calvin was the dictator of Geneva. Calvin, so this ill-informed view goes, enforced his will on the Geneva council and literally ran the city. McGrath points out, however, that Calvin's:

> . . . influence over Geneva was exercised indirectly, through preaching, consultation and other forms of legitimate suasion. Despite his ability to influence through his moral authority, he had no civic jurisdiction, no *right*, to coerce others to act as he wished. Calvin could and did urge, cajole and plead; but could not, however, command (p. 109).

Allied with the myth of Dictator Calvin is the myth that Calvin was the prosecutor in the trial that led to the burning of Servetus, the heretic who had already been condemned by the Roman church. In discussing Calvin's role in the Servetus affair, McGrath first notes the historical context:

The sixteenth century knew little, if anything, of the modern distaste for capital punishment, and regarded it as a legitimate and expedient method of eliminating undesirables and discouraging their imitation. The city of Geneva was no exception: lacking a long-term prison (short-term prisoners were held captive, at their own expense, while they awaited trial), it had only two major penalties at its disposal—banishment and execution (p. 115).

Today, we may find it incomprehensible that people were executed because they didn't believe in the trinity or the deity of Christ or some other article of the Christian faith. McGrath, however, explains why heretics in the 16th century were seen as significant social threats. He cites the bloody siege at Munster in which Anabaptists tried to overthrow lawful authority and establish their own government. Anabaptists were those who insisted that infant baptism was invalid and that every Christian had to be re-baptized—immersed—based on a profession of faith. Here's what McGrath says about the impact of the revolution at Munster on the civic order throughout Europe.

> The radical wing of the Reformation, also known as Anabaptism, was primarily characterized at the religious level by its rejection of infant baptism: at the social level, however, its views were radically anti-authoritarian, often including important hints of communism. Events at Munster, which came under that radical control in 1534, confirmed the serious threat which that radical wing of the Reformation posed to existing social structure. Although Protestant and Roman Catholic city councils might differ on many matters, they were united in their belief that heresy threatened the stability and hence the existence of their cities. The fate of Munster—which had to be retaken by a protracted and bloody siege—brought home the fact that heresy concerned far more than mere ideas: it posed a serious menace to urban existence. No city could afford to allow such a destabilizing influence within its bounds (p. 118).

Heresy in 16th century Europe was a serious matter, and when Servetus appeared in Geneva, he posed a threat to civic order. Unfortunately, and according to McGrath erroneously, the common myth has been that Calvin did his utmost to prosecute Servetus, and ultimately was virtually solely responsible for the faggot being laid on Servetus' death stake. Yet McGrath tells us that Calvin's role in Servetus' trial was "that of a technical advisor or expert witness, rather than prosecutor" (p. 119). The city council of Geneva, in fact, consulted with other cities allied to it about how to deal with Servetus, and all the cities unanimously agreed that Servetus should be burned alive. In fact, McGrath notes, "Calvin himself attempted to alter the mode of execution to the more humane beheading; he was ignored" (p. 120).

I have provided details about Calvin and his times because those details offer powerful reasons to reject the myths that Calvin was the dictator of Geneva, that Calvin, single-handedly, prosecuted poor, helpless Servetus, who, by the way, willingly traveled to Geneva and openly made himself known. I have taken time to dispute myths about Calvin because those myths keep people from considering the virtues of Calvin and Calvinism. And what are those virtues? Listen again to McGrath:

"If any religious movement of the sixteenth century was world-affirming, it was Calvinism. Yet Calvinism affirmed the world in order to master it, addressing its specific situation rather than luxuriating in abstract speculation" (p. 219). Odd, isn't it, that one of the common complaints about Calvin and Calvinism is that both are examples of arid intellectualism?[2] "Calvin's 'secularization of holiness' (Henri Hauser) involved bringing the entire sphere of human existence within the scope of divine sanctification and human dedication. It is this sanctification of life, of which the sanctification of work is the chief pillar, which stamped its impression upon Calvin's followers" (p. 220).

The believer is called to serve God in the world. Calvin's insistence that the individual believer could be called by God to serve him in every sphere of worldly existence lent a new dignity and meaning to work. The world is to be treated with contempt to the extent that it is not God, and is too easily mistaken for God; yet, in that it is the creation of God, it is to be affirmed. 'Let believers get used to a contempt of the present life that gives rise to no hatred of it, or ingratitude towards God' (*Institutes* III.xi.3). 'Something that is neither blessed nor desirable in itself can become something good for the devout' (III.xi.4). Christians are thus to inhabit the world with joy and gratitude, without become trapped within it (p. 232).

Manual labor was not simply the norm at Geneva; it was the religiously sanctioned ideal. For the first time, the ordinary everyday activity of even the most petty producer was given a religious significance (p. 233).

These quotations tell us that the focal point of Calvin and Calvinism was the believer's engagement with the world under the aegis of theology. Thus, works become the evidence of election. A child of God can know that he or she is God's child by worldly activism as evaluated by Scripture (p. 240). The child of God shows love to God by "whole-hearted commitment to serve and glorify God by labouring in his world" (241). Niebuhr, in *Christ and Culture,* is correct in classifying Calvin and Augustine as two theologians who believed that Christ is the transformer of culture. And Calvin's legacy of transforming culture is enormous. In fact, McGrath says, "The transformation of the status of work from a distasteful and degrading activity, to be avoided if possible, to a dignified and glorious means of affirming God and the world he created is one of the most important contributions of Calvinism to western culture" (p. 245). Abraham Kuyper is an example of a Calvinist who had an indelible imprint on the Netherlands in

---

[2] Even a casual reading of Calvin's *Institutes* will provide abundant evidence to support the contention that Calvin is the theologian of the Holy Spirit, a premise that is virtually unknown among wide segments of those who classify themselves as Charismatics or Pentecostals. In fact, B. B. Warfield says that Calvin is "preeminently the theologian of the Holy Spirit. In point of fact it is from him accordingly that the effective study of the work of the Holy Spirit takes its rise, and it is only in the channels cut out by him and at the hands of thinkers taught by him that the theology of the Holy Spirit has been richly developed" (pp. 107-02). Indeed, the *Institutes*, the central work that should be the focal point of debate about Calvin and Calvinism, not only affirms a vital religion in a believer's day-to-day existence in the world but also stresses the necessity of believers' relying upon the Holy Spirit to maintain that walk. I wonder how many critics of Calvin and Calvinism, those who accuse both the man and his theology of arid intellectualism, have taken the time to read, much less study, the *Institutes*.

various capacities, including his work as Prime Minister. His life is the embodiment of the Calvinist ideal to transform culture. In his *Lectures on Calvinism,* Kuyper affirms that Calvinism is devoted to cultural transformation, based on regeneration of the human heart. He says, "Thanks to this work of God in the heart, the persuasion that the whole of a man's life is to be lived as *in the Divine Presence* has become the fundamental thought of Calvinism" (p. 23).

I pause now to ask this question: What is so hideous, so malignant, so distorted about the believer living the whole of his or her life as in the Divine Presence? Isn't that exactly what Scripture teaches?[3] But I'm begging the question. Broadly, then, what does Scripture teach about the believer's role in culture?

Covenant

To provide a framework for discussing Scriptural teaching about the believer's role in culture, I appeal to the ancient concept of covenant, which is foundational to an understanding of the Bible. O. Palmer Robertson in *Christ and the Covenants* says that a covenant is a "bond in blood sovereignly administered." In other words, a covenant is a matter of life and death, and God sovereignly administers the conditions of the covenant. Here's an example of a covenant.

In the garden, God told Adam that the day he ate of the tree of the knowledge of good and evil, Adam would die. God's prohibition was a life and death matter, a bond in blood. But God's covenant with Adam was more than a personal obligation that Adam was required to fulfill. As Romans 5:12 tells us, the entire human race fell when Adam fell, and, thus, all of Adam's posterity are born in sin. Puritan children memorized the little ditty, "In Adam's fall, we sinned all," to remind them of the original sin they inherited from their father Adam and that was transmitted directly to them by their biological parents. The importance of covenant theology is that it provides a framework for understanding biblical doctrines such as the fall, the solidarity of the human race, the need for a mediator, and the eschatological hope of ultimate redemption, body and soul. Covenantal or Reformed theology, which can be traced through Augustine and Calvin, stresses the hopelessness of human kind because of imputed sin. We are not capable of good works as sinners. Augustine argued long and loud in repudiating the theology of Pelagius, a theology that invested fallen men with a pre-fallen Adamic nature, and Augustine argued from a biblical foundation when he repudiated Pelagius. Likewise, I believe the repudiation of semi-Pelagianism at the Synod of Dort is valid because it is based on biblical teaching about the corruption of Adam's nature so that Adam and his offspring not only do not seek God after the fall but they hate God; they are God's

---

[3] Calvin's *Institutes* provide profound insights into Scriptural teaching and do so with élan and charm. Indeed, in the *Institutes,* Calvin's reputation as a scholar of the highest order is justified. His scholarship is replete with citations from the Fathers to support his contention that his theological thinking is in line with historic orthodoxy, particularly Augustine's soteriology. I wonder how many, particularly evangelicals who descry Calvin's theology, have taken time to read Calvin's major theological treatise?

enemy. Even in a cursory reading of Romans 3, one would have trouble missing the fact that "No one does good, not even one. No one seeks for God."

This view espoused by covenant theology doesn't sell well in Detroit, Pittsburgh, San Antonio, Boston, Atlanta, San Diego, Honolulu, Chicago, Oklahoma City, Denver, Ann Arbor, Des Moines, Topeka, Atlanta, New Orleans, Dallas, Phoenix, Las Vegas, Sacramento, Boise, Portland, Minneapolis, New York, Bangor, Newark, Charlotte, Nashville, Birmingham, Indianapolis, and Little Rock, just to mention a few places where Calvinism is generally seen as an undesirable religious posture. Why doesn't it sell well? To be fair, brothers and sisters in Christ who hold to a semi-Pelagian or Arminian theology just don't think the Bible teaches what Calvin and his followers think it teaches. Some of these brothers and sisters are biblical scholars; most are just folks who know they have been changed by God and want to follow Jesus.

This is not the place—and definitely not the time, seeing that my 30 minutes are running out quickly—to analyze all the biblical data for the Calvinistic understanding of the covenant, but it is the place to affirm that the biblical data, in the opinion of Calvinists, confirms that salvation is entirely a gift of God. Calvinists do not believe in prevenient grace, the grace that enables the rebel to make his or her own choice to serve God, the grace that woos the rebel to lay down his or her arms but in no way causes the rebel to submit to Christ's authority. Rather, Calvinists believe that God alone changes the human heart from stone to flesh, enabling a person to believe, indeed, guaranteeing a person's faith and repentance. Regeneration, for the Calvinists, precedes faith and repentance. Regeneration, for the semi-Pelagian, follows faith and repentance. The difference between the two positions is profound and cannot be treated as a mere difference of theological opinion.

According to the Calvinist, the covenant that God unilaterally enacted with Adam in the garden before the fall is a covenant of works. If Adam had fulfilled the conditions of the covenant, he would have inherited eternal life—and so would all of his posterity, because Adam acted as a public figure, not as a private individual. Thus, all, except Christ, are born under Adam's headship, and all are condemned to eternal punishment. And why are they condemned? Because in Adam they broke God's righteous law. Their only hope is for God to provide a new covenant head, one who can satisfy the requirements of the law on their behalf. God has done that by making a covenant with His Son to redeem a people for Himself. All who come to Christ are freed from the condemnation of the covenant of works that Adam violated in the garden. And once a person comes under the headship of Christ, he or she is forever in union with Christ and can never be called to account by God as one who has violated the covenant of works. Why is it that all whom God calls to Himself will not fall away? Because Christ perfectly fulfilled the law, and those in union with Christ have also perfectly fulfilled the law and can never be accused of being law breakers again. Thus, Augustine, in his *City of God*, spoke of two types of people, those who love God and those who love themselves. Those who love God are citizens of the City of God, and those who love themselves are citizens of the City of Man. Two cities, one for those who are under the broken covenant of works and one for those who are under the covenant of grace. Two diametrically opposed views of life. One view promotes a works righteousness, that is, doing good in defiance of God's covenant of grace, doing good works on the premise that such works have intrinsic value. For instance, we hear people count a work as good when it is done with a sincere heart, not realizing that sincere hearts are exceedingly rare. As the author of *Ecclesiastes* notes, "There is not a righteous man on earth who does good and never sins." In fact, sincerity is an illusive term that seems to mean, "If I feel that my actions are based on pure motives, my actions are based on pure motives." The other view of life sees good works as the works Christ does. His work alone is sufficient to count as good.

The Cultural Mandate

The covenant as an expression of relationship between God and man has another dimension, the cultural mandate, which is found in Genesis 1:28:

> God blessed [Adam and Eve] and said to them, "Be fruitful and increase in number; fill the earth and subdue it. Rule over the fish of the sea and the birds of the air and over every living creature that moves on the ground."

One commentator says this about Genesis 1:28:

> Man goes forth under this divine benediction—flourishing, filling the earth with his kind, and exercising dominion over the other earthly creatures. Human culture, accordingly, is not anti-God (though fallen man often has turned his efforts into proud rebellion against God). Rather, it is the expression of man's bearing the image of his Creator and sharing, as God's servant, in God's kingly rule. As God's representative in the creaturely realm, he is steward of God's creatures. He is not to exploit, waste or despoil them, but to care for them and use them in the service of God and man. (NIV Study Bible)

Notice that Genesis 2:15—"The Lord God took the man and put him in the Garden of Eden to work it and take care of it"—is a fulfillment of the cultural mandate of Genesis 1:28. Work, as Calvin noted, is to be offered as praise to God because humankind is God's vicegerent and was created to represent God to the creation. King David understood this. In Psalm 8 he wrote:

> When I consider your heavens, / the work of your fingers, / the moon and the stars, / which you have set in place, / what is man that you are mindful of him, / the son of man that you care for him? / You made him a little lower than the heavenly beings / and crowned him with glory and honor. / You made him ruler over the works of your hands; / you put everything under his feet; / all flocks and herds, / and the beasts of the field, / the birds of the air, / and the fish of the sea, / all that swim the paths of the seas. / O Lord, our Lord / how majestic is your name in all the earth.

Man's rule is a gift from God, necessary to fulfill the cultural mandate.

But what happened after the fall? Is the cultural mandate withdrawn? God's curse upon Adam and Eve suggests that the cultural mandate is not revoked; rather, humankind's ability to fulfill the cultural mandate is vitiated. The woman will be fruitful and multiply, but her childbirth will be attended with pain. Adam will continue to cultivate the ground, but his toil also will be painful and he now must contend with thorns and thistles. The fallen human race is in the untenable position of living and working in a world that is cursed while continuing to be responsible to fulfill the cultural mandate. In other words, humans cannot do what they are required to do; nevertheless God's mandate remains intact. God still requires fallen humans to be perfectly obedient, and not only are humans not able to obey perfectly (that is, to obey at all because to disobey is to violate the entire law) but they also continue to disobey by their sinful attempts to fulfill the cultural mandate. The situation was bleak when God cursed our first parents, and it remains bleak, or rather hopeless, for everyone who lives under a broken covenant of works and attempts to fulfill the cultural mandate. But the situation is glorious for those who are in Christ who has fulfilled the covenant of grace and enables His people even now, while they struggle with sin in this life, to genuinely participate in fulfilling the cultural mandate, and who will one day, in their glorified state, see the cultural mandate fulfilled in the eschaton, the recreated earth in which God's people will dwell.

Implications

My time is evaporating, and yet I want to discuss implications of the Calvinistic theology I have outlined, particularly in relationship to the cultural mandate.

The implications of the Calvinistic understanding of covenant and the cultural mandate are profound, in my view, because theology should inform practice, and if we grasp the significance of Calvinism's understanding of the covenant and the cultural mandate, we will recognize that salvation is always by works. Either fallen humanity works in futility to build a culture that cannot please God or redeemed humanity accepts the work of Christ as sufficient to build a culture that will please God. Either people establish their own works as sufficient to create a world that pleases them (and some of those people hope that their part in building that world might please God) or people forsake their own attempts to please themselves and rest in the assurance that God's son by His work of redemption has pleased the Father, and the Father can never be more pleased with anyone than He is with His son. Christians, then, do not work to find favor with God. They work because God has favored them with salvation. Christians work out of gratitude, not out of obligation to satisfy God. If a person calls him or herself a Christian and works to please God, then such works are idolatrous, offerings made to a concept of God that does not fit the Biblical data about who God is.

Perhaps it is apparent now why Calvinism is quite different theologically from semi-Pelagianism. The semi-Pelagian believes that a person has the innate ability to lay down his or her arms and agree to a truce with God. People, according to the semi-Pelagian, have the ability to choose God, if they but will. The flip side of this is that a person can also choose to unchoose, to take up arms against God again and again become His enemy. Psychologically, it seems not unfair to say that the semi-Pelagian considers the work that Christians do as a continual effort to maintain one's salvation. Thus, the work a Christian does, under the semi-Pelagian view, is akin to the work of those who labor under the broken covenant of works. For the semi-Pelagian, the efforts of both the denizens of the City of God and the City of Man are based on works that are designed to satisfy God. But God's wrath has been appeased in the once-for-all sacrifice of Christ, and God is thus satisfied with the work—the passive and active obedience—of His son, His only son, who by His work of new birth creates other sons of God.

I hear barely muffled objections to my analysis, and I think it prudent at this point to hope that my time is running out and to suggest that semi-Pelagians may indeed live better than their theology allows them to live. That is, Christians who hold to a semi-Pelagian viewpoint really do have better motivations for service to Christ than their theology permits them to have. They really must subscribe to a Calvinistic view of resting in the work of Christ for their salvation, and they can rest in Christ when they seek to fulfill the cultural mandate as they are called as Christians to fulfill it. But they must overcome the theological error in their system to subscribe in practice to Calvinistic theology, and if they don't overcome the theological error, their attempts to satisfy the cultural mandate are doomed because they are idolatrous.

I have pointedly contrasted Calvinistic with semi-Pelagian views of the covenant and the cultural mandate because the issue of works righteousness has a tremendous impact on the way we evaluate the work Christians are called to do. Consider, for example, the way Christians often consider what counts for spiritual success. Is a small church with little growth in membership a successful church? To define "success," let's just look at the tremendous efforts that have been put into writing books about church growth as a sign of God's blessing. Or listen to ministers of the health and wealth movement explain how you, too, can receive all that God has for you. Or read the literature by those who tell Christians to name it and claim it. These major movements in Christendom help define what constitutes a "good work" and therefore what constitutes the fulfillment of the cultural mandate. I suggest that all such movements are based on the principle of idolatry, the attempt to have a relationship with God by manipulating Him, by defining human works as the basis of blessing, whether those works be faith, prayer, or some other action grounded in an effort to gain acceptance with God in the hopes of getting something from God, whether that something is eternal salvation or temporal blessing.

As Christians, we can forget that we are servants of God and that we are not vicegerents because we are good or capable. We are vicegerents because God has restored us in Christ and given us a new chance to participate in fulfilling the cultural mandate in the strength and wisdom of Christ. As Christians, we really do have a duty to do good, because our Lord did good and we are His disciples, but we cannot do good in and of ourselves. This paradox is resolved when we realize that as Christians we are in union with Christ; all the spiritual blessings He has gained by His work of redemption are ours. We share in the life of Christ by virtue of His merits imputed to us. At the same time, we really do have to die to ourselves if we are going to participate in fulfilling the cultural mandate in our time and place, but, again, we cannot die to ourselves unless God enables us to put to death the old nature. But because we are in Christ, we do have the strength to die to ourselves because Christ died to Himself. If we don't die to ourselves, our aspirations—our hope to do the works we want to do—will very likely interfere with doing the works we should do.

Another implication of the Calvinistic position I have advocated is that Christians should reject the TGIF—Thank God It's Friday—mentality as sub-Christian. Work is our service to God; to demean work and to prize leisure is to call into question God's wisdom in giving the cultural mandate.

The Calvinistic position also frees the Christian to pursue with all his or her strength the divine command to subdue the world. All work that is done in Christ has redemptive value, not because work redeems, but because God has ordained human work as the means to achieve His purposes of election. Not only do Christians demonstrate their union with Christ by their works, but they also provide the means God has ordained to build His kingdom. How you and I work is a statement about our Lord's work in us. If we conduct our daily work in the Divine presence, in times of crisis—either the testing of others or ourselves—we will have logged in the necessary hours to be sterling examples of what it means to live according to Christ's ethics in the midst of intense pressure to do otherwise.

A corollary to the sanctification of work as the way to demonstrate union with Christ is the freedom to engage in various types of work. Christians can and should subdue the political systems, and training in law is perfectly acceptable. Christian artists are needed. Calvinism knows nothing of the secular-sacred dichotomy that often attends semi-Pelagianism. In fact, Christians should aspire to be Christian intellectuals because the realm of ideas is God's possession. Christians should bring—indeed, are called to bring—to bear the full force of the covenant of grace in critiquing those laboring under the broken covenant of works. The sanctification of the professions—from plumber to college president, from secretary to U.S. Senator—also means that the focus of labor is not evangelism. Calvinism firmly rejects the eschatological view that the primary role of the church is to rescue souls from this present wicked age and then to teach those rescued souls to rescue other souls. While acknowledging the necessity for evangelism (see J. I. Packer's *Evangelism and the Sovereignty of God*), Calvinism notes that *all* of life is to be lived in the Divine presence. To privilege evangelism (and often then privilege the vocation of ministers because they are the church's chief evangelists from their pulpits) is to promote a secular-sacred dichotomy and to market an eschatology that denigrates the world as a place that can *only* be transformed in individualistic spiritual terms. The Biblical presentation of covenant, however, presents humanity in terms of familial relationship, not individualistic terms.

These implications I have outlined lead me, finally, to provide a working definition of the Christian's covenantal role in culture. The role of the Christian in culture is to provide a model of covenantal relationship based on the work of Christ, to live a transformed life in the nitty-gritty details of life in order to transform culture. I doubt that evangelical semi-Pelagians would quibble with me about the definition I have offered, but the thrust of my argument is that semi-Pelagianism bases its agreement of this definition on a world-and-life view grounded in a theology of works righteousness because, according to the semi-Pelagian, people have the ability to choose to do good works—works that can please God.

Conclusion

Do I hear time's winged chariot loudly approaching—or is the chariot departing? Whether I have missed my ride, I do not have time to consider, but I do have a moment to conclude, and I conclude with a challenge. Let's assume that the position I have presented is in error, not only because it isn't Biblical but also because it just won't work. Calvinism, someone might say, cuts the nerve of any real motivation for transforming culture.

Actually, the assumption that Calvinism won't work is the assumption that controls much of contemporary Christian thinking. As I noted earlier, covenant theology doesn't sell well in Detroit, Pittsburgh, San Antonio, Boston, Atlanta . . . and so forth. Thus, the ruling theological paradigm in evangelical America is semi-Pelagianism. So let's look at American culture and see the impact of semi-Pelagianism.

You needn't worry that I am going to spend yet another 30 minutes cataloging the eddies in the cesspool of American culture. Even secularists have cried out against the dominant paganism of our time. If Christians are supposed to be salt and light to the culture in which they are located, I need not go on and on about the tastelessness of evangelical semi-Pelagianism. Yet Calvinism has demonstrated that it can transform the culture. McGrath concludes his book by showing how powerful Calvinism was in revitalizing a culture in the mire of works righteousness, a culture laboring under the broken covenant of works.

Many believe that American culture is on a collision course with destruction, and already the carnage of this course is scattered about us, sometimes knee deep. Opportunities for reformation of our culture, indeed, seem to be running out, so isn't this an opportune time to reconsider the Biblical power of Calvinism to transform our culture? I would to God, that whether in a short or long time, all who hear me this day, might become such as I am—a Calvinist—because we are called to redeem the time.

References

Augustine, Saint. *The City of God.* Trans. Marcus Dods. In *A Select Library of the Nicene and Post-Nicene Fathers*, ed. Philip Schaff. Grand Rapids, MI: Eerdmans, 1956.

Kuyper, Abraham. *Lectures on Calvinism.* Grand Rapids, MI: Eerdmans, 1931.

McGrath, Alister E. *A Life of John Calvin.* Oxford: Blackwell, 1990.

Niebuhr, H. Richard. *Christ and Culture.* NY: Harper & Brothers, 1956.

NIV. New International Version Study Bible. Grand Rapids, MI: Zondervan, 1984.

Robertson, O. Palmer. *The Christ of the Covenants.* Philipsburg, NJ: Presbyterian and Reformed, 1980.

Warfield, Benjamin B. *Calvin and Augustine.* Philadelphia, PA: Presbyterian and Reformed, 1956.

Nicene/Calcedonian Theological Reflection and Inclusive Language for God in Post-Modern Western Culture

W. E. Knickerbocker, Jr.[*]

Nicene/Chalcedonian theological reflection is understood as reflecting the light of Christ and the Holy Trinity—as revealed in Scripture and Tradition interpreted through our reason, conscience, intuition, imagination, and will—upon human experience (which includes but is not limited to memory, passions, affections, emotions, and sexuality). In this reflection Christ incarnates our reason, conscience, intuition, imagination, will, and experience, and, because they are too small to hold Christ, Christ takes them into Himself and through Him into the Holy Trinity and redeems them. Philosophically Nicene/Chalcedonian theological reflection assumes an eternal relationship of metaphysics, epistemology, and ethics in which metaphysics is the primary determinant of epistemology, and metaphysics mediated through epistemology is the primary determinant of ethics.

This way of theological reflection is grounded in the Doctrines of the Incarnation and the Trinity. The Doctrine of the Incarnation teaches that in Jesus Christ the Divine entered the human and because the human is too small to hold the Divine the Divine takes the human into itself and redeems it. The Incarnation includes the incarnation of human language. In the Incarnation of human language God takes the familial human terms of Father and Son to refer to Himself in a revelatory way. We do not name God; God names Himself for us.

At the Council of Nicea (325), the First Ecumenical Council of the Church, the bishops were concerned with the proper understanding of the relationship between Jesus, the Son of God, and God, the Father of Jesus. While there were other titles given to Jesus in Scripture, such as Son of Man, the Word, Messiah (Christ), and Emmanuel, it was the name, Son of God, which became central in the way that the Early Church understood Jesus. The name, Son of God, was understood as the name which included in itself the various other titles given to Jesus. The Council used a baptismal creed from the Church in Caesarea as the basis for their deliberations and removed the designation of Jesus as Word of God in that creed and put in its place the designation of Jesus as Son of God (Kidd, II, 30). While there are other titles given to God in Scripture, such as Maker,

---

[*] W. E. Knickerbocker, Jr. is a Roman Catholic layman; a husband, father, and grandfather; and Professor of Church History at Memphis Theological Seminary where he has been teaching Church History and Christian Spirituality for twenty-eight years. He holds the B.A. degree from Washington and Lee University and the B.D. and Ph.D. degrees from Emory University. He and his wife, Sandie, are spiritual directors of "The Household of the Holy Family," a private lay association in formation in the Marianist/Benedictine tradition in the Catholic Church, which encourages Christian family spiritual formation. He is a poet whose published poetry includes the volume: *New Eden: Poems for Living in Community with God's Holy Family.*

Husband, and Rock, it is the name, Father, which became central in the way that the early Church understood God. In fact, "Father" is more than a title for God. In the Old Testament the word "Father" is used to refer to God eleven times, and in these contexts "Father" can be understood as a metaphor for God, i.e. the Old Testament writers were using their human understanding of fatherhood to speak of God. However, in the New Testament, in which God is called "Father" 261 times, this is no longer only a metaphorical way of referring to God but is understood as being the revealed name of God, the name of God revealed to His followers by Jesus, the Son of God (Allison, 160). Jesus not only instructs His followers to address God as "Our Father," but also instructs them to say "hallowed be your name" (Mt. 6:9; Lk. 11:2) (See Rolnick, 271-272). The names "Father," "Son of God," and "Jesus" are paralleled in the Old Testament by the name "Yahweh." Pronouns used to refer to the First Person of the Trinity are masculine because God is Father, not because He is male (See Miller, 42). For the Early Church the central proclamation of the New Testament is that Jesus is the Son of God the Father who, through His Birth, Life, Death, Resurrection, Ascension, and High-Priesthood, saves us from sin, death, and Satan; and the Early Church called God "Father" because Jesus called Him "Father" and taught His disciples to do the same (See Jeremias, 21).

As Patrick Reardon reminds us, before the First Person of the Trinity is our Father outside the Trinity, He is the Son's Father within the Trinity (See Jn. 20:17) (Reardon, 108). Moreover, in the Incarnation He reveals who He always is for us: our Father. A human father is a person before he becomes a father. God the Father is a Person precisely because He is always Father. As an eternal Father, He has an eternal Son. There was never a time when they did not exist together. Thus, the Son and the Father are One (Jn. 10:30), and when we have seen the Son we have seen the Father (Jn. 14:8). No one comes to the Father but through the Son (Jn. 14:6). Anyone who comes to God must come to One who is Father, and as Father He always has His Son.

The Third Person of the Trinity, the Holy Spirit, through Baptism continues the Incarnation of human language by claiming us as adopted daughters and sons of the Father and sisters and brothers of the Son, again using familial language in a revelatory way (see Mk. 10:30, Rom. 8:23, II Cor. 6:18, Gal. 4:5-6). This adoption is proclaimed in the soteriology expressed in the doctrine of *theosis*, a soteriology which influenced the addition by the Council of Constantinople (381), the Second Ecumenical Council, of the affirmations about the Holy Spirit to the original Creed of Nicea. In our adoption "in Christ" we become "partakers of the divine nature" (II Pet. 1:4) (Reardon, 110). This is the theological reflection which produced the Nicene-Constantinopolitan Creed.

Finally, the Mother of the Family of God, named in the Nicene-Constantinopolitan Creed as the Virgin Mary, is also named *Theotokos*, "God-bearer" (*Mater Dei*, "Mother of God") in the doctrinal statement of 433 which settled the disputes of the Council of Ephesus (431), the Third Ecumenical Council—a name ratified in the Chalcedonian Christological Definition, a commentary on the second clause of the Nicene-Constantinopolitan Creed issued by the Council of Chalcedon (451), the Fourth Ecumenical Council. Here again is a familial term used by the Holy Spirit in a revelatory way to name the maternal human face in the Family of God (See Montague, 69-143).

This Nicene/Chalcedonian way of theological reflection and the Doctrines of the Incarnation and the Trinity were developed in the Church's struggle with heresies, especially with the heresy of Arianism in the Fourth Century. Arian theological reflection begins with reflection on human experience and moves through reason, conscience, intuition, imagination and will to Scripture and Tradition. Ancient Arianism reflected on the relationship of the First and Second Persons of the Trinity from the perspective of the ordinary human experience of the relationship of a human father and a human son. Because a human father exists before his human son exists and is a human being before he is a father, the First Person of the Trinity existed before the Second Person of the Trinity existed and is a Being before He is a Father. Thus, "once there was no Son," and, therefore, the First Person of the Trinity is not eternally Father (See Kidd, II, 14-15). He can be named with names other than the name Father.

Contemporary proponents of the use of inclusive language for God by their conclusions seem to indicate a method of Arian theological reflection in that they assume that the way we refer to God arises out of the cultural experience of humankind. They assume that since the cultural experience of the Early Church was patriarchal, so the ways to refer to God by Christians in that culture were patriarchal. Our post-modern, Western culture is becoming less patriarchal, so we should refer to God in less patriarchal ways, including referring to God as "mother." Like Ancient Arianism, the proponents of the use of inclusive language for God begin their theological reflection with human experience. This is post-modern Arianism arguing against ancient Arianism. As in ancient Arianism, in post-modern Arianism the First Person of the Trinity is not eternally Father. Therefore, He can be named by other names. It is true that there are other titles for God in Scripture and Tradition, but the familial terms of Father and Son enshrined in the New Testament and the Nicene-Constantinopolitan Creed are normative, for they are not simply titles for God but are names for the First and Second Persons of the Trinity. Proponents of the use of inclusive language in referring to God, because of a way of theological reflection which is Arian, do not acknowledge the norms and, therefore, claim the right to name God.

Like ancient Arianism, post-modern Arianism denies that the First Person of the Trinity is eternally "Father;" denies that the Second Person of the Trinity is eternally the Father's Son, thereby denying the divinity of the Son and the Incarnation of God in Jesus of Nazareth; and denies that the mission of the Holy Spirit is to take us into the eternal life of the Son and through Him to the Father, for the Son is not eternal and the Father is not eternally Father.

The result of this post-modern Arian theological reflection is false teaching, which, if accepted, changes the Christian religion into another religion.

References

Allison, C. Fitzsimmons. *The Cruelty of Heresy: An Affirmation of Christian Orthodoxy.* (Harrisburg: Morehouse Publishers), 1994.

Jeremias, Joachim. *The Central Message of the New Testament.* (New York: Charles Scribner's Sons), 1965.

Kidd, B.J. *A History of the Church to A.D. 461*, 3 Vols. (Oxford: Clarendon Press), 1922.

Miller, John W. "Rays of Fatherhood Shining Forth—Why We Call God Father: Biblical and Cultural Considerations," *Touchstone*, 14:1 (Jan./Feb. 2001), 40-46.

Montague, George T. *Our Father, Our Mother: Mary and the Faces of God.* (Steubenville, OH: Franciscan University Press), 1990.

Reardon, Patrick Henry. "Father, Glorify Thy Name," *Reclaiming the Great Tradition: Evangelicals, Catholics, and Orthodox in Dialogue*, ed. James S. Cutsinger. (Downers Grove, IL: InterVarsity Press), 1997, 101-114.

Rolnick, Philip A. "Fatherhood and the Name of God," *Names*, 40:4 (Dec. 1992).

Is Naturalism Self-Defeating?: Plantinga's Critique of Naturalism

Larry Lacy[*]

Section One: Introduction and a Dialectical Difficulty

One very pervasive strain in our culture is naturalism, the view that (i) the only things that exist and have not been caused to exist by something else are the entities which compose the natural world, i.e., the fundamental physical entities, and (ii) all other entities are either composed of or produced by the fundamental physical entities.[1] If naturalism is true, then there is no God, and there are no supernatural persons. All persons will be embodied and will either consist of or will have been produced by the fundamental particles and/or fields of force. Given the complexity of such organisms as the human body, if naturalism is true, then it is rational to believe in something like neo-Darwinian evolution and irrational not to believe in something like neo-Darwinian evolution. It is this naturalistic evolutionary view of things which is such a pervasive feature of our culture. With regard to this particular aspect of our culture, the only Christian attitude is Christ against culture.

Alvin Plantinga has mounted an important argument against the rationality of accepting this naturalistic evolutionary view of things.[1] Let us refer to naturalism by N and neo-Darwinian evolution by E. If N&E are true, then it is rational to believe (and irrational not to believe) that our cognitive faculties have been produced and fundamentally shaped by the process of naturalistic evolution. The question Plantinga poses is this: what would be the probability that our cognitive faculties were reliable, given that they were produced and primarily shaped by a naturalistic evolutionary process? To say a cognitive faculty is reliable is to say that most of the time the outputs of that faculty are true. Let R be "Our cognitive faculties are reliable," and let K be background knowledge. Then, using the symbolism of the proposition calculus, we can express Planting's question as follows: What is the value of P(R/N&E&K), i.e., what is the probability of R given N&E&K?

The heart of Plantinga's argument is his claim that P(R/N&E&K) is either low or inscrutable. (I will not present Plantinga's argument for this claim, but I will present an

---

[*] Larry Lacy is Emeritus Professor of Philosophy at Rhodes College in Memphis, Tennessee.

[1] The natural world is the world that would be revealed by a perfected natural science. For present day naturalists, the most reasonable view of the natural world is that it consists of fundamental physical particles, and/or fields of force, and the various things whose existence consists in or has been produced by a certain arrangements of such fundamental particles and/or a certain configuration of fields of force.

[2] I will be dealing with the version of the argument to be found in Alvin Plantinga, *Warranted Christian Belief* (Oxford: Oxford University Press, 2000), pp. 231-240.

alternative to his version of the argument.) If P(R/N&E&K) is either low or inscrutable, and if S believes N & E, and S comes to rationally believe that P(R/N&E&K) is either low or inscrutable (say as a result of encountering Plantinga's argument), then S would have a rationality defeater for any belief produced by his/her cognitive faculties. The concept of a rationality defeater is to be explained as follows: if S believes P, then Q is a *rationality defeater* for S's belief that P, if (i) S would not be rational if S did not believe Q, and (ii) if S believes Q and is rational, S will reject P. Now if S has a rationality defeater for any of his/her beliefs, then S has a rationality defeater in particular for N. If S believes N, then to be rational, S must believe E. It would follow (if Plantinga's argument that P[R/N&E&K] is low or inscrutable is sound) that no one (having being convinced of Plantinga's argument) can rationally believe N. Thus N is self defeating.

By contrast, says Plantinga, consider the epistemic situation of the Christian Theist. Let CT stand for the conjunction of basic Christian beliefs. P(R/CT&K) is not low; it is reasonably high. It is probable that the God who is worshipped by Christians would have designed our faculties such that when they function properly in the kind of cognitive environment for which they were designed, then they will be reliable, for it is probable that God would have aimed them at truth and would have successfully aimed them at truth. In order to avoid irrationality and yet to hold the kind of beliefs most of us hold in common, we must, then, also hold either Christian beliefs, CT, or some other beliefs about supernatural person(s).

Now there is, I believe, a problem with this argument as it stands. If Plantinga's argument gives the person who believes N&E a rationality defeater for *any* belief he/she may form, then it also gives him/her a rationality defeater for the belief that P(R/N&E&K) is either low or inscrutable. So the argument appears to be self-defeating. Plantinga does not accept this claim that his argument is self-defeating. It is exceedingly difficult to see whether he is right about this. Rather than debate this issue with Plantinga, I propose to modify his argument in a way that avoids what I will call this dialectical difficulty and then attempt to construct a Plantinga-like argument that N is self-defeating. (My argument can only be Plantinga-like, for the initial reform I make in Plantinga's argument requires other important changes—though due to the time constraints, I will be unable to explain that point.)

Section Two: Dealing with the Dialectical Difficulty

The alteration to P's argument needed to avoid the dialectical difficulty requires us to introduce the distinction between transparent and opaque cognitive faculties. If a cognitive faculty produces a belief which we can see to be true, then I will call that faculty, in so far as it produces that belief, a transparent cognitive faculty. If a cognitive faculty produces a belief we cannot see to be true, then I will call that faculty, in so far as it produces that belief, an opaque cognitive faculty. I believe that sense perception, in all of its deliverances, is an opaque cognitive faculty. I cannot just see that "There is a computer terminal before me" is true; I could be just a brain in a vat with my neurons being stimulated in such a way that I have computer terminal-like sensations. On the other hand reason, for at least some of its deliverances, is a transparent cognitive faculty.

I can just see that 2+2=4, and hence I can infer that when reason operates within the range of such self-evident outputs, reason is reliable. However, reason, for some of its deliverances, may be an opaque faculty. Suppose it is a deliverance of reason that "Every event has a sufficient cause." I do not think we can just see this to be true. Hence, reason, qua yielding this belief (if it does), would be an opaque cognitive faculty.

Having made this initial revision, we need to reformulate the central question. Let Rocf stand for "Our opaque cognitive faculties are reliable." The reformulated central question is: what is P(Rocf/N&E&K)? I will argue below that some beliefs that would be essential to establishing N as a rational belief are the products of an opaque cognitive faculty and I will argue that the probability of the reliability of this opaque cognitive facultiy is low or inscrutable, given N&E. The important point is that (or so I claim) the cognitive faculty I employ in conducting this argument, i.e., reason operating within a certain range, is a transparent cognitive faculty. This initial revision of Plantinga's argument, thus, saves the argument from the charge of being self-defeating.

Section Three: Reformulating Plantinga's Argument

With this modification to Plantinga's argument, let us see how we can construct a Plantinga-like argument that Naturalism, N, is self-defeating. First, it is not rational to believe N as a basic belief; N is the kind of proposition that requires evidence for belief in it to be rational. What would constitute adequate evidence for N? I think two things are required: (i) evidence that the fundamental entities composing the natural world are not personal in character (i.e., that they are physical) and that all persons either consist of such fundamental physical entities or have been wholly produced by them, and (ii) appeal to the principle of simplicity to block positing the existence of anything other than physical things. Let S stand for the principle of simplicity. The naturalist will argue that science has shown that the things in nature (including us) are physical in nature or have been wholly produced by that which is purely physical in nature. Putting together the results of science and S, we get, "Nothing exists except those entities studied by science." This is the thesis of N.

This principle of simplicity, S, can be taken in either of two ways: (i) as a *metaphysical* principle—i.e., it is more likely that ultimate reality contains fewer rather than more different kinds of things), or (ii) as a principle of *rationality*—i.e., it would be irrational to posit additional beings, unless there is good reason to do so. Consider S first as a *metaphysical* principle. Taken this way, it would be a deliverance of reason, but one that is not self-evident; we cannot just see that this is how reality is. Further, this metaphysical principle would be far different from what Thomas Nagel calls "simple coping beliefs."[3] I see no hope for showing that this metaphysical belief would have survival value. If a belief has survival value, that is presumably because the proposition believed is true and believing this true proposition allows the organism to cope more successfully with the physical environment. For example, a human organism with cognitive faculties which in the presence of a tiger produces the beliefs, "There is a tiger"

---

[3] Thomas Nagel, *The Last Word* (Oxford: Oxford University Press, 1997), p. 135.

and "Tigers are dangerous" will have a survival advantage over a human organism which does not in the presence of a tiger produce such true beliefs. I fail, however, to see how believing "It is more likely that ultimate reality contains fewer rather than more different kinds of things," even if this is true, would allow an organism to cope better with its physical environment. Therefore, if N&E are true, then the probability that reason, in yielding this sweeping metaphysical principle is reliable, is either low or inscrutable. Suppose, however, Christian Theism is true, and reason, functioning properly, yields S. Christian Theism satisfies S as well as does N. According to Christian Theism, there is only one kind of ultimate reality (something which does not depend on something else), God. According to N the only kind of ultimate reality is physical things. If Christian Theism is true and if our reason when functioning properly produces the belief in S as a metaphysical principle, then it is more likely than not that reason when producing this belief is reliable.

Suppose we take S not as a metaphysical principle but as a principle of "rationality"—it would be irrational to posit additional beings, unless there is good reason to do so. Then the naturalist could reason this way: science has shown that all the things we know about are physical or are produced by the physical; therefore, we ought not to posit any additional being, any non-natural being. Therefore, it is rational to believe N and irrational not to believe N.

S, as a principle of rationality (rather than a metaphysical principle), does not require that we refrain from positing new beings. (If it did we could never be rational to posit electrons to explain certain phenomena.) All S says is that we should not posit additional beings *without good reason*. But the Christian Theist might believe that there are good reasons to posit that in additional to the physical world, God exists (or at least one very powerful, very intelligent supernatural person exists—which is enough to make N false). Perhaps the two most powerful reasons are (a) the apparent fine-tuning of the physical universe to produce intelligent life, and (b) the manifest fact of our capacity to discern evidential relations (to "see" that P makes Q probable). The claim of the proponent of the view that there is at least one supernatural person might be that these two facts cry out for explanation, and SP (there is at least one supernatural person) provides a better explanation of these facts than does N. Of course, the naturalist will deny this. But let's look at a judgment the N must rely on in response to the first of these two facts. The naturalist must hold, "Though we cannot see how neural complexity could produce the capacity to discern evidential relations, nevertheless this is possible." Call the faculty which yields this belief X (perhaps X is reason operating beyond the range of self-evident truths). What is the probability that X is reliable, given N&E? First, X is not transparently reliable. Next, I see no reason to believe that this metaphysical belief, if true, would have survival value, or that it is a deliverance of the faculties which produce our coping beliefs. So it seems to me that the probability that it is reliable, given N&E, is low or inscrutable. But then the naturalist cannot appeal to the above belief to rule out a good reason to posit a supernatural person. But it is only if the naturalist can show that there is no good reason to posit a supernatural person, that the naturalist can invoke S (as a principle of rationality) to argue for N.

Consider the second theistic argument—the argument from the apparent "fine-tuned" character of the physical universe to produce intelligent life. One way to account for the apparent "fine-tuning" of the physical universe is to posit either that there are a vast number of universes or a vast number of phases to this one universe such that in each universe (or each phase of this universe) the constants in the basic laws and the constants which describe the initial conditions of the universe (or a particular phase of the universe) are randomly generated (perhaps by quantum flux when the universe or phase of the universe is very small and dense). Given a large enough number of universes (or phases of this universe), it would not be improbable that all these constants in some universe (or phase) would be just right to produce intelligent life. I think there are two problems with this response. (a) The present evidence seems to tell against there having been a vast number of phases of this universe before the big bang of 15 or so billion years ago, and to posit vastly many universes would violate the principle of simplicity as a principle of rationality. (b) There is a price to be paid for the naturalist who makes this move. For, if we postulate a large enough number of universes (or phases) we need not think our well-ordered train of sensations has an external cause (physical things). For though this complex consistent ordering of our sensations (assuming they are not caused by physical things) is enormously improbable, given that this is the only universe (or phase of our universe), given a large enough number of universes (or phases), this order, occurring without a cause, would not be improbable. So if the naturalist appeals to this way of evading the argument for a supernatural person from the apparent fine-tuned character of the physical universe, he/she undercuts any reason he/she has to think the universe is physical, and hence undercuts any reason to adhere to naturalism. Perhaps the most fundamental things are minds and sensations. With no physical bodies to explain the emergence of finite minds, perhaps the best explanation involves an appeal to a supernatural person.

Section Four: Summary and Conclusion

The result of all of this suggests that N&E is, as Plantinga says, self-defeating. N cannot rationally be believed as basic. To argue for N the naturalist must appeal to (i) the success of physical science in showing that the things of nature are physical or are wholly produced by the physical, in conjunction with (ii) the principle of simplicity, S. S must be accepted either as a metaphysical principle or a principle of rationality. To be rational in accepting it as a metaphysical principle, the probability that the cognitive faculty qua producing this belief is reliable must not be either low or inscrutable. But given N&E, the probability of the reliability of this cognitive faculty qua producing this belief would be either low or inscrutable. Suppose, on the other hand, the naturalist accepts S as a principle of rationality. This will not help the naturalist unless he/she is also able to resist arguments by the Christian theist that SP gives a better explanation of some facts that cry out for explanation than does N. To rationally resist this claim the naturalist must regard a certain faculty, qua producing a certain belief, as reliable. The probability that this faculty, qua producing this belief, is reliable is low or inscrutable, given N&E. The upshot of this line of argument is that the person who accepts N&E cannot rationally trust the faculties which yield the beliefs which are required to make belief that N is rational.

But if N, then E; therefore, N cannot be rationally accepted. Therefore, N is self-defeating. Plantinga would argue that Christian Theism is not self-defeating in this way, and hence that, unless Christian Theism has an intellectual liability as serious as being self-defeating, Christian Theism is more rational than N.

A Consistent Ethic of Life Critique of Christian Complicity in a Culture of Death

Peter R. Gathje[*]

I. Introduction

A quick review of various church statements with regard to abortion, euthanasia and the death penalty reveals how churches in the United States apparently lack a consistent ethic on "life issues." A consistent ethic of life sees a similarity between these issues and stands in resistance to all three practices. It is not just the official church statements which indicate a lack of this consistent ethic of life. Even more so, poll data on these issues reveal that Christians of all denominations reflect essentially the same divisions as those evident in the broader society on these issues.

In order to simplify things I will focus upon the life issues of abortion and the death penalty. Here the incoherence of moral vision within the Christian churches is readily apparent. For example, the Southern Baptist convention stands in opposition to abortion, but supports capital punishment. This is also true of many independent churches that might be classified as "fundamentalist." On the other hand, the opposite pattern is evident in most of the so-called mainline churches, such as the United Methodist Church, the Episcopal Church, the United Church of Christ, and Presbyterian Church U.S.A., among others.[1]

---

[*] Dr. Peter R. Gathje is Associate Professor of Religion and Philosophy and Chair of the Religion and Philosophy Department at Christian Brothers University in Memphis, Tennessee. He received his Ph. D. in theological ethics from Emory University in 1994. He is the author of two books, *Christ Comes in the Stranger's Guise: A History of the Open Door Community* (1991) and *A Work of Hospitality: The Open Door Reader* (2002), as well as numerous articles, primarily in the area of Christian social ethics. His research interests include Catholic social teaching, nonviolence, just war, capital punishment, and New Testament ethics.

[1] A number of liberal and mainline Christian churches and religious organizations have publicly stated that abortions are sometimes an acceptable option, and should continue to be legal. According to lists prepared by The Secular Web and the Religious Coalition for Reproductive Choice, they include: American Baptist Churches-USA; American Friends (Quaker) Service Committee; American Jewish Committee; American Jewish Congress; Central Conference of American Rabbis; Christian Church (Disciples of Christ); Council of Jewish Federations; Episcopal Church; Federation of Reconstructionist Congregations and Havurot; Moravian Church in America-Northern Province; Na'Amat USA; National Council of Jewish Women; North American Federation of Temple Youth; Presbyterian Church (USA); Reorganized Church of Jesus Christ of Latter Day Saints; Union of American Hebrew Congregations; Unitarian Universalist Association; United Church of Christ; United Methodist Church; United Synagogue for Conservative Judaism.

From the perspective of John Paul II, we might say that these churches have become captive to a culture of death and have betrayed a more coherent Christian vision that urges the respect for the dignity of all human life as created and redeemed by God. But in order to begin that argument we must first be clear what a culture of death is and how it differs from the faith and moral vision of the Gospel of life that supports a consistent ethic of life. We can then in turn consider how abortion and the death penalty reflect the culture of death. With all this in mind we may then make the argument that most churches in the United States are in cultural captivity with regard to life issues, such as abortion and the death penalty, rather than living in the liberating power of the Gospel. I will leave that argument to our discussion time.

II. What Is a Culture of Death?

John Paul II in his encyclical letter *Evangelium Vitae* (EV) or "The Gospel of Life" has identified three major characteristics of a culture of death.

A first major characteristic of the culture of death is an over-emphasis upon individual freedom to the neglect of solidarity with the vulnerable and/or those in need of redemptive healing. John Paul writes of:

> a new cultural climate [that] is developing and taking hold, which gives crimes against life a new and—if possible—even more sinister character, giving rise to further grave concern: broad sectors of public opinion justify certain crimes against life in the name of the rights of individual freedom, and on this basis they claim not only an exemption from punishment but even authorization from the state, so that these things can be done with total freedom (EV par. 4).

John Paul uses the Cain and Abel story to illustrate the enduring importance of answering "yes" to Cain's question, "Am I my brother's keeper" (Genesis 4:9). He writes, "Yes, every man is his 'brother's keeper', because God entrusts us to one another. And it is also in view of this entrusting that God gives everyone freedom, a freedom which possesses an inherently relational dimension"(EV par. 19). Created by God for community, we flourish as God's creatures in relation with each other. Our very salvation is not even an individual matter, but rather is tied into our participation in the Body of Christ and being that Body of Christ in our relations with others.[2]

John Paul intertwines the relational quality of human freedom with his insistence that true freedom is grounded in adherence to truth that transcends the individual. It is the denial of such truth and its replacement with a kind of moral relativism in which morality is determined by majority vote that is the second characteristic of a culture of death. John Paul writes:

> When freedom, out of a desire to emancipate itself from all forms of tradition and authority, shuts out even the most obvious evidence of an objective and universal

---

[2] This is of course a major theme in Paul's letters, in particular First Corinthians and Romans. In particular see I Corinthians 12 and Romans 12.

truth, which is the foundation of personal and social life, then the person ends up by no longer taking as the sole and indisputable point of reference for his own choices the truth about good and evil, but only his subjective and changeable opinion or, indeed, his selfish interest and whim (EV par. 19).

John Paul sees the denial of this truth as emerging from a denial of God. He writes:

the eclipse of the sense of God and of man, [is] typical of a social and cultural climate dominated by secularism ... Those who allow themselves to be influenced by this climate easily fall into a sad and vicious circle: when the sense of God is lost, there is also a tendency to lose the sense of man, of his dignity and his life, in turn the systematic violation of the moral law, especially in the serious matter of respect for human life and its dignity, produces a kind of progressive darkening of the capacity to discern God's living and saving presence (EV par. 21).

Again, in elaborating upon this characteristic, John Paul turns to the Cain and Abel story. Cain's sense of sin is due to his awareness of God. God further affirms the continuing dignity of Cain as a human being in both holding Cain accountable for his sin, thereby affirming the relational freedom of Cain, and in redemptively addressing Cain's sin. God is redemptive in not only holding him accountable for the murder of Abel but also providing a context for conversion by protecting his life.

Without a sense of truth larger than oneself, without a sense of God, John Paul sees that the conditions are ripe for individualism, utilitarianism, and hedonism. In these, he identifies the third major characteristic of the culture of death, an inordinate drive for efficiency that eliminates those who are weak, vulnerable, or considered a blight upon humanity. John Paul writes:

The values of being are replaced by those of having. The only goal which counts is the pursuit of one's own material well-being. The so-called 'quality of life' is interpreted primarily or exclusively as economic efficiency, inordinate consumerism, physical beauty and pleasure, to the neglect of the more profound dimensions—interpersonal, spiritual and religious—of existence (EV par. 23).

The result of this, John Paul states, is that "The criterion of personal dignity—which demands respect, generosity and service—is replaced by the criterion of efficiency, functionality and usefulness: others are considered not for what they "are," but for what they "have, do and produce" (EV par. 23).

John Paul sees this kind of cultural climate "as a veritable structure of sin" which he believes is "actively fostered by powerful cultural, economic and political currents which encourage an idea of society excessively concerned with efficiency." "It is possible," he continues:

to speak in a certain sense of a war of the powerful against the weak: a life which would require greater acceptance, love and care is considered useless, or held to be an intolerable burden, and therefore rejected in one way or another. A person who, because of illness, handicap, or, more simply, just by existing compromises the well-being or life-style of those who are more favored tends to be looked upon as an enemy to be resisted or eliminated. In this way a kind of 'conspiracy against life' is unleashed (EV par. 12 see also par. 64).

Also part of this cultural climate that stresses efficiency and production is the failure "to perceive any meaning or value in suffering, but rather considers suffering the epitome of evil, to be eliminated at all costs" (EV par. 15).

These three factors—emphasis upon individual rights to the neglect of human solidarity, the separation of freedom from transcendent truth and responsibility, and the placing of efficiency above human dignity—together form the culture of death. The culture then comes to be practiced in a variety of moral evils, three of which John Paul especially addresses in this encyclical letter, namely abortion, euthanasia, and the death penalty.[3] In each of these practices John Paul II sees that there is a denial of human solidarity, the severing of freedom from truth and responsibility, and a denial of human dignity as grounded in what we are as children of God.

III. What Is a Consistent Ethic of Life/Gospel of Life?

In contrast to this culture of death, John Paul II and other Catholic leaders, thinkers, and activists have urged a vision of the Gospel of Life or, as it is sometimes called, "a consistent ethic of life." Influenced by John Paul II, the U.S. Catholic Bishops Conference gave a clear expression of this ethic when they stated:

> Because victims of abortion are the most vulnerable and defenseless members of the human family, it is imperative that we, as Christians called to serve the least among us, give urgent attention and priority to this issue of justice…This focus and the Church's firm commitment to a consistent ethic of life complement each other. A consistent ethic, far from diminishing concern for abortion or equating all issues touching on the dignity of human life, recognizes the distinctive character of each issue while giving each its proper role within a coherent moral vision."[4]

Thus, as understood by the U.S. Catholic Bishops, a consistent ethic of life does not exclusively focus on the abortion issue, but recognizes its connections with other justice issues in which the respect for the dignity of human life is at stake. A consistent ethic of life recognizes that there are common theological or faith convictions at stake in the issues of abortion, the death penalty, and euthanasia.

---

[3] John Paul gives a long listing of other evils that he sees as reflecting a culture of death (EV par.10).

[4] U.S. Catholic Bishops, *Pastoral Plan for Pro-Life Activities: A Reaffirmation*, 1985.

If we turn to John Paul II's encyclical, *The Gospel of Life*, it is possible to sketch some major theological convictions crucial to the consistent ethic of life and its moral vision.

John Paul II argues for a respect for human life that is grounded in the theological conviction that God is both Creator and Redeemer of human beings. It is this theologically grounded respect for human life that John Paul identifies as the "Gospel of Life." In his encyclical letter, the central biblical story around which John Paul develops his discussion of the Gospel of Life is the Cain and Abel story. We have already seen that this story was important in his discussion of the culture of death. But how does it function in arguments for the Gospel of Life?

A key insight in the letter that John Paul returns to again and again is that God is for life and stands opposed to death. He quotes from the Book of Wisdom, "God did not make death, and he does not delight in the death of the living. For he has created all things that they might exist ... God created man for incorruption, and made him in the image of his own eternity, but through the devil's envy death entered the world, and those who belong to his party experience it (Wis 1:13-14; 2:23-24)" (EV par. 7). John Paul thus grounds the Gospel of Life in the faith conviction that God creates human beings in the image of God and through the redemption in Christ humans have as their "destiny" a "full and perfect life" (EV par. 7).

John Paul stresses that death entered the world through sin, and in particular "death entered it in a violent way, through the killing of Abel by his brother Cain" (EV par. 7). In this murder and God's response to it, John Paul finds many insights that support a Gospel of Life. In support of his later point that the culture of death involves the denial of God that in turn leads to a denial of respect for the dignity of each human being, John Paul notes that "man's revolt against God in the earthly paradise is followed by the deadly combat of man against man" (EV par. 8). John Paul observes that "At the root of every act of violence against one's neighbor there is a concession to the 'thinking' of the evil one, the one who 'was a murderer from the beginning' (Jn 8:44)" (EV par. 8).

But this story is not only about the power of sin expressed in death, it is also a story that gives us what John Paul sees as a biblical pattern of accountability and redemption that reflects God's insistence upon human dignity. John Paul notes that God never stops God's dialogue with Cain. Rather, God "admonishes him, reminding him of his freedom in the face of evil" (EV par. 8). This freedom is an enduring aspect of human existence, and as we noted earlier in our discussion of the culture of death, John Paul also sees in this story that our freedom entails responsibility within our relationships given that we are created by God for community.

Thus, in connection with Cain's human freedom, God holds Cain accountable for his sin against Abel, "Cain is cursed by God and also by the earth... He is punished" (EV par. 9). "And yet," John Paul immediately adds,

God, who is always merciful even when he punishes… gave [Cain] a distinctive sign, not to condemn him to the hatred of others, but to protect and defend him from those wishing to kill him, even out of a desire to avenge Abel's death. Not even a murderer loses his personal dignity, and God himself pledges to guarantee this. And it is precisely here that the paradoxical mystery of the merciful justice of God is shown forth. (EV par. 9)

John Paul then quotes from Saint Ambrose whose commentary on this same story stated, "God who preferred the correction rather than the death of a sinner, did not desire that a homicide be punished by the exaction of another act of homicide" (EV par. 9).

It is in connection with our social nature that God responds to Cain's question, "Am I my brother's keeper?" God's answer is "yes" because we are created as relational beings who can only flourish as individuals within our lives lived with each other. Likewise, we can only truly be free insofar as we accept truth, namely God, as the guide for our lives. John Paul urges that if we lose the sense of God in our lives, our sense of human dignity:

is also threatened and poisoned, as the Second Vatican Council concisely states, 'Without the Creator the creature would disappear… But when God is forgotten the creature itself grows unintelligible'. Man is no longer able to see himself as 'mysteriously different' from other earthly creatures; he regards himself merely as one more living being… Enclosed in the narrow horizon of his physical nature, he is somehow reduced to being 'a thing' … He no longer considers life as a splendid gift of God, something 'sacred' entrusted to his responsibility and thus also to his loving care and 'veneration'. Life itself becomes a mere 'thing', which man claims as his exclusive property, completely subject to his control and manipulation. (EV par. 22)

In sum, in terms of the creation and God as Creator and in relation to the Cain and Abel story, John Paul identifies several important grounds for human dignity. First, we are created in the image of God, and this relationship with God is never lost or diminished no matter the stage of human life or what human beings do or fail to do. Second, we are created as social creatures, responsible for the good of each other. Third, we are created to live according to the truth and we are free to respond to the truth in our lives. Fourth, we have a transcendent destiny, namely union with God, and thus we are persons deserving of respect and not mere things.

But for John Paul it is not only our creation as God's children that grounds human dignity, the redemption is also crucial. He begins his discussion of the redemption with the Cain and Abel story. John Paul writes that it is not only the blood of Abel that cries from the ground, but "The blood of every other human being who has been killed since Abel," and indeed it is "the voice of the blood of Christ" (EV par. 25). But this blood of Christ is redemptive. John Paul writes that "it expresses and requires a more radical 'justice', and above all it implores mercy… it is the source of perfect redemption and the gift of new life" (EV par. 25). John Paul urges that "by contemplating the precious blood of Christ, the sign of his self-giving love (cf. Jn 13:1), the believer learns to recognize and appreciate the almost divine dignity of every human being" (EV par. 25).

Additionally, John Paul sees that "Christ's blood reveals to man that his greatness, and therefore his vocation, consists in the sincere gift of self. Precisely because it is poured out as the gift of life, the blood of Christ is no longer a sign of death… but the instrument of a communion which is richness of life for all. … It is from the blood of Christ that all draw the strength to commit themselves to promoting life" (EV par. 25). By the power of God in Christ the cross as an instrument of death has been transformed into the means of redemption. Thus it is that "The unconditional choice for life reaches its full religious and moral meaning when it flows from, is formed by and nourished by faith in Christ… who became man and dwelt among men so 'that they my have life, and have it abundantly' (Jn 10:10)" (EV par. 28).

In sum, the redemption picks up and amplifies themes already seen in creation regarding human dignity and respect for human life. John Paul points out that in the redemption "The Christian truth about life becomes most sublime. The dignity of this life is linked not only to its beginning, to the fact that it comes from God, but also to its final end, to its destiny of fellowship with God in knowledge and love of him." And he affirms, "The life which Jesus gives in no way lessens the value of our existence in time; it takes it and directs it to its final destiny: 'I am the resurrection and the life… whoever lives and believes in me shall never die' (Jn 11:25-26)" (EV par. 38).

The crucial points here are that in recognizing God as our Creator we see that our lives are from God and for God, and therefore we are to regard our own lives and the lives of others as belonging to God. Human life is entrusted to us; this is the truth of our existence. When we deny this truth, we kill others and we self-destruct. When we accept this truth, we care for the lives of others and we flourish. In terms of the redemption, we are to live in our relations with others in order to share with them what God has freely given to us, namely redemptive and healing life in the place of death-dealing vengeance. We are to love as God loves us. We are to practice justice as God is just with us. We are to be gracious, as God is gracious with us. We are not to crucify others in imitation of the ways of sin and death, rather we are to raise others to new life in anticipation of the resurrection.

In terms of abortion, this means first of all that we need to recognize that all human life at all stages of development is from God. This nascent life, like all human life, does not belong to us, "because it is the property and gift of God the Creator and Father" (EV par. 40). A Christian community that does not welcome new life as the good gift of God the Creator and does not recognize the obligation to care for this new life is abrogating to itself the role of creator. One can see that abortion is thus, in some sense, related to a kind of idolatry. At the same time, a Christian community sees that welcoming and caring for new human life is frequently difficult and requires the work of the whole community to support the primary care-givers. The Christian community is especially called to be a place in which mothers and new human life are to be welcomed no matter the circumstances of the pregnancy or birth.

Likewise, the death penalty is a denial of the truth that human life belongs to God. Given that such violence is not necessary for the protection of society and the punishment of the wrongdoer, we should seek " a system of penal justice ever more in line with human dignity and thus, in the end, with God's plan for man and society" and thus a system without the death penalty. John Paul calls for public authority to fulfill "the purpose of defending public order and ensuring people's safety, while at the same time offering the offender an incentive and help to change his or her behavior and be rehabilitated" (EV par. 56). We can see here John Paul's two-fold account of God's justice, holding persons accountable for wrong-doing, but for the purpose of redemption.

IV. The Culture of Death, the Practice of Abortion and the Death Penalty

In the support of both abortion and the death penalty there is ample evidence of a culture of death in the United States. In both cases there is, first of all, the denial of human solidarity, of community, in favor of a kind of individualism. In abortion, this comes out in the pro-choice rhetoric of the right of the woman to decide what to do with "her body." Left out in this language of choice is the recognition that pregnancy involves not only two persons, the mother and the father (not to mention a third—the unborn), but also that the whole society is responsible for the care of new life. Also left out in this language is the recognition that pregnancy involves God. All of the debates about when human life or personhood begins and the denial of such a status prior to a certain point miss the crucial affirmations that all life is from God and God gives to each human life a purpose or destiny that is not subject to human decision-making. In the individualism evident in abortion rights there is inherently the claim that this new life is an object to be disposed of as one sees fit, and this denies that this new life is from God and for God.

In capital punishment the individualism is expressed in at least three ways. First, there is the denial of any social responsibility in relation to the person who did the murder. The tendency in our society is to deny that society in any way shares responsibility with a person who commits the horrible act of murder. Murder and crimes of all kinds are simply seen as individual moral failure. The relation between crime and the failure of society to consistently make available quality education, care for the mentally ill and mentally retarded, and to address ongoing racism and poverty (among other factors that contribute to crime) is routinely dismissed in public discussions on holding criminals accountable.

Second, there is the dehumanization of the person convicted of murder so that he is described as "an animal," or "mad dog," or "beast" or worse. In this language there is the attempt to separate this human being from being human, and thus to deny any solidarity with him as a fellow human being and as a child of God. This kind of dehumanizing is also typical of pro-choice rhetoric in which the unborn child is described as a "parasite" or "invader" or "merely a blob of tissue."

Third, there is also individualism in the legitimacy given to individual cries for vengeance. As someone who works against executions, I often hear persons who are for executions state, "What if your mother was killed? Or "What if someone raped and killed your daughter?" Such questions reduce the social policy of capital punishment to individual redress of wrong and they also imply that the state's criminal justice system should function as a vehicle for individual vengeance. The perhaps natural first response to the crime of murder—vengeance—is institutionalized and turned into a social policy justified by appeals to the rights of the victims. Again the individual right of the victims is pitted against the individual rights of the perpetrators.

In terms of the second characteristic of a culture of death, the separation of freedom from truth and responsibility, it is evident that the practice of abortion urges that the freedom and moral autonomy of women require access to abortion. This insistence is related to the individualism already discussed. However, there is also in this case the emphasis that moral autonomy requires that the decision be made by each woman apart from the law or other authority. This is a common argument in pro-abortion circles that "only the woman has the right to decide." Lacking in such statements is an appreciation of a standard of truth that transcends the individual, and that in fact, it is often the individual who is closest to the decision who is least capable of making an informed and truly free choice. More tragically, there is also in this view of autonomy the notion that one's freedom can be gained through the destruction of innocent life. Put bluntly, but I think accurately, by Sidney Callahan, "Women will never climb to equality and social empowerment over mounds of dead fetuses, numbering now in the millions."[5]

In the case of capital punishment, the second aspect of a culture of death, the separation of freedom and truth is evident in two ways. First, there is the denial of the possibility of the freedom of those persons convicted of murder. What I mean is the denial that a person has the freedom to change; and further that a person who has murdered is therefore to be denied the chance at conversion and to have his conversion recognized and accepted by society, and so be welcomed back into society. Another way to put this is that capital punishment is unconcerned about rehabilitation, or in theological terms, redemption. Capital punishment assumes that for at least some people the state will decide that they can never change, and thus also that God's grace can never work within them. Although Jesus said, "You will know the truth and the truth will set you free," the state, echoing Pilate, says in capital punishment, "What is truth?"

Second, in the practice of capital punishment in the United States it is not truth that the state is after, rather it is the confirmation of power of the system to execute. The Supreme Court has ruled that a person may be executed even if innocent if the proper procedural requirements have been fulfilled. Further, despite a 68% reversal rate in capital convictions, and nearly 100 people freed from death row since the late 1970's, the

---

[5] Callahan in Paul T. Jersild, et. al., eds., *Moral Issues and Christian Response*, (New York: Harcourt Brace, 1998): 401.

state still persists in insisting that it can be trusted to not put innocent people to death.[6] The state in effect makes the claim to be God, or to stand in for God, not only claiming that it has the right to decide who lives and who dies, but also claiming that it can infallibly determine guilt and innocence.

In terms of the third aspect of the culture of death, the placing of efficiency above human dignity, we see a culture that treats human beings instrumentally, that is as means rather than ends. With abortion, the inconvenient pregnancy is taken care of with a medical procedure that pro-choice arguments describe as analogous to ridding oneself of a parasite or a removal of a cancer or other tumor. As John Paul described it, this emphasis upon efficiency denies the value of suffering and goes to any length, even killing another human being, to avoid suffering. In terms of abortion it is the suffering of the pregnant woman that is to trump the life of the unborn. To accept an unwanted pregnancy within this type of culture is to be seen as either heroic or oppressed by a false consciousness.

In capital punishment the concern for efficiency is seen in the state's justification for killing; it rids society of someone who is unwanted. Capital punishment is reserved for society's losers, and losers are best disposed of like garbage. The poor, racial minorities, the mentally retarded and the mentally ill populate death row. The irony is that society sought to ignore them for most of their lives, and then spends millions of dollars seeking to execute them. But even as execution is sought, people argue that it is important to have executions because it will save money (even though factually this is wrong). But this use of other persons as means to an end is also evident in that politicians continue to support capital punishment because it is a politically easy way to appear tough on crime. Support for capital punishment is politically expedient. Politicians use capital punishment to promote their electoral chances and popularity while denying the truth that capital punishment is not a deterrent, is more expensive than life imprisonment, and is applied in ways that reflect racial and class biases.[7]

V. The Cultural Captivity of the Churches

Standing against the cultural attitudes and practices of death is the coherent and

---

[6] See for example remarks made by two Catholic political leaders, Governor Frank Keating of Oklahoma and Supreme Court Justice Antonin Scalia at the Pew Forum, "A Call for Reckoning: Religion and the Death Penalty," January 25, 2002. Both argued for the state's authority to execute and both dismissed concerns about the execution of the innocent. Their remarks are available at www.pewforum.org/deathpenalty/resources. One may also add here President George W. Bush's dismissal of concerns regarding execution of the innocent in Texas despite serious flaws in capital cases in that state. See Stephen Bright, "Death in Texas," at http://schr.org/death-penalty-info.

[7] On these points see Garner C. Hanks, *Against the Death Penalty: Christian and Secular Arguments Against Capital Punishment*, (Scottdale, PA: Herald Press, 1997), The National Coalition to Abolish the Death Penalty, www.ncadp.org, and T. Richard Snyder, *The Protestant Ethic and the Spirit of Punishment*, (Grand Rapids: Eerdmans, 2001).

consistent Gospel of Life that affirms human dignity as grounded in our creation and redemption by God. It is the absence of this vision that is evident when churches in the U.S. either support abortion and oppose the death penalty, or oppose abortion and support the death penalty. Until Christians become converted to this vision Churches will continue to reflect the split within the larger society that justifies the killing of people who are vulnerable and/or in need of healing or redemption. In the practice of both abortion and the death penalty there is a failure of moral imagination in terms of the Gospel of Life. Churches and Christians that support abortion fail to imagine the unborn as God's gift of new human life, as human persons. Churches and Christians that support the death penalty fail to imagine the convicted killer as made in the image of God and redeemable through the grace of God, and fail to imagine the convicted killer as us standing before God as judge. In both abortion and the death penalty, these failures reveal the need for the Churches and Christians to be liberated from their cultural captivity through conversion to the God of life who sent Jesus into the world that we "may have life and have it abundantly" (Jn 10:10).

On the Purpose of Christian Art

Scot Lahaie[*]

It is my intent in this essay to explore the purpose of Christian art. Historically, the Christian artist has left a significant legacy. The vast majority of the artists working during the Italian Renaissance expressed personal faith in God through the Catholic Church (Schaeffer 19). These artists and others like them in other ages have created some of humanity's best art: paintings full of passion expressing a rich human experience; sculpture dynamic in form and full of symbolic meaning; tapestries that seem to reflect the very mind of the creator. Christian artists working in our contemporary age, however, have often played "second fiddle" to artists who have not tasted the saving knowledge of Jesus Christ. But why? Why have Christian artists lost their influence in our present age? I ask this question because I believe the answer will enlighten our understanding of the purpose of Christian art and the function of the Christian artist.

Let me begin with an examination of the term "Christian artist." The word "Christian" here is used as a type of title to distinguish one type of artist from another. It is strange that we seldom hear about Christian engineers, or Christian computer programmers, or even Christian hygienists. Are there no Christians working in these fields? On the contrary, there are many such folk. Any Christian who works as an engineer, or programmer, or hygienist will tell you that they honor Christ by fulfilling their work with great care and honesty. They often quote the New Testament where we are reminded to "work as if unto the Lord."

I also find it strange that we often hear people talk of Christian nurses and doctors. They describe such people as full of compassion and mercy, but in doing so they imply that doctors and nurses who are not Christians do not possess compassion and mercy for their patients. Say this out loud at a medical convention and see how many people set you straight. So why should we make this distinction if it is really not accurate? Are they not really just health care professionals who have given their hearts to Jesus and seek to serve him with their lives?

In very recent months the news media have been reporting on physician led prayer for the sick, which is portrayed as a new medical trend. The fact that patients heal faster when their treatments are combined with prayer has surprised many people in the news media (ABC News). Prayer has had such an impact on healing in recent years that many research groups have begun doing controlled studies on the subject. Indeed, several

---

[*] Scot Lahaie is Assistant Professor and Director of Theater at Gardner-Webb University in Boiling Springs, North Carolina. He holds a Masters of Arts in Theater History and Dramatic Criticism and a Masters of Fine Arts in Stage Directing. Professor Lahaie is also co-founder of the Horton Foote Society, and a former Artistic Director of the Keller Theater in Giessen, Germany, where he co-translated and produced the first English version of Coubier's classis German comedy, *The Beloved*.

medical schools, most notably those associated with private religious colleges, now offer at least one class on the role of the spirit and Christian prayer in treating the sick. Could doctors or nurses who pray with their patients be called "Christian doctors" or "Christian nurses"? Perhaps, but should anyone else standing in the hospital hallway stop and pray for a sick person, we would simply call him a Christian. So what purpose does the distinction of "Christian doctor" serve? So let us agree that the artist, like the engineer, programmer, hygienist, doctor, or nurse, is simply a person that can be, or not, a Christian. Like the engineer, the artist is about the task of designing and creating. This is the very heart of what an artist does day-to-day. Like the programmer, the artist is concerned about code, organization, and structure. A work of art is seldom a totally spontaneous creation. It consists of many rules and systems that allow the work to speak in the manner designed by the artist. All in all, the work of the artist does not change because he has given his life to follow after the Lord Jesus. So it becomes an easy conclusion that a Christian artist is nothing more that an artist who is a Christian.

But many argue that they mean more than just that. These people tell us that a Christian artist is an artist who creates "Christian art." This sounds reasonable at first, but again we must ask what is signified by the term "Christian art"? If we can validate the term "Christian art," then we might be able to accept this notion.

Let's start again from the beginning. If a Christian artist is an artist who has given his life to Christ, then by comparison Christian art must be a work of art that has given its life to Christ and experienced salvation. This is, of course, foolishness. The logic of our comparison does not hold. We obviously mean something different by "Christian art" than we mean by "Christian artist." There are, in fact, only two plausible applications of this phrase. We must either mean that Christian art is art made by a Christian, or we must mean that Christian art is art that reflects Christian thought and ideas. I believe that we must reject the idea that "Christian art" is art made by a Christian for the same reasons that we would reject the idea that a doctor could prescribe "Christian medicine." In short, not everything that a Christian artist makes reflects a religious theme. This leaves us with the idea that Christian art is indeed art that reflects a Christian theme.

This is indeed a wonderful idea. Many of the greatest works of art in the history of humanity are on religious themes. Michelangelo's Sistine Chapel comes immediately to mind. I am sure that you could name several more. But if Michelangelo had painted a painting of a beautiful sunset without a religious motif, would it be any less beautiful? Would his brush strokes be any less inspired? Or would his use of color or his composition be any less brilliant? I think not. We must simply acknowledge that an artist's inspiration, talent, and technique are not dependent upon the subject matter of his work.

Most of us belong to the non-artist category. A few of us are artists, but have never experienced the kind of inspiration and talent that made Michelangelo great. There may even be someone reading this essay that has experienced such a gifting. Most of us can only gawk from afar at the creations of such inspired artists and wonder. But from where does this gifting come? What is its nature?

Let me guide your attention to what the Bible has to say about Christian artistry. Many are surprised to discover that God's word has any concern for artists or their art. Assuredly, God's word is very illuminating about the purpose of art and the role of the artist in the community of the faithful. In Exodus, chapter thirty-one, Moses stands before God on Mount Sinai. It is here that God gave Moses the tablets of stone, and here he instructed Moses about the work of the tabernacle. Beginning in verse two, God tells Moses that he has called and prepared a man named Bezaleel (among others) to help Moses in preparing the complete furnishings of the tabernacle.

> And the LORD spake unto Moses, saying, see, I have called by name Bezaleel . . .: and I have filled him with the spirit of God, in wisdom, and in understanding, and in knowledge, and in all manner of workmanship, to devise cunning works, to work in gold, and in silver, and in brass, and in cutting of stones, to set them, and in carving of timber, to work in all manner of workmanship . . . and in the hearts of all that are wise hearted I have put wisdom, that they may make all that I have commanded thee . . ..

The things that these artists and artisans made were for the tabernacle of the congregation, and included the ark of the testimony, the mercy seat, all the furniture of the tabernacle, the candlestick, and the altars of incense and of burnt offering, and the cloths of service and the holy garments for the priests.

This is an amazing passage. We should never again look at an artist of any kind and think that he does what he does because of his genetic code. On the contrary, we must look to heaven and recognize that the Creator of heaven and earth has "filled him with the Spirit of God, in wisdom, and in understanding, and in knowledge, and in all manner of workmanship, to devise cunning works." This is in itself a revelation. We now can say with confidence that we know the source of creativity and artistry. But what function should this artistry serve?

In this particular passage pertaining to the tabernacle we are led to believe that inspired art is to be used in service to God's work—in our case, the Church. There are two common thoughts about how art might serve the church. The first is related to an appreciation of beauty. Like all art lovers, we seek out paintings to hang on our walls or the walls of our church building. I believe that fine art is a matter of taste. You should hang on your wall the kind of art you like. It is, after all, your wall. But I also want to issue a call that we not use the simplistic criteria of Christian art versus secular art to distinguish between acceptable and non-acceptable art. Rather, let us buy, display, and enjoy art that is perceived to be good, while we shun art that is poorly designed or shabbily made. The reality is that there will be art of religious theme in both categories.

This idea is not new. Indeed, it is similar to the "art-for-art's-sake" argument made by Oscar Wilde at the end of the nineteenth century. Franky Schaeffer repeated it again in

Christian terms during the 1970s in his inspiring book *Addicted to Mediocrity*. Schaeffer's position is extreme in demanding that no utilitarian restraints be placed upon the Christian artist whatsoever. This argument is sound to a degree, but ultimately strips art of any purpose apart from the expression of beauty.

The second common thought is that art can be enlisted to help with the task of evangelism. Again, I want to draw your attention to the scriptures: First Corinthians, chapter one, verse twenty-one, where it is written that it "pleased God by the foolishness of preaching to save them that believe." This passage tells us that God planned to reconcile a lost world to himself through one method—the preaching of the Good News. This is important because nowhere in the Bible does it say that God uses art to bring men unto himself. It is not sanctioned by heaven for that purpose. Nor can we construe art as a silent or static or even visual preaching of the gospel; it is not. For our modern church to force art into such service is wrongheaded and denies the power of proclamation.

Let me take a moment to address this further. As a young man I spent many years as a tent-maker missionary in Europe. Because of my study of theater and my talents in performance, I employed art and drama in street evangelism efforts. Although we attracted much interest from those we encountered, the art and drama itself never led anyone to Christ. We could not accredit even one conversion to our creative efforts. At the very best, we could say that these presentations so engaged the minds of our hearers as to open doors for us to share our faith through personal testimonies and the preaching of the word.

Although not for evangelism, I do believe that art is given to the church for a purpose. It is here that I believe that art must go beyond just the expression of beauty. I believe that art has the ability to help humanity (both lost and saved) to understand the fallen world in which we live. When used correctly, art is one of the tools that the church has at its disposal to be salt and light to a lost world. It is not for our self-edification alone. Art can make our world a better place to live. Regardless of the medium, whether visual, dramatic, or musical, art has the power to speak against the ills in our fallen world, such as the atrocities of war, or the violence of urban gangs, or the national tragedy that abortion has become, or teen violence in our nation.s schools, or date rape, or drug abuse, or school drop-out rates. Art is capable of speaking strongly to all these ills, while offering hope for a better way of living. This is the same purpose behind all social ministries of the local church: pregnancy crisis centers, homeless shelters, soup kitchens, teen outreach centers, runaway shelters, battered spouse shelters, and other similar programs. Most of us would have been slow to include galleries of Christian art or Christian drama presentations in this list of social outreach ministries, but the truth is that they all invoke change in the fabric of our society and thereby make our world a better place to live. They have the effect of being salt and light.

In many ways, non-believing artists have known this principle for years, although the change that these artists wanted to invoke has traditionally been political. Bertolt Brecht is perhaps the finest example in dramatic literature. Brecht's entire Epic Theater project was based in Marxist ideology with the purpose of altering the mindset of the proletariat.

In a similar way, the Soviet Union supported an entirely new style in the visual arts during their nation's rise to world power—Socialist Realism. The subject matter reflected in this visual medium was always the proletariat seen in happy and productive scenes of overcoming, which reflected the ideology that *"Arbeit macht frei."*

It does not surprise me that art should serve the same function in the church that it served in the world. What does surprise me is that art (especially theater) has been considered suspect by the church for so long that few are willing to entertain the idea of supporting Christian artists who wish to change the world for the better. Indeed, the church has on the whole abandoned its artistic and creative brothers and sisters in their "Spirit filled work" of making the world a better place. Let me remind you of Bezaleel and how the Lord "filled him with the spirit of God, in wisdom, and in understanding, and in knowledge, and in all manner of workmanship, to devise cunning works . . . ."

Let me summarize. First, I believe that the "Christian artist" is an artist who is a Christian, and not just an artist who creates Christian art. Second, "Christian art" is art that expresses a religious theme, although that criteria does not guarantee its quality. Third, the very source of all artistry is the "Spirit of God, in wisdom, and in understanding, and in knowledge, and in all manner of workmanship." Fourth, art cannot replace the preaching and proclamation of the Good News because it was not ordained for that task. And finally, Christian artists must be free to challenge the injustices and ills of our society in order to be salt and light in a fallen world, being more akin to outreach ministry. Only then will Christian artists rise above "second-fiddle-status" in a world desperate for the salt of the church and the light of the gospel.

References

ABC News. "Can Prayer Heal? Scientists Suggest Recovery May Be the Hand of God at Work."
http://abcnews.go.com/sections/Downtown_010813_remotehealing_feature.html

Schaeffer, Franky. *Addicted to Mediocrity*. Illinois: Crossway Books, 1981.

Pope John Paul II, *Fides et Ratio*:
A Challenge and a Declaration of Hope

Pamela Werrbach Proietti[*]

On September 14, 1998, Feast of the Triumph of the Holy Cross, Pope John Paul II published *Fides et Ratio*, his most radical encyclical to date, an encyclical essay far more radical than the counter-cultural *Evangelium Vitae*. In the previous encyclical, John Paul confronted the "culture of death." In the most recent encyclical, he declared his opposition to the dangerous trends of modern philosophy, and even denounced modern philosophy itself for having gone off in the wrong directions: an "undifferentiated pluralism," which culminates in a moral relativism "based upon the assumption that all positions are equally valid"; historicism, which denies the enduring validity of truth; positivism or "scientism," which limits absolute truth to the findings of the positive sciences and dismisses moral values as mere products of the emotions; utilitarian pragmatism, which favors majority rule over any countervailing concept of the common good or of any other moral good (a nihilistic approach to the judicial interpretation of law that has influenced many judges and legal scholars); and the various forms of atheistic humanism, which gave rise to modern totalitarian systems of horrific and pitiless inhumanity (sections # 5, 46, 47, 54, 86-91).

All of these trends in modern philosophy have degraded human reason. Modern philosophy has abandoned the quest for knowledge about Being and the Good that characterized the philosophy of ancient Greece and Rome and the Medieval Christian philosophy of Saint Thomas Aquinas. Philosophy and theology have both been diminished by these developments in the philosophy and culture of the modern and the post-modern worlds (section # 48, 81-83).

The pope describes all of these trends as leading toward nihilism; and the temptation to despair (sections # 46 and 90). According to some post-modern thinkers, the time of certainties is irrevocably past, and the human being must now learn to live in a horizon of total absence of meaning. There has been a collapse of that optimistic world-view we may call post-Kantian and post-Hegelian rationalist optimism, which had viewed history as the triumphant progress of reason. John Paul laments the widespread collapse of trust in the power and dignity of human reason, whether in the work of contemporary philosophers or theologians. While the former have abandoned the passion for ultimate

---

[*] Pamela Werrbach Proietti has studied at Dominican University, River Forest, Illinois, and Boston College, where she is ABD in political philosophy. She has taught at the University of Dallas and Saint John's College, Santa Fe, as well as the University of Memphis. Her earlier research took a reasoned and unusual because moderate approach to the controversy over the status of women in the traditional classics of philosophy. Much of her work has focused on John Locke and the British Enlightenment. More recently, she has begun studying the relation of the Enlightenment philosophers to the Scholastic tradition that preceded them.

truth, the latter have failed "to recognize the importance of rational knowledge and philosophical discourse...for the possibility of belief in God" (sections # 55 and 56).

The pope seeks to restore for mankind a proper understanding of the true nobility of human reason; and he also seeks to restore the proper interdependence of philosophy and theology, since each without the other is impoverished and enfeebled. He describes a philosophy that has been marginalized in our times and replaced by mere instrumental conceptions of rationality (section # 56). Modern theology, in response to modern philosophy's abandonment of the search for truth, has likewise lost sight of the true dignity of reason; theology now attempts to ground itself in mere transitory and individual experiences and feelings, whereas both Plato and Saint Thomas had grounded their philosophies in the ennobling horizon of universal, objective, and transcendent truth (sections # 43-45, 81-83).

Just as he had challenged our modern cultural assumptions in his *Gospel of Life*, so the pope challenges the complacent assumptions of the various schools of modern philosophy. Where his earlier encyclicals had criticized cultural prejudices that contradicted and undermined moral truths, especially the truth of the sanctity of life, this encyclical also challenges Western culture, but this challenge takes place on the very deepest level. John Paul recognizes the importance of philosophy as both the cause and effect of culture. Philosophy can inspire people to discover both their capacity to know the truth and their deepest yearning for the ultimate and definitive meaning of life (sections # 1-4, 16-18). Philosophy is often the necessary ground for understanding and dialogue between believers and unbelievers (sections # 64-72). Such a dialogue is essential to resolving critical issues facing humanity—threats to peace, dangers of environmental pollution, and the barriers to co-existence of different races and cultures. Christians must solve these problems with members of other religions and with all those who care about the renewal of humanity.

The pope's underlying purpose in the encyclical is to remind his readers of the nobility of human reason, which by necessity rests upon the foundation of the possibility of the existence of truth (sections # 24-34, 55-62). The title given to his introductory remarks is "know thyself"(sections # 1-6). This title itself reminds the reader of Socrates and the noble grandeur of ancient Greek philosophy. The opening sentences also remind the reader of the ecumenical perspective that this Pope has encouraged. The pope refers to the teachings of Confucius, of Lao-Tze, of the Buddha, and to the sacred texts of Hinduism, as well as to the ancient Greek poets and philosophers. "In both East and West, we may trace a journey which has led humanity down the centuries to meet and engage truth more and more deeply. The more human beings know reality and the world, the more they know themselves in their uniqueness" (section # 1).

The pope reminds his readers that the most fundamental human desire is the desire to know the truth about human life and about Being itself; the ancient Greek philosophers have described the passion that moves the philosopher as a love that is born out of the natural human capacity to wonder (sections # 21-34). From this beginning in natural philosophic wonder, Plato's philosopher ascends the "ladder of love," as he progresses toward an ever-greater understanding of the truth about eternal Being. However, contemporary philosophy has emphasized the limitations of human knowing and is increasingly pessimistic about the power of reason; the possibility of discovering any sort of transcendent meaning for human life is cast into doubt. Modern man faces an abyss as he seeks to understand the meaning of death and to discover some possible meaning of human life (sections # 81-82).

Both Christian revelation and ancient philosophy can guide the modern man who seeks to answer the most fundamental human questions. The classical conception of philosophical inquiry provides far deeper reflections on the meaning of human life than can be found in modern philosophy (sections # 36-45). Ancient thought also understood the close ties between philosophy and natural science; when modern natural science became the prevailing view of man's relation to the natural world both around and within him, the ties between philosophy and natural science were severed. Ancient philosophy had presented the authentic human life as a journey that allows no rest, a journey in search of wisdom—or knowledge of the truth about Being and about the meaning of human life. The triumph of the modern scientific worldview resulted in a less lofty understanding of the goals of philosophy and a mistrust in the power of the human mind to discover truth. While modern medicine, the many discoveries of the modern natural sciences, and many developments in modern technology have all served to make the material lives of contemporary man more comfortable, many have ignored the spiritual crisis that has accompanied this material prosperity in the lives of men and women in the West.

While the pope writes with an enthusiastic admiration of the ancient Greek philosophers, two corrections of the ancient understanding are provided: Firstly, ancient intellectual elitism, or the fundamental distinction between philosophers and all other men, must be rejected in Christian thought. Non-philosophers are not assigned an inferior status (section # 38). And all forms of human reason have been distorted by human sinfulness, and are therefore imperfect (section # 22, 37).

And, secondly, philosophy is not properly understood to be self-sufficient in its search for truth (sections # 16, 36-44, 72-79). Ancient philosophy had maintained the absolute separation of philosophy from all conventional or traditional teachings about how one ought to live. Both Plato's Socrates and the later (Roman) Epicurean and Stoic philosophers sought to discover the truth about nature and to seek to understand the nature of the good life for a human being. For the true philosopher, all traditional ideas must be challenged; religious beliefs should not limit the philosopher in his quest to discover the truth about being and the good life. However, ancient philosophy remained open to the possibility of the supernatural in its search for truth within the natural order (sections # 40-44, 75-78). Modern philosophy later closed off this possible harmony between theology and philosophy, as it also closed off the ancient philosopher's belief in rational access to the truth about Being.

Theology has also suffered from this radical separation of theology and philosophy. Theology needs philosophy as a partner in dialogue in order to confirm the intelligibility and universal truth of its claims. Both theology and philosophy have been caught in a crisis of meaning and a pervasive pessimism with respect to the power of human reason (section # 81). This situation makes the search for meaning difficult and often fruitless...and can lead to skepticism, indifference, or the modern forms of nihilism. The pope reminds readers that ancient philosophy, down through the "enduring" philosophic legacy of Saint Thomas, maintained a faith in the possibility of the Unity of Knowledge and the belief that the human mind can arrive at a unified and organic vision of Truth.

On the other side of the argument, the pope argues for the indispensable aid that faith provides to human reason. This aspect of the pope's argument is decisively grounded in the pope's faith in the truth of Biblical revelation. According to this Christian understanding, faith alone allows for human reason to overcome the obstacles imposed by sin and to reach toward the truth about God. Without the guidance of faith, human reason would likely remain darkened by sinfulness. It is only because of sin that we do not reach God with ease through natural reason (section # 22). And it is only through Christ that reason is freed "from the shackles in which it had imprisoned itself" (section # 23). The pope emphasizes the necessity for faith and the weakness of human reason, mired in sin, without it (section # 22).

The pope discusses the universal human experience of death, but does not conclude that this experience leads on toward some sort of existentialist embrace of "authenticity." The individual human being is confronted with the question, "Does life have a meaning?" Each of us then seeks a certitude in which he can anchor his life. The pope concludes that the search for ultimate truth is so deeply rooted in us that it is unthinkable that it should be useless. Both Augustine and Aquinas, along with the ancient Greek philosophers before them, had all reached the same conclusion: that human love in not a longing aiming toward nothing. Each human being is a philosopher, because each of us longs most deeply to understand the truth about Being and to know the purpose of human life.

The logic of the encyclical distinguishes three basic modes of truth: 1) truths confirmed by experience, and therefore proper to both everyday life and scientific research; 2) truths of philosophy and religion—which provide answers to the question of life's meaning; and, 3) the truth revealed in Jesus Christ (mysterious truths of the Christian faith) (section # 30; also # 15-23). This final truth is the most decisive for John Paul; the philosopher would not agree with John Paul's designation of the revealed truth of Sacred Scripture as "the lodestar" of the human quest for meaning.

The second category of truth is an implicit rejection of the moral and ontological assumptions of modern philosophy. The pope admires the openness of ancient philosophy to the supernatural; and he openly rejects the self-sufficiency claimed for philosophy "by some modern philosophers." One can usefully contrast this particular claim of late-modern philosophers with the early-modern rationalist philosophy of

Spinoza. Spinoza had argued that the world of nature can be adequately understood by human reason, without ever resorting to any superstitious claims about the role of supernatural forces. Yet even Spinoza felt compelled to concede that he could not rationally demonstrate the nonexistence of the Biblical Creator-God. (Nor could he have demonstrated the impossibility of miracles). Contemporary philosophy has been both less logically rigorous and more radical in attacking all forms of religious doctrine.

Because we human beings devote so much time to expanding our knowledge of both ourselves and the world around us, we understand that it is the true nature of the human being to seek the truth, both scientific and practical truth. And we all seek that ulterior truth which would explain the meaning of life (sections # 25-30). At this point in the encyclical, the argument takes what at first appears as a decisively non-philosophical turn; John Paul develops his "personalist" philosophy in the context of this question of the meaning of life. The truth that the human being seeks is attained not only by way of reason, but also through trusting acquiescence to other persons who can guarantee the authenticity and certainty of the truth itself. Here, the implied subject would appear to be the truth of Biblical revelation, which teaches the centrality of both human and divine love, and grounds the original human experience in the love of Adam and Eve. However, to the surprise of the reader, the pope goes on to describe the Platonic emphasis on friendship as the context for sound philosophical enquiry (section # 33). Reason needs to be sustained in all its searching by trusting dialogue and by sincere friendship.

What is the correct link between the two most fundamental orders of human knowledge, between the knowledge provided by revealed truth and that knowledge possible through philosophical learning?

Faith gives reason a higher goal and frees it from the limitations deriving from sin. And reason can affirm for the believer the rationality of faith. Their relation is compared to a circle (section # 73). The pope clearly believes that the proper relation between philosophy and theology was developing from ancient times up until the philosophy of Aquinas. Sadly, after Aquinas, later philosophers imposed a fateful separation between reason and faith, until modern philosophy came to assume that there was no common ground and no common interest that could unite faith and reason (section # 45). Modern theologians eventually embraced the same position; they mostly deny the rationality of Christian faith (section # 55).

The Pope warns of the dangers to both philosophy and theology in this false separation of theology and philosophy. Will this encyclical have an impact on modern philosophy? Probably not. The ideas in this encyclical would be far more likely to influence modern theology, particularly Roman Catholic theology. John Paul also expresses his hope that modern Christian philosophy might have an expanding influence upon popular culture. In this challenging encyclical, John Paul II joins forces with other modern thinkers who have observed that the ideas of Plato and Saint Thomas might be instructive for modern theologians and philosophers. Yet some hope remains for a revival within Western culture of an appreciation for the true nobility of philosophy and reason;

the pope expresses hope for some sort of spiritual renewal within Western culture. Just as Thomas Aquinas successfully led a Christian philosophic renewal of the ancient wisdom of Aristotle, so the pope might lead the way toward yet another rediscovery of the possible harmony between philosophic and Biblical wisdom.

References
All of the above notes are to sections of *Fides et Ratio*, by Pope John Paul II and published by *L'Observatore Romano*, English Edition, 14 October 1998.

Christ, Creed, and Culture

Bill Jenkins[*]

I am hardly going to tackle H. Richard Niebuhr and try to suggest ways in which his *Christ and Culture* is somehow flawed or failed. Not only has the usefulness of his taxonomy proved itself, but world class theologians like Paul Howard Yoder, Stanley Hauerwas, and Karl Rahner have used a much of their considerable mental power to critique and resituate the terms that Niebuhr popularized. Instead, I want to speak more provisionally out of my personal commitments and pedagogical experiences to offer some suggestions and assertions having to do with how Christ must be mediated through the ancient creeds, especially the Nicene Creed, before we can understand the relationship between Christ and Culture. We can only begin to utilize Niebuhr's paradigm—or anyone else's—after we decide which Christ we are relating to culture. The Christ of orthodox Trinitarian adoration, the Christ of neo-pagan appropriations such as those of Sophia worship, the Christ of rationalist demystification such as that advocated by Bishop Spong and his intellectual predecessors, the Christ as therapist of bourgeoisie anxieties—these versions of Christ now vie with one another, each dominant among certain social and intellectual classes. Bluntly stated, I claim that only the orthodox Trinitarian understanding of Christ is the correct one; this is the Christ we must situate within discussions of Christ and Culture.

Here at the beginning of the third millennium (Y2K already seems so long ago!), Christianity retains little of the cultural status is possessed fifty years ago when Niehuhr published *Christ and Culture*. Gone with that status was the easy fit between Christian theologizing and Western ascendancy in its Enlightenment mode. For instance, the Liberal Christianity of Niebuhr's day seemed to dwell comfortably within Modernity's rationalistic ambience. The genteel academic habits of Christian gentlemen scholars, the rhetoric of empirical plausibility, and the unquestioned assumption of Protestant Christianity's cultural dominance all formed a fairly unified and intact subculture that called the shots academically. How could those folks at Union Theological Seminary have foreseen the hyper-sexing of Christianity in their Mainline denominations, or the return of archaic forms of spirituality, or the embracing of irrational forms of argumentation to promote blatantly anti-Christian ideas? What would Niebhur and his cohorts have done with a recent reformulation of the Trinity, which states: "God is the union of Eros, Possibility, and the Good" (Cauthen)?

Conservative Protestantism has fared no better, although statistics crunching seems to prove that there are more evangelical than liberal Christians sitting in pews. Modern deracinated evangelicals are sinking in their own theological swamps. Hysterias and

---

[*] Bill Jenkins is Assistant Professor of English at Crichton College, Memphis, Tennessee. His research interests include the writers Annie Dillard, Willa Cather, and Walker Percy. He is interested in using Trinitarian theology to examine modern culture, especially the ways in which the modern Church interacts with culture.

obsessions abound in middle class American mega-churches as much as in urban cathedrals promoting labyrinths and gay union liturgies. In such cases, it does not make much sense to discuss Christ and Culture since what people mean when they speak of Christ seems so foreign to one another as well as to the ancient creedal understanding. As Anglican theologian Edith Humphrey writes, "It is not simply that a different 'Jesus' is being preached, teaching which we can correct by appeal to apostolic witness. It is that many have come to believe that there is no one Jesus at all, and indeed that Jesus himself is one among a number of human mediators of life, if in fact the individual requires such mediation."

The dominant use of Christ today seems to be one of emotional and psychic enhancement regardless of how one defines "liberal" or "conservative." Even if the Bible is accorded inspiration, its texts seem to serve more as aids for stimulating personal happiness rather than as richly diverse narratives that cohere Christologically. As Lutheran theologian Carl Braatan puts it, for most Christians today, "History itself is nothing but a resource of symbols to stimulate certain moods and feelings according to each person's private fancy. Worship means getting together in small groups of kindred spirits to hear one another's stories." If, however, the end of all humankind is participation in the life of the Trinity, then the contemporary Christs of so much American Christianity can do little to generate a vibrant, obedient culture. Instead we seem stuck with postmodern Christs, pastiche Christs drawn from our own nomadic consumer and psychological desires. Such Christs might be personally meaningful, but they do little more than mirror middle-class needs and desires.

I am interested in how creedal Christianity ensures the survival of Christ culturally. I am interested in how this Christ generates fullness of faith in every dimension, even if that fullness is sometimes fugitive or eclipsed—either hounded out of churches or ignored as an embarrassing anachronism. I am interested in how creedal ignorance spawns again and again amazing Gnostic mutations and cultural Christianities. I assert here without offering a substantial enough defense that without a Trinitarian understanding of Christ, then the operative paradigm of a congregation or denomination will always shift towards model number two in Niebuhr's terms, that is, the Christ of culture.

For instance, scanning religious television, one can see quickly how far from orthodoxy modern Christians can roam. Creflo Dollar subtitles his show "Changing the World" but this apparent nod to the cultural mandate merely certifies that what such "ministries" intend by change is gaining the economic and mental well-being of suburban middle class pagans. The obviously misnamed Trinity Broadcasting Network typifies the urge to be spiritual aside from any sacramental life that would have grown out of Trinitarian worship. Each show is a clone of the other, all failing to provide any reference to the Trinity or any discussion of Jesus as the pre-existent Logos, or any eucharistic embodiment of Jesus. The name "Jesus" becomes a rhetorical cue. Jesus more than Christ turns into a religiously charged figure who remains rather indistinguishable from the Holy Spirit. The Spirit becomes the de facto star of such show biz religion because the "Spirit" is amenable to treatment as a force, a kind of energy that Christians can socket into. Through the Gnostic—at times even Shamanic—guidance of the pastor, the aspiring adepts can ascend to higher levels of spiritual awareness and obtain the principles of financial success, good family life, effective communication, or whatever. Local independent congregations tend to replicate at least some features of this rootless Christianity because the message sells so well.

What's lost, of course, is exactly the culturally transformative power of Trinitarian orthodoxy. Evangelical Protestants in general and not just the obviously heretical versions on television will remain trapped within an environment stripped of all transcendence as long as it fixates on Jesus, or in some cases the Spirit, merely as a source of moral, mental, and economic upkeep. The standard décor of church interiors will continue to reflect the values of 1990s secular suburbia as long as the divine Trinity remains absent from worship. Dense symbolism becomes foreign to the life of a church, replaced instead with flattened symbols of secular value, especially those having to do with size. The symbolically stale mega-church is a logical cultural spin-off of a theology that ignores the Trinity even if the church claims to be conservative in its faith. Huge suburban churches grow seamlessly into the tentacular sprawl radiating away from cities. The SUVs, Lexuses, and BMWs in the parking lot signal the values and aspirations of the congregation along with the disappearance of liturgical space and language. In fact, most mega-church building designs conscientiously seem to avoid visual and verbal references to traditional faith, although now and then elements that create a nostalgic effect are noticeable, much in the way that the detritus of previous generations finds its way onto the walls of a Cracker Barrel restaurant. The implicit—and sometimes explicit— Christology expressed in these churches is thoroughly Arian or Modalist, resulting in the evacuation of Eucharistic vision with all that that implies about the value of material creation.

Many Christians have become suspicious of the obsessions nourished by some mega-church theologies. Though not all of these Christians are young people, the revolt against largeness and comfort in church going appears frequently in those around college age. Yet as one listens to this suspicion of a commodified Christianity, one can hear an all too familiar populist rhetoric: the older generation has got it all wrong; our parent's Christianity is hopelessly conformist; all traditional discourse must be scrapped; history only proves how corrupt the institutional church was; Trinitarian doctrine is too complicated and irrelevant; liturgy kills the spirit of true worship, and so on. Rather than seeing the revolt against Boomer gigantism as a principled discipleship sustained by mature reflection on Scripture, we should probably interpret our students' rebellion as part of a long-standing American social text. Christians who turn away from Suburbia's congregational culture in their pilgrimage to a more authentic "relationship with Jesus" in fact might be merely playing out a very traditional script. The urge to repristinate the church and to turn religious experience back to a kind of primal unmediated encounter with Jesus is nothing other than an urge to replay yet one more time a narrative that has consistently structured much American evangelicalism for almost two centuries. In the voices crying for "real" Christianity, one can hear echoes of older condemnations of organized religion made by the likes of Ralph Waldo Emerson, William Ellery Channing, Joseph Smith, and Alexander Campbell.

The cultural fallout of this disdain for history and creedal affirmation isn't too hard to see because there isn't much culture there. Denominations arising from Back to the Bible orientations are not known for their great musical compositions, novels, poetry, or painting. Neither have they generated long-lasting contributions to political thought or philosophy. One cannot deny the very real moral earnestness of many people who commit to a Bible-only interpretation of Jesus. The anonymous multitude of holy lives who even today thrive within the parameters of a Christianity that is essentially blind to the Nicene creed indicates that God can sustain a faithfulness that actively spurns ancient orthodoxy. Nevertheless, good moral intentions cannot sustain truly Christian engagement with culture. A faith limited by piecemeal Biblicism ends up drawing only on the resources of the immediate environment to interpret that environment. Such a perspective sees church history as a failed project launched by arrogant people who fiddled with the purity of the church. This philosophy cannot engender a distinct contribution to the debate concerning Christ and Culture in contrast to previous orthodoxies. The Trinitarian view of Christ requires liturgical embodiment, which in turn opens up the incarnational and creational implications of Christ for culture. The loss of Trinitarian worship profoundly affects culture outside the church. The material embodiment of a Christianity that avoids the Nicene understanding of Christ usually remains immanent in expression.

In terms of personal and public morality, for example, evangelical Christendom couldn't be farther from liberalized Protestantism, yet both are Siamese twins in their rejection of Trinitarian thought. Both dimensions of modern Christianity refuse patristic authority. One side cries, "Back to the Bible," and the other belligerently identifies the Bible as only an ancient document useful for its source material along with other religious texts. Both sides claim that the fullest understanding of Christ and culture must derive from aggressively updating the Gospel. But neither side succeeds in engendering a transmissible intergenerational culture.

The balancing act of "Christ and culture" will perpetually frustrate Christians who perceive their task as always streamlining the faith so that it will move easily with the times. Historically, the creedal definitions of Christ ran tandem with the developing Biblical canon, and this consensual orthodoxy has proven itself viable in many different cultures and civilizations even to this day. Paleo-orthodoxy, to use a term popularized by Thomas Oden, is the matrix for maintaining long term encounter with and creation of culture. Genuine Christian culture has always grown from Trinitarian worship in its sacramental health. One only has to look at the icons of the early church or hear the music of the Lutheran Reformation or view the paintings inspired by Calvinist theology to see the point. Ignorance of creedal adoration of Christ has cultural ramifications. The Nicene vision of Christ is much more than a dogmatic safeguard that we can usually ignore as we turn to what we define as more immediate concerns. Whatever the complex social and historical reasons for the present day refusal to think and worship in Trinitarian wholeness, Christians who promote the relevance of Christ to the modern and postmodern world without this Triune vision will produce only simulacra of relevance.

One contemporary scholar of Trinitarian orthodoxy is the Episcopalian traditionalist C. FitzSimmons Allison. Allison argues that blindness to the heresies that the ecumenical orthodox church identified means that these heresies will merely resurface throughout history: "There is scarcely any heresy that does not have a modern expression or a modern heresy that we have not seen before in the church's history." Christianity in the late twentieth century witnessed an especially fertile growth of such heresies, partly because, as Allison puts it, these perennial denials of Christ "pander to our deepest fallen desires." An Episcopal church that celebrates Samhain instead of All Saints Day and an independent charismatic congregation whose pastor regularly receives a word from God to teach about prosperity have both turned away from rightful worship of the second person of the Trinity. In attempting to enact some kind of dialectic between Christ and culture while refusing to proclaim Christ of the creed, the church either anxiously or blandly reflects modernity's own preoccupations. Even if these preoccupations are sincerely spiritual, the church slides toward heterodoxy and amnesia.

An interesting example is the current bizarre fascination with the Gospel of Thomas. A few congregations have actually experimented with incorporating readings from Thomas into the lectionary. Religion professor Marvin Meyer has translated a new edition of Thomas and maintains a Gospel of Thomas website. Traffic on the site surged almost ten times its normal rate just after release of the movie *Stigmata*. Thus, the confluence between popular culture and increasingly popular non-Christian forms of spirituality surfaces in churches once dedicated to influencing the culture for Christ. In the environment of late Modernity, churches raid metaphors and symbols either from secular capitalism—Jesus is my CEO, —or from other religious traditions. As Allison points out, when we avoid the Christ of the creed, we sink into the gravitational clutches of our own fallen desires, even if we dress up those desires as spiritual.

A Rushed Conclusion
Nothing here really alters Niebuhr's typology, and there is no need to guess what shape a renewed Christian civilization might take or which Christ and culture paradigm could best sustain it. We can't specify because the providential cycles of genuine renewal in the church have always surprised us, though each renewal has also maintained continuity with Trinitarian and therefore sacramental worship. Even so, l am willing to risk making one assertion. A Trinitarian recovery will entail a rediscovery of the category of the Beautiful, both as a moral category and as a material one. The recovery must begin first within the worshiping church, but it will also enlarge into an analysis of our circumambient culture with its fixation on trashiness. What in the world would Niebuhr say to our current civilization, drenched as it is with pornographic images and consumerist paganism, a place where young girls from suburbia dress and act like prostitutes and young men from inner cities rove as super-predators? As with a previous Dark Age, devotion to the Triune God can sustain a vision of human dignity and creational delight that will work its way beyond the walls of a church building.

Anglican theologian Peter Toon has written much recently on how the devolution in worship reflects a church pandering to secular culture. He claims: "The doxological character of liturgical syntax and vocabulary disappears, effacing the transcendent nature of worship. The immanent dimension appears to be all, demanding expression in language that fits well the secularized therapeutic culture of consumption." When the church adapts to the materialism of the modern world it no longer possesses the tools for transformation of the world. A concept like the beauty of holiness disappears into frenetic activity labeled "ministry." The leverage needed to keep "Jesus" from becoming a cipher into which we inject prevalent desires born of unconscious idolatries is the Jesus of eucharistic worship born of Trinitarian orthodoxy. Lutheran Homiletics professor Richard Lischer critiques contemporary Christianity this way: "When we listen to what passes for religion, what we hear is the vocabulary of common sense, peace of mind, competition, success, democracy, tolerance, and family" (178). How far we have descended into an immanent vision of Christ with a concurrent loss of cultural impact is easily seen when we compare the categories listed by Lischer and Toon with the luminous words of Gregory of Naziansus:

> The Word of God Himself, who is before all worlds, the Invisible, the Incomprehensible, the Bodiless, the Beginning of beginning, the Light of light, the Source of Life and Immortality, the Image of the Archetype, the Immoveable Seal, the Unchangeable Image, the Father's Definition and Word, came to His Own Image, and took on Him Flesh for the sake of our flesh, mingled Himself with an intelligent soul for my soul's sake.

We can argue until we are blue in the gills about which of Niebuhr's categories for Christ and culture provides the most Biblical model for cultural obedience. Roman Catholic and Reformed thinkers, for instance, can still put on a pretty good show. Or, we can argue with similar energy that his schema depends on error-ridden assumptions and must be scrapped in favor of another. Whatever. My thesis is that something more fundamental stands behind such categories, and that is that we must first throw in our lot with the Christ of ecumenical orthodoxy before we can begin to discuss any plausible configuration of Christ and culture.

References

Allison, C. FitzSimons. "Heresy is Cruel: The Contemporary Dangers of Docetisim and Ebionism." <http://www.tesm.edu/missmini/alli-crd.htm> (See also his *The Cruelty of Heresy: an Affirmation of Christian Orthodoxy*. Harrisburg, PA: Morehouse Publishers, 1994.)

Brataan, Carl E. (It is with some embarrassment that I confess I cannot track down the source of this quotation. This paper originated as a conference paper, and I had no intention originally of working it over for publication. My apologies for the slipshod scholarship.)

Cauthen, Kenneth. "God, Trinity, and Creation: God as Masculine and Feminine." 22 Feb. 2001 http://www.frontiernet.net/~kenc/speculat.htm

Gregory of Naziansus. *Second Paschal Oration*, 9.

Humphrey, Edith. "God's Treasures in Jars of Clay." 7 March 2001 http://www.magma.ca/~inrig/olst/humphrey.htm

Lischer, Richard. "Interrupted Sermon." *Interpretation*. 50.2 (1996): 169-181.

Toon, Peter. "Simple Sentences—Are They Appropriate For Divine Liturgy?" 7 July 2000 http://justus.anglican.org/resources/pbsc/caun0046.htm

Gabriel Marcel and The Spirit of Teaching:
Reflections on Presence and Transcendence

Gray Matthews[*]

A man cannot be free or remain free, except in the degree to which he remains linked with that which transcends him, whatever the particular form of that link may be: for it is pretty obvious that the form of the link need not reduce itself to official and canonical prayers. I should say that in the case particularly of the true artist in paint, or stone, or music, or words, this relationship to the transcendent is something that is experienced in the most authentic and profound way.

-- Gabriel Marcel

What I have in mind with this essay is a brief foray into what I consider to be the heart and soul of teaching. More precisely, my focus is upon *the teacher*, a being whose chief work is accomplished through a special kind of participation with other beings. I am not at all concerned with pedagogical techniques here, which in my estimation have nothing to do or say about the *heart and soul* of a teacher. Quite the contrary, techniques can often serve to increase a teachers' existential frustration and function as impediments to genuine learning. I want to focus, instead, upon the spiritual experience of teaching, on the practice of teaching as a calling or vocation, and the unique obstacles one may confront in such work. I want to illuminate the work of teaching from a spiritual perspective, regardless of the subject or content of course material taught, and regardless of whether one teaches in a secular or religious institution.

For assistance in this task I have turned to the writings of Gabriel Marcel (1889-1973), and would like to highlight some key concepts in his philosophy that I think are highly relevant to the act of teaching and to being a teacher. Although Marcel is not especially noted for his pedagogical viewpoints, his ideas about communication, being, presence, spirit, creativity and freedom, as well as how these can become degraded, are of the utmost value, relevance and utility for understanding the heart and soul of being a teacher.

In my view, the core of the experience of teaching, as Marcel has helped me to identify it, is this: *Teachers and students are whole persons opened toward one another and Mystery, who are intertwined in a living process of mutual education.* The purpose of this essay is to illuminate this phenomenon as well as share some reflections on how such a potentially in-spirited experience can become degraded or *dispirited*. After first exploring some of Marcel's fundamental philosophical concepts, I will turn to address the

---

[*] Gray Matthews is Assistant Professor in the Department of Communication, The University of Memphis, where he has been honored with the university's Distinguished Teaching Award. His research has been published in the *Southern Communication Journal* and *The Merton Annual*. Dr. Matthews serves as coordinator of the local chapter of the International Thomas Merton Society.

problem of dispiritedness in education, and then conclude the essay by integrating these concepts into a working pedagogical perspective.

Fundamentally, my words stem from a personal, spiritual experience of working in a secular institution that is often opposed to the intellectual legitimacy of the sacred. My ultimate vocation—my calling, as I see it—is to be a witness to the Transcendent. The college classroom, in essence, is the space wherein I most experience the joys and frustrations, the graces and curses, of such a vocation. It can truly be a rewarding profession, but it is also a job that, frankly, has me often in the throes of despair to the point that I am not infrequently confronted with temptations to withdraw or resign. Yet ultimately, I must confess, this brief essay is a testament to hope—to the endurance of hope as well as to the hope of endurance.

Gabriel Marcel and the Mystery of Being

Gabriel Marcel is typically tagged as an existentialist, a label he never accepted and always railed against. It has stuck, I suppose, because of three factors: (1) his philosophical writings focus on concrete human situations and the situatedness of the human existent; (2) he was writing at a time in which existentialism was making a tremendous mark on the intellectual and literary worlds; and (3) he personally interacted with Sartre, Jaspers and Heidegger as colleagues, correspondents and fellow critics. Yet, Marcel's philosophy and writings clearly subordinate existence to essence, for Marcel's orientation began with the concept of being and then examined being in-situations, markedly different from the perspective of Sartre and Heidegger.

Due to his conversion to Catholicism in 1929, some observers tend to classify Marcel as a *Christian* or *religious* existentialist. Still, the label cannot adhere, convincingly. Although Marcel repudiated the existentialist label, he could not deny working from a fairly traditional Christian outlook. What is most interesting here, though, is that his conversion did not have a dramatic *conversionary* impact on his thinking; that is, his perspective and arguments did not substantially change. His writings, before and after his religious conversion, are consistent with each other. This is not to say that his conversion did not have an effect, for it did; rather, Marcel's religious shift served better to fulfill and substantiate his philosophical musings, or better yet, to complete his own thinking. In short, his conversion was a logical consequence of his philosophy.

Marcel's own preference, if forced to apply labels, was Neo-Socratic. His reasons for accommodating this identifying mark are particularly what make him relevant to the art of teaching and to the crafting of this essay. Marcel was a Neo-Socratic in the sense that he: (1) highly valued the reasoning powers inherent in authentic dialogic communication; (2) placed self-knowledge as the starting point of any true philosophical work; and (3) believed philosophical thinking must be worked out in relation to others. In sum, if we are to get anywhere in figuring out who we are and what we are doing here, we had better begin with our concrete life situations and the reciprocal unfolding of selves through communion with others.

In reading Marcel, therefore, I am literally forced to reflect upon my own life situation, and particularly on the daily concrete situation of entering a college classroom as a professor. As a so-called academic professional, I have certain duties and responsibilities to fulfill; but as a Christian, I have duties and responsibilities beyond my specific job role. Hence my most interesting days as a teacher seem always to be the ones in which I experience some kind of tension between being a professor and being a *confessor*. This is less a problem to me, however, than it is a mystery with which I am engaged.

Problem and Mystery

Marcel is, perhaps, most noted for emphasizing the distinction between a problem and a mystery. This distinction is helpful to keep in mind as a teacher. A problem is any source of difficulty, stress or perplexity that exists outside oneself; a problem can be objectified and characterized because it is separate from us. A mystery, however, "encroaches upon its own data, invading them"; it is something I am a part of, intimately involved in, to the degree that I cannot separate myself from it (Marcel 1956, 19). For example, I cannot step outside of my own life in order to study it; thus, in a very real sense, I do not *have* a life, I simply live.

We cannot analyze mysteries as we do problems: We meet mystery. This meeting, or encounter, is one in which "I cannot place myself outside it or before it; I am engaged in this encounter, I depend upon it, I am inside it in a certain sense, it envelopes me and it comprehends me—even if it is not comprehended by me: (Marcel 1956, 22). Mystery is beyond problem, and is termed the "meta-problematical" by Marcel. One encounters mystery through a particular form of "secondary reflection" or recollection, in which one approaches mystery as a whole person. This notion of mystery as applied to the practice of teaching may be better understood after examining other emphases in Marcel's perspective.

Being and Presence

Running consistently through Marcel's philosophy is the theme of how we relate to the world in which we live. Marcel perceives two modes of relation or orientation: being and having. Problems ensue whenever the having mode overtakes or dwarfs the being mode. A "having" orientation to life resides in the felt need to possess and control, limiting reality and ones' experience of it to something outside of self to be manipulated for one's advantage. A being mode of relating to the world deepens one's appreciation for mystery and our participation in the mystery of life.

In regard to the act of teaching, we can see how these two modes of relating to students and to knowledge might be conceived in Marcellian terms. A having mode would view students as objects to be molded, controlled and referred to as "my students." Knowledge would be something one *has* that one may politely share with another person if they so choose; the teacher possesses a degree that (falsely) entitles one to think of whole courses of study as "my courses" or "my classes." On the other hand, the being perspective would view students and knowledge as something one is in relation to, and not as something one has. *Being* a teacher, then, means participating in a mystery of engagement with others that cannot be completely conceived of as outside of oneself. Such a perspective naturally, for Marcel anyway, leads to an ethic of care or love. In fact, Marcel claims that love and intelligence cannot be divorced; in order to do so, one must abstract them from being, as something we have. In as much as teachers and students are involved in a pursuit of intelligence, we are exhorted by Marcel to undertake this task guided by love.

This discussion leads us necessarily to the concept of *presence*. Beings have presence, but here "having" must not be thought to connote possession. We can be present to each other in meeting, in encounters with other beings as beings and not as objects. Marcel's view of presence is very similar to Buddhist notions of mindfulness, of being here now, fully present and attentive to the immediate situation. Presence is communicated in a way that brings beings into communion with one another. Often enough, a teacher may be in the classroom, but not present to the students; and vice versa. Yet, the opposite can happen: "when somebody's presence does really make itself felt, it can refresh my inner being; it reveals me to myself, it makes me more fully myself than I should be if I were not exposed to its impact" (Marcel 1950, 205). Such an understanding, if applied to teaching, would transform a classroom of people into a being mode of relation. Marcel explains that "when we say that a presence must not be thought of as an object, we mean that the very act by which we incline ourselves towards a presence is essentially different from that through which we grasp at an object; in the case of a presence, the very possibility of grasping at, of seizing, is excluded in principle" (Marcel 1950, 207-8).

Availability and Freedom
Now we come to two more critical terms in Marcel's philosophy that can be applied to the heart and soul of being a teacher: being available and being free. According to Marcel, "availability" is, unfortunately, merely an adequate translation of the French term he utilizes: *Disponibilite*. Marcel wishes "*disponibilite*" to imply a combination of openness and handiness, a permeable availability, and refers to a giving of oneself—of being present whenever needed. A self-centered person is an unavailable person, a captive soul, incapable of being present to others. Furthermore, Marcel argues that the unavailable person:

> will be incapable of sympathizing with other people, or even of imagining their situation. He remains shut up in himself, in the petty circle of his private experience, which forms a kind of hard shell round him that he is incapable of breaking through. He is unhandy from his own point of view and unavailable from the point of view of others (Marcel 1950, 163).

Upon deeper reflection, Marcel claims that the act of giving oneself, of making oneself available to others, could appear as a form of sacrificial madness; however, he writes that "if a man were to shirk from such madness, he would be falling below himself" (1950, 166). In other words, we become more human by being more present, and therefore can help others become more human and present along with us. It is a kind of perpetual open invitation to communion with others.

I think it is instructive to link the idea of availability to Marcel's perspective of freedom. First, it is interesting to note how Marcel describes the unavailable person: he or she is "incapable" of doing certain things. In a sense, being incapable is similar to lacking a kind of freedom. The unavailable person is held back, unfree, and closed to creative development and the power to act as a subject.

In the opening chapter of his critique of technology and mass culture, *Man Against Mass Society,* Marcel raises the fundamental question of what it means to be a free person, and how one loses such freedom. It is important to recall that Marcel understands a human being to be an ontological mystery; thus when we lose touch with ourselves and our participation in the mystery of being, we lose our freedom to not only be available, but to be our true selves. Marcel urges us to remain reflective of this precarious situation—precarious because we live in a society anchored in a having, rather than being, mode of existence.

Marcel opposes what he calls "techniques of degradation" that train the human person to lose touch with oneself, to become one who "tends progressively to be reduced to the status of a mere *thing*" (1956, 19). I interpret Marcel to be issuing a charge to educators, especially when he calls his readers to the deeply reflective task of being awake to the internal and external forces that threaten to weaken our relations to mystery and the freedom of being present: "Between the physical destruction wrought by the atomic bomb and the spiritual destruction wrought by the techniques of human degradation there exists, quite certainly, a secret bond; it is precisely the duty of reflective thinking to lay bare that secret" (1956, 14).

Before we investigate more closely what Marcel means by "techniques of degradation," we need to explore one more significant theme: Our link to the transcendent.

Transcendence
Marcel declares that we have an "urgent inner need for transcendence," that our own reality is bound to something greater than ourselves (1950, 48). Mysteriously, we are severely alienated from ourselves when our link to the transcendent is ignored. To meet this inner need, Marcel claims that we must appeal to "a level of being, an order of the spirit, which is also the level and order of grace, of mercy, of charity" (1952, 22). "What we have to do," he says, "is to proclaim that we do not belong entirely to the world of objects to which men are seeking to assimilate us, in which they are straining to imprison us" (1952, 22). As stated in the opening epigraph, "a man cannot be free or remain free, except in the degree to which he remains linked with that which transcends him" (1952, 23). It must be noted that the transcendent is not separate or outside us; rather, it is "conceivable in terms of a participation in a reality which overflows and envelopes me, without my being able to view it in any way as external to what I am" (1964, 144).

For Marcel, we appeal to the transcendent by our openness, which is a sign of both our freedom and creativity as human beings. Being creative, says Marcel, "always implies the idea of being open towards others" (1952, 24). Thus Marcel beautifully connects the manner in which we relate to each other as human beings to the manner in which we relate to the transcendent. Although he does not equate *transcendent* with *God*, the association is easily and perhaps justifiably inferred, particularly when Marcel employs the use of capitalization—in the context of discussing the transcendent—when making references to "Other," "One," or "Him." In this way, Marcel is prompting us to simply reason from a position of deep reflection, rather than argue from a position of dogma, regarding insight into the depths of being.

Ultimately, Marcel reminds us, "we do not belong to ourselves: this is certainly the sum and substance, if not of wisdom, at least of any spirituality worthy of the name." These illuminating words of Marcel can be found in his foreword to Kenneth T. Gallagher's (1962) fine analysis of Marcel's philosophy, a study in which Gallagher helps us realize more clearly that, for Marcel, "we do not withdraw from others in order to ensconce ourselves within being. The self to which being is present is not an insular ego which abuts upon a transcendent. The experience of being arises in communion...there is no self except so far as there is communion. My self apart from other selves quite simply is not. It comes to be in communion" (Gallagher, 8). Hence communion is the key to the paradox: "If we can reach the transcendent, then the transcendent is already immanent in our own experience" (Gallagher 1962, 4). The transcendent is the other side of the mystery of our being, and "try as we will, we will only awake to being within being" (Gallagher, 4).

To realize our communion with the transcendent is to be a witness, one who can supply testimony to the experience of participating in the mystery of being. It is the realization of being alive with others. Unfortunately, there are many ways in which such an experience can be numbed, in which the light can be darkened.

Dispiritedness and the Techniques of Degradation
Before applying the above sketch of Marcellian themes to the practice of teaching, we must detour to examine those variables that can counter or squelch the spirit of teaching. Here I want to lead a brief excursion into the land of dispirited teachers in order to identify certain "techniques of degradation" that function to block reflection, being, presence, communion and participation in mystery.

The classroom seems always to be a site of contest between spirit and dispirit. By the terms "spirit" and "dispirit" I do not mean Christian and non-Christian, nor even sacred or profane; rather, in following Marcel, I wish to call attention to the battle between the forces that work to either celebrate or denigrate what is essentially the spirit of being human, that ontological link between the person and the Transcendent. This contest is made manifest through the communication practices of teacher and student, which can be in-spiriting or dis-spiriting in actuality. Regardless of subject matter, the classroom is fundamentally grounded in communication behaviors and the maintenance of relationships. In short, who we are and how we are with others greatly affects what is taught and learned.

The classroom, however, is not constructed in a vacuum or void, but is simply another part of an educational system that is involved in its own battle between spirit and degradation. The educational system, in turn, is embedded in social, economic and political contexts in which the battle is more often likened unto a cultural war. At stake is whether education can be used to enhance or impede the spiritual development of human beings. In question are our pedagogical practices and techniques.

Simply stated, Marcel's notion of techniques of degradation refers to anything that can reduce being to a having orientation. The effects of degradation are alienation and despair—these are the real enemies of education, not ignorance or prejudice, which are merely the fruits of an unreflectiveness toward one's alienated and despairing situation. Thus we are to be watchful regarding any techniques of instilling alienation and despair; from propaganda to genocide to technological progress, techniques of degradation invade our lives threatening "to substitute satisfaction at a material level for spiritual joy, dissatisfaction at a material level for spiritual disquiet" (Marcel 1952, 57).

Marcel highlights two techniques, in particular, as special concerns: the spirit of abstraction and the reduction of being to function. Both of these techniques, again, stem from a having mode of relating to the world. When in operation, they squeeze the soul out of students. Thus what the spiritually sensitive teacher is exhorted by Marcel to do is to assist students in becoming more aware of their spiritual dignity as human beings. Such a pedagogical goal, however, cannot possibly be reached by any arsenal of techniques, but only by being fully present as a person in communion with the transcendent. Therefore, what is most primary and essential is the assistance teachers can provide through encouraging a genuine depth of reflectiveness in learning. What we must fight, then, are those techniques of degradation that reduce the contemplative nature of reflectiveness to abstract thinking.

In his introduction to Marcel's brilliant "existentialist diary" entitled *Being and Having*, James Collins summarizes Marcel's view of the person as "a reflecting exister, whose hold on the real is also his token of participating in being and having the capacity to enter freely into communion with God" (Marcel 1965, xiv). Perhaps the source of all techniques of degradation lies in an active resistance to our ontological need to truly reflect upon our condition. Marcel criticizes a postmodern, post-Christian society as one that increasingly "denies the place of contemplation and shuts out the very possibility of contemplation, such a civilization, I say, sets us inevitably on the road towards a philosophy which is not so much a *love of wisdom* as a *hatred of wisdom*: we ought rather to call it a misosophy" (1952, 65). Marcel adds in another work: "This almost complete vanishing away of the contemplative activity in the modern world has something, at least, to do with the terrible evils from which mankind is suffering" (1952, 122).

Time and space does not allow a full treatment of Marcel's views on the necessity of contemplation, but it must be noted in passing that he identifies contemplation with participation and contrasts the contemplative participant in life with the spectator who merely watches life go by from an alienated vantage point. To the spectator, life is an abstract object. To the contemplative, life is to be lived. To the degree that teachers can make these ideas concrete is the degree to which education for life takes place.

Presence and Reflection in Teaching

The concepts discussed thus far will now be integrated through my sharing of personal reflections on teaching creatively from a Marcellian perspective. I intend to present, albeit briefly, some of the ways that I think we can apply Marcel's wisdom in helping students, and teachers, defend themselves against the techniques of degradation while simultaneously encouraging them to discover their own links to the transcendent. In this way, I hope to more clearly address the conference theme of Christ and Culture.

I would suggest at least four primary steps (not techniques) that teachers can take to hearten and enliven the educational experience of students. The first step is the teacher's willingness to be present to the students. This does not mean that one is continuously at the students' beck and call, but it does mean that one is spiritually available when needed. To be present as a teacher requires the courage to face the freedom and vulnerability of being oneself, openly, in the presence of others. Being present, however, can never be a mere act—it simply cannot be faked.

The second step is creative fidelity. For Marcel, "fidelity" is the "active perpetuation of presence, the renewal of its benefits" (1956, 36). The teacher practices fidelity by recognizing the presence of the students, by seeing the students as beings with presence. The notion of "creative" fidelity refers to the many ways one can be responsive to the presence of others. Marcel strikes an aesthetic parallel here: "If artistic creation is conceivable, it can only be on condition the world is present to the artist in a certain way—present to his heart and to his mind, present to his very being" (1956, 36). Creative fidelity, on the part of the teacher in a classroom, is a form of commitment to a faithful relationship with the students as fellow human beings. Marcel is suggesting something more than an informal pact or agreement to cease hostilities and sit down as peaceful friends; he is referring to the mystery of being in which we must recognize and honor our communion with others. Similar to a marriage vow, what God has joined together let no man or educational system pull apart.

The third step is to encourage what Marcel has termed "secondary reflectiveness," of which contemplation is probably the best example. This may sound easier than it is. Most students have endured a schooling system that has trained them in abstract, critical and analytical thought—and not in contemplative thinking. Most students have been prodded to "get the point" instead of wondering about it. More disconcerting are the typical job constraints facing teachers, especially those in higher education where greater emphasis is placed upon production techniques associated with research, publications, conferences and grant-writing, and not the seemingly unproductive work of contemplating one's existence and meaning in life. Yet, when a teacher allows such reflectiveness—when it is encouraged and rewarded—one realizes through witnessing the students' satisfactions in contemplation just how right Marcel really is when he says we have an urgent inner need for the transcendent.

The fourth step is to be aware of the soulful dimensions of pedagogy, and to guard against utilizing techniques of degradation. By this I mean that we should be conscious of all that we teach and how, and not just what we intend to teach in the abstract. The act of teaching affects souls, not mental banks or knowledge containers. Students attend to what we do not say as much, if not more, as to what we say. Teaching is direct and indirect, blatantly obvious and submerged. Accompanying every lesson plan are "teachings" about what constitutes knowledge and truth, the nature of being and having, the value of openness and availability, and the mystery of the transcendent. The Marcellian inspired teacher will be particularly sensitized to the relationships between mystery, wonder and reverence; and between contemplation, truth and love.

In sum, these four steps involve a pedagogy of freedom fostered by an ethic of care for personal beings. The Marcellian teacher seeks to assist students in the spiritual process of waking up to their own lives, an existential attempt "to trade numbness for awareness" so that one feels "the intensity of moral involvement. It is to feel *personally* about life, to feel the meaning of *personal* answerability, to *personally* care about the increase of good in the world" (Morris 1966, 50). "A really alive person," writes Marcel, "is not merely someone who has a taste for life, but somebody who spreads that taste, showering it, as it were, around him; and a person who is really alive in this way has, quite apart from any tangible achievements of his, something essentially creative about him" (1950, 139).

Conclusion

To summarize, I have attempted to trace a few fundamental themes in the philosophy of Gabriel Marcel that were selected for their potential value and relevance to the heart and soul of teaching. I briefly examined some of the possible insights to be gained regarding the spiritual nature of teaching when we conceive of such an educational practice steeped in an awareness of the ontological mystery of being, the power of presence and availability, and our communal linkage to the transcendent.

From a perspective of the conference theme, Christ and Culture, this essay has sought to offer one interpretation of how to negotiate the tensions of being a Christian intellectual in a culture of unreflective and sometimes hostile noise with no room for mystery. Marcel does not write as a theologian or an evangelist, but I must agree with Sam Keen's high estimation of the value of Marcel's contribution to our understanding of spiritual living: "Awareness of the mysterious character of being and the sacredness of life may not lead to belief in any particular religion, but it does create a spirit of openness within which the word of faith may be heard" (1967, 50). To pause, to be quiet, to contemplate truth and one's existence in a meaning-full universe is a radical venture in a noisy culture, and tantamount to genuine spiritual adventure—an adventure this author hopes leads the wayfarer into the Light. Marcel captures the spiritual essence of genuine education, and the heart and soul of teaching, in these words:

> It might be said that the true questions are those which point, not to anything resembling the solution of an enigma, but rather to a line of direction along which we must move. As we move along the line, we get more and more chances of being visited by a sort of spiritual illumination; for we shall have to acknowledge that Truth can be considered only in this way, as a spirit, as a light (1950, 13).

References

Gallagher, Kenneth T. 1962. *The Philosophy of Gabriel Marcel*. NY: Fordham.

Hanley, Katharine Rose, Trans. 1998. *Gabriel Marcel's Perspectives on The Broken World*. Milwaukee: Marquette University.

Keen, Sam. 1967. *Gabriel Marcel*. Richmond, VA: John Knox.

Marcel, Gabriel. 1965. *Being and Having*. NY: Harper and Row.

---. 1965. *Three Plays*. NY: Hill and Wang.

---. 1964. *Creative Fidelity*. NY: Noonday.

---. 1956. *The Philosophy of Existentialism*. NY: Citadel.

---. 1952. *Man Against Mass Society*. Chicago: Gateway.

---. 1950. *Mystery of Being, Vol. I*. Chicago: Gateway.

Morris, Van Cleve. 1950. *Existentialism in Education*. NY: Harper and Row.

Hermeneutical Adequacy:
A Brief Case for Reading Scripture as *Scripture*

Dan Wilson[*]

Introduction

Man is the measure of all things, of things that are in so far as they are and of things that are not in so far as they are not. Concerning the gods, I cannot know either that they exist or that they do not exist; for there is much that prevents one's knowing: the obscurity of the subject and the shortness of man's life. (Diogenes Laertius 9.5)
                                                                    Protagoras

All Scripture is God-breathed and is useful for teaching, rebuking, correcting and training in righteousness, so that the man of God may be thoroughly equipped for every good work. 2 Timothy 3:16-17 (NIV)
                                                                    Paul

While it is obvious that the agnosticism of Protagoras and the Christian theism of the Apostle Paul stand in stark distinction, it is also axiomatic that their respective positions determined their hermeneutic and their hermeneutical goals. The skepticism, relativism, and even playfulness of the classical Greek sophists like Protagoras have become pervasive again in the universities of the Western world.[1] Reminiscent of the attitudes and experience of the early sophists, contemporary literary theorists opt for a hermeneutic of deconstruction that rejects logocentrism[2] and belief in absolute truth. In the title of his

---

[*] When Dr. Wilson presented this paper, he was a Ph.D. candidate at Mid-America Baptist Theological Seminary in New Testament and Greek. He was serving as an adjunct teaching a full-time load in the Classics Section of the Foreign Languages and Literatures Department of The University of Memphis and as an adjunct Greek instructor at Mid-America Baptist Theological Seminary. At present, Dr. Wilson is Assistant Professor of Christian Studies, specializing in the New Testament, at Bryan College. In addition to the field of hermeneutics, Dr. Wilson's research interests lie in classical rhetoric and rhetorical theory, cultural anthropology of ancient Mediterranean peoples, contemporary cultural studies, and Christian apologetics. His dissertation was entitled *Jesus' Rhetoric of Authority in the Temple Conflict Narrative: A Rhetorical Analysis of Matthew 21-23*. He can be reached at wilsonda@bryan.edu or www.bryan.edu.

[1] George A. Kennedy, *Classical Rhetoric and Its Christian and Secular Tradition from Ancient to Modern Times*, 2d revised and enlarged (Chapel Hill, NC: University of North Carolina Press) 37-38. See also Steven Mailloux, *Rhetoric, Sophistry, Pragmatism*, (New York: Cambridge University Press, 1989).

[2] *Logocentrism* is a catchall term for Western thinkers' preoccupation with meaning, rationality, and truth.

book Stanley Fish posed the question, "Is There a Text in This Class?", thus typifying this intellectual move.[3]   Christians, however, hold the Bible as the "text," and this clashes with the current intellectual climate of postmodernists like Fish. Postmodern literary theorists find no place and no grace for Christians who read Scripture as Scripture.

This Graceless Age: Postmodern Hermeneutics—Undoers and Unbelievers

Gone are the days when Christian humanists and secular humanists really waged war over the truth, philosophical or otherwise, in an effort to *get it right*, i.e. to get the correct interpretation of a text. Ushering in this graceless age, Nietzsche, Feuerbach, de Saussure, Foucault, Derrida, Rorty, and Fish undermined the old metaphysical and epistemological givens of Modernity, especially as they relate to interpreting authors and their texts in general and the Scriptures in particular.

Why has the faith been undone that authors actually could be understood, intentions grasped, and proper interpretation made? The answer lies in the metaphysical position taken by Postmoderns and their forerunners, and that is the position of non-realism. The presupposition of non-realism surfaces in a telling way in Jacques Derrida's theory of language, for to him, "There is nothing outside the text." This means that all language and all thought, every word and every concept, is part of a worldwide web of signifiers. Derrida, following de Saussure, holds to differential, not referential, linguistics. In such a contingent language system there is an endless interplay of signifiers but there is no "reality" there, just differences.

From the non-realist position, it follows then that words do not mean things and that "things" as we conceive of them are really indeterminate and mere projections of reality. Derrida, more than any other postmodern figure, dismantles the figure of the author and the author as determiner of meaning, which is the lynch pin of the metaphysical scaffolding of Western philosophy.[4] As a hermeneutical non-realist, there is no such thing as an absolute or God's-Eye-View of reality, only a number of finite and fallible human perspectives. If, therefore, philosophy is merely a genre of literary rhetoric, then the method of deconstruction (strangely) follows. Kevin Vanhoozer summarizes Derrida's critical sentiment:

---

[3] Stanley Fish, *Is There a Text in This Class? The Authority of Interpretive Communities*, (Cambridge MA: Harvard University Press, 1980).

[4] Kevin J. Vanhoozer, *Is There a Meaning in This Text?: the Bible, the Reader, and the Morality of Literary Knowledge*, (Grand Rapids: Zondervan, 1998), 48. This work is the magisterial critique of postmodern hermeneutics, taking much from Anthony Thiselton's thought even further and in a more user-friendly way. In addition to critique, Vanhoozer proffers a stout philosophical and theological defense of hermeneutical realism and adequacy.

Now neither priests, who supposedly speak for God, nor philosophers, who supposedly speak for Reason, should be trusted; this "logocentric" claim to speak from a privileged perspective (e.g. Reason, the Word of God) is a bluff that must be called, or better, 'deconstructed.'[5]

Now when a Christian utters the phrase, "the Bible says . . . ," he or she is not met with an opponent differing over points of fact but with a deconstructionist saying, "How dare you tell me what this text means or what I should be interested in or what to do with a text!" In particular, Fish holds that interpretive communities must be free of "correct interpretations" to pursue their own interests. (But how stable is the notion of community as a locus for meaning?) The neo-pragmatist is, hermeneutically speaking, pro-choice. Neither the author nor even the notion of truth has any authority for a deconstructionist. Truth gets a demotion from being timeless and absolute to "what is good for us to believe here and now" or "what works for me in this situation."

Now the job of the literary critic is "to identify point of failure in a system, points at which it is able to feign coherence only by excluding and forgetting that which it cannot assimilate, the absolute indigestible, that which is 'other' to it."[6] The metaphysical assault on authors and authorial intention bleeds over to the status of texts as texts. Along the same lines Richard Rorty asks, "Can the ubiquity of language even really be taken seriously?"[7] Rorty added:

> For all we know or should care, Aristotle's metaphorical use of *ousia*, St. Paul's metaphorical use of *agape*, and Newton's metaphorical use of *gravitas*, were the results of cosmic rays scrambling the fine structures of some crucial neurons in their respective brains. . . . It hardly matters how the trick was done. The results are marvelous. There had never been such things before.[8]

This eliminates the distinction between interpreting texts and using them—there is no "getting it right." Fish states this total shift from the traditional locus of meaning: "I now believe that interpretation is the source of texts, facts, authors, and intentions."[9]

---

[5] Ibid., 22.

[6] Elizabeth Castelli, Stephen D. Moore, eds. et al, *The Postmodern Bible*, (New Haven: Yale University Press, 1995), 120.

[7] Richard Rorty, "Philosophy and Pragmatism," in *After Philosophy: End or Transformation?*, edited by K. Baynes, J. Bohman, and T. McCarthy, (Cambridge, MA: MIT Press, 1987), 57.

[8] Rorty, *Contingency, Irony, and Solidarity*, (Cambridge: Cambridge University Press, 1989), 16.

[9] Fish, *Is There a Text?*, 16.

Interpretation can now be a hostile act in which interpreter "victimizes" the text, since authors, their intentions, and their texts are not really theirs but really ours, our projections. Howard Felerpin concludes:

> The new reader sounds very much like the old Author whose death he is announcing, his authoritarian tone itself symptomatic of the authority vacuum left by the demise of the Author and the communal sanctions that authorize Him.[10]

The Postmodern Bible: Hermeneutical Agnosticism—Allegorists and Gnostics

Even if postmodern interpretation had not entered directly into Biblical and theological studies,[11] the deconstruction of orthodox Christian belief and traditional Biblical interpretation must be defended from this hermeneutical crisis rampant in the humanities. The title "G/god's H/holy and indeterminate W/word(s)" spells disaster for Christianity, especially as it tries to influence culture as salt and light.

Is the Biblical text a lamp to our feet and a light to our path, or an unending labyrinth that leads everywhere and nowhere at once? When interpreting the Bible, postmoderns insist that the meaning of texts is undecidable—"there is more that one way to skin a text."[12] What is left of literary criticism if there are no facts, only playful interpretations which are mere power plays? "The prime rule for [postmodern] hermeneutics, as in real estate, is 'location, location, location.'"[13] The context of the hermeneut, not the text, is determinative of meaning. The interpretation of Moses and the Exodus varies with the location of the interpreter, whether the act of interpretation happens among contemporary Orthodox Jews, seventeenth century Puritans, Latin American Catholic Marxists, or an African American Sunday School class.

Who or what is "Luke"? The Biblical scholars have had their answers. When couched in the age of Modernism, higher critical and liberal scholars made a rather pessimistic conclusion that the documents called the *Gospel According to Luke* and *The Book of Acts* were definitely not written by Luke, the dear physician, supposed companion of the Apostle Paul. On the other hand, conservative and evangelical scholars have robustly defended the proposition that this Luke actually penned *Luke* and *Acts* in

---

[10] Howard Felerpin, *Beyond Deconstruction: The Abuses of Literary Theory*, (Oxford: Clarendon, 1985), 203.

[11] See Stephen D. Moore's, *Literary Criticism and the Gospels: The Theoretical Challenge*, (New Haven: Yale, 1989); and *Poststructuralism and the New Testament: Derrida and Foucault at the Foot of the Cross*, (Minneapolis: Fortress Press, 1994).

[12] Vanhoozer, 111.

[13] Ibid., 112.

the A.D. sixties. Which of the two basic options is correct? Couched in the unsettling age of Postmodernism, the question is entirely moot! The postmodern critics say: "'Luke' is the name we give to our best interpretation; 'Luke' is a projection of our desire for a unifying center and ground to textual meaning, 'Luke' is an expression of the reader's will; I am 'Luke.'"[14] In critique, Kevin Vanhoozer notes that such a postmodern move is remarkably similar to the interpretive patterns of Gnostics of old and the allegorists from the Alexandria School or Medieval times.

Vanhoozer thinks that both the Gnostics and postmoderns bear the burden of a radical dualism: Gnostics held to a dichotomy of body and spirit while postmoderns hold to a radical dichotomy of language and the world. Gnostics and postmoderns deny the Incarnation—the preeminent Christian premise that the Word became flesh.[15] (So, its *deja vu* all over again.)[16] Just as in the Gnostic view, salvation is gained through the right special knowledge, so too are postmoderns liberated (saved) by a certain kind of knowledge—the knowledge of *différance* (to use Derrida's term). This salvation is the liberation from totalizing and oppressive systems. This knowledge of the secret way language works does not come by rationality but by something akin to gnosis—"quasi-mystic intuition."[17] Describing Scripture as the ineffable rhetoric of the Divine, incomprehensible to humankind, is the tendency of postmodern hyperspiritual and hypertextual Biblical interpretation. Is there no alternative between absolute and anarchic interpretation, or between a Gnostic appeal to hidden meanings and an agnostic abandonment of the quest for meaning?

This Enabling Grace: Christian Hermeneutics—Charity, Humility, and Dignity

Vanhoozer builds a compelling defense for hermeneutical realism and adequacy by first showing the fundamental error in postmodern hermeneutics. The error is a theological one and must be fixed theologically. He holds that, "the contemporary malaise on postmodern literary theory ultimately stems . . . from this non-realist denial of the created order."[18] The logical fruit of the death of God movement is the disappearance of absolute truth, univocal meaning in world history, and the authority of the Author and human authors. Atheism or radical agnosticism has had its effect on the theory of general hermeneutics. One postmodern literary thinker admitted this crucial link. The refusal to assign fixed meaning either to the world or to texts "liberates an activity we may call countertheological, properly revolutionary, for to refuse meaning is

---

[14] Ibid., 88.

[15] Ibid., 121.

[16] Anecdotal aphorism attributed to Yogi Berra, baseball manager and lay philosopher.

[17] Ibid., 122.

[18] Ibid., 49.

finally to refuse God."[19] Derrida's, et al, deconstruction of the author is more or less direct consequence of Nietzsche's announcement of the death of God.

Christians, however, know God is not dead, for he exists, he speaks, and he acts in a saving way. Here is where Vanhoozer's philosophical description of hermeneutics provides both a mode of critiquing postmodern literary theory and a positive theological formulation of an adequate Christian hermeneutic. Vanhoozer states, "Implicit in the question of meaning are questions of the nature of reality, the possibility of knowledge, and the criteria of morality."[20] Thus, any theory of hermeneutic consists of a triad: metaphysics, epistemology, and ethics.

Vanhoozer rightly espouses an unabashedly Augustinian approach. Augustine's *credo ut intelligam* (I believe in order to understand) makes as an act of faith the assumption that there is meaning in texts. Instead of a hermeneutic of suspicion, a Christian hermeneutic is one of charity. This follows from the recognition of the divine origin and gift of language. Vanhoozer's triadic framework reflects his view of the role of the Trinity in communication and understanding.

> God's very being is a self-communicative act that both constitutes and enacts the covenant discourse: speaker (Father), Word (Son), and reception (Spirit) are all interrelated. Human communication is a similarly covenantal affair, though we cannot pour ourselves into our communicative acts and ensure their effects as God can through his Word and Spirit.[21]

It is only this theistic assumption that underwrites a realistic and coherent account of the capacity of human speech to communicate meaning and feeling. Reading is something more than just the play of signs. I concur with Vanhoozer who declares: "I believe in hermeneutical realism, I believe in hermeneutical rationality, and I believe in hermeneutical responsibility."[22] God as Creator insures that authors can speak as communicative agents, made in his image. The Incarnation insures that, like God, humans can communicate ideas and intentions through speech acts signified not just through signs. The Spirit insures that readers can understand adequately.

What Vanhoozer endorses is not a hermeneutic of glory; he is not avowing a return to the "intentional fallacy" symptomatic of a hermeneutical absolutism. Rather, out of a

---

[19] Roland Barthes, "Death of Author," in *The Rustle of Language*, trans. Richard Howard (New York: Hill and Wang, 1986), 54.

[20] Vanhoozer, 19.

[21] Ibid., 456-57.

[22] Ibid., 31.

hermeneutic of charity comes humility. "Humans have the dignity of communicative agency, though not its perfection."[23]

This resounds like an amended version of the great doctrine of the perspicuity of Scripture made famous by Martin Luther. Luther maintained that although God is inscrutable, he has not left himself incomprehensible. While the Nicene Creed says, "God spoke through the prophets . . . ," this does not mean a Christian interpreter claims to understand perfectly. Interpretation does not have to be an all-or-nothing affair, and, since we are not God, we need not choose between a meaning that is wholly determinative and a meaning that is wholly indeterminate.[24]

Besides humility, the Christian hermeneutic of charity includes dignity. "What the deconstructor finds objectionable about Christology is the claim that Jesus is a reliable sign of God's own being and presence."[25] Yet it is the dignity rooted in the grace gift of language that allows for our adequate understanding of Jesus as a reliable sign of God's redeeming work. The deconstructor's skepticism of signs begins to look indistinguishable from the vice of pride. But it is the dignity and humility of grace that guard against both old types of pride (the old hermeneutical absolutism) and new types of pride (the new hermeneutical relativism). What deconstructors miss, or dismiss, is that their hermeneutical relativism is actually a new, and backhanded, expression of *hermeneutical absolutism*.[26]

Deconstructors show themselves to be inconsistent in the practice of their hermeneutic of suspicion for they sometimes encounter something other than their own projections in texts. It is also odd that deconstructors do not see that the ethical assertion, "There are absolutely no absolutes," is self-refuting and absurd. They likewise miss the problematic nature of their position on literary ethics (i.e. the ethics of reading). Without a qualm they assert, "There is absolutely no meaning in this text except for the meaning that I declare it has."

---

[23] Ibid., 457.

[24] Take, for example, the issue of metaphors. Metaphors may have a relatively determinate meaning without being exhaustively specifiable. Understanding God as Father may not yield a single correct sense, and it surely does not yield a literalistic sense, but it does give rise to a relatively stable model that exercises a "regulative" function for subsequent language and thought about God." In certain respects (in terms of origin or creation, care, and providence), God is our Father. See Janet Martin Soskice, *Metaphor and Religious Language*, (Oxford: Clarendon, 1985).

[25] Ibid., 86.

[26] The only absolute is that there are none, nor are there any proper or adequate interpretations of reality—whether intentions or texts of authors.

The truth, however is that we are not masters of language nor slaves to the indeterminacy of language, but rather citizens of language. Augustine was right; things are as they are because we live in the City of God. Therefore, in view of the covenant of communication and understanding, we ought to be humble while holding to our dignity as we make sense of texts. We are made adequate for this by grace. Thus we can read texts and understand authorial intent adequately as well as read and understand Scripture as *Scripture*.

> *You then, my son, be strong in the grace that is in Christ Jesus. And the things you have heard me say in the presence of many witnesses entrust to reliable [sufficient] men who will also be qualified [adequate] to teach others.   2 Timothy 2:1-2 (NIV)*

Alexander Hamilton, Montesquieu and the Humanity of the Modern Commercial Republic

John Stack[*]

What are we to make of the fact that modern life is shot through with commerce? In coming to grips with such a fundamental question, it behooves us to turn to the thought of Alexander Hamilton, one of the primary architects of the American commercial republic. It is generally acknowledged that, with the possible exception of James Madison, Hamilton did more than anyone to defend and explain the United States Constitution. In light of his tremendous influence on the American founding and the subsequent development of the American political regime, it is worth considering why he championed the commercial way of life. To this end, I first explore the connection Hamilton saw between the commercial republic and a type of virtue and attempt to defend him against the charges that he promoted avarice and that he scorned merchants. I then argue that to the extent that the modern commercial republic ameliorates some of antiquity's harsh inhumanities, that republic is more conducive than was the ancient martial republic to a culture of life. The many other fundamental disagreements between the ancient and modern political philosophers, some of which may also bear on the culture of life, are beyond the scope of this article. The totality of ancient thought may be more compatible with the culture of life than are most modern teachings. I argue that the modern embrace of commerce, though, appears to be more affirming and supportive of a culture of life than is the ancient alternative.

The Commercial Republic Nourishes Commercial Virtues

Hamilton viewed himself as practicing a statesmanship aimed at inculcating and preserving sufficient virtue among his fellow citizens for self-government. To be sure, he realized that it would utopian to expect more than a few citizens to exercise a virtue of a higher order, so he and other founders took care to establish, and even to rely heavily upon, institutional that republican government "presupposes the existence" of civic virtue to a greater extent than does any other contrivances and "effectual precautions" to help

---

[*] John Stack, Providence Academy, Plymouth, MN. An earlier version of this article was published in the *Catholic Social Science Review*, Vol. V, 200, pages 81-94. This revision is published with permission of *CSSR*. Some of the ideas presented in this article were drawn from research conducted during the time the author had a Calihan Research Assistance Fellowship, sponsored by the Acton Institute for the Study of Religion and Liberty, Grand Rapids, MI.

protect liberty.[1] They also realized, however, political regime.[2] Hamilton publicly acknowledged that "[t]he institution of delegated power implies that there is a portion of virtue and honor among mankind, which may be a reasonable foundation of confidence."[3] Associating a "portion of virtue and honor among mankind" with one of the institutions of republican government that increases the likelihood that such government is also free, Hamilton would have been loath to undermine what he proclaimed to be a "reasonable foundation for confidence."

Hamilton thought the modern commercial republic and the commercial virtues it fosters such as diligence, thrift, foresight, sobriety, prudence and strenuous enterprise would help to maintain "a portion of virtue and honor among mankind." He never denied that some people have higher callings than to practice the virtues that lead to commercial prosperity, but he figured that as America was by no means a "nation of philosophers," most Americans most of the time would be better off practicing the commercial virtues.[4]

Some scholars assert that in championing a commercial republic, Hamilton promoted avarice. This assertion is worth taking seriously because, if true, it would be hard to avoid the conclusion that Hamilton's vision of America had a tendency to undermine virtue by promoting vice. Marc F. Plattner asserts that "[f]ar from encouraging public spirited virtue, it [Hamilton's praise of the political utility of commerce] promotes what traditionally has been considered a vice—namely avarice."[5] In a similar vein, James F. Pontuso writes that Hamilton "unabashedly appealed to the avarice of his fellow citizens."[6]

---

[1] *Federalist* No. 57, p. 384. (Unless otherwise indicated, *Federalist Papers* quoted in this essay were written by Hamilton). No. 57 was written by Madison. In other essays, Hamilton observes that statesmen should not expect citizens to exercise "superior virtue," "stern virtue," or "superlative virtue" (*Federalist* No. 22, 73 and 75; pp. 142, 493, 505). All parenthetical page citations from *The Federalist* refer to Jacob E. Cooke's edition of the work (Middletown, Connecticut: Wesleyan University Press, 1961).

[2] *Federalist* No. 55, p. 378 (Madison).

[3] *Federalist* No. 76, p. 514.

[4] *Federalist* No. 49, p. 340 (Madison).

[5] "American Democracy and the Acquisitive Spirit," in Robert A. Goldwin and William A. Schambra, eds., *How Capitalistic Is the Constitution?* (Washington, D.C.: American Enterprise Institute for Public Policy Research, 1982), p. 8.

[6] "Constitution-Making and the 'New Political Science': Alexander Hamilton's America," p. 3. The paper was delivered at the 1999 Annual Meeting of the American Political Science Association, Atlanta, Ga., September 2-5, 1999 and can be accessed at http://pro.harvard.edu/abstracts/062/062001PontusoJam.html.

A careful analysis of *The Federalist* calls these assertions into question.[7]

The term "avarice" appears a dozen times in the work, each time it is used by Hamilton, and in nearly every instance (with two possible exceptions considered below) the term is employed in an unambiguously negative sense. Typical examples of its usages include the first *Federalist* essay, where Hamilton lists avarice second among four motives that are "not . . . laudable" (p. 5), and *Federalist* No. 6, where he identifies avarice as one of the "irregular and violent propensities" (p. 32) and remarks that the Duke of Marlborough's avarice prolonged the War of the Spanish Succession "beyond the limits marked out by sound policy" (p. 33). Also, in *Federalist* No. 15 Hamilton writes: "I have unfolded to you a complication of the dangers to which you would be exposed should you permit that sacred knot which binds the people of America together to be severed or dissolved by ambition or by avarice, by jealousy or by misrepresentation" (pp. 89-90). Hamilton nowhere mentions how "that sacred knot" was established. He presupposes that it exists, and assumes it is worth preserving. He lets it be known that whether the "sacred knot" will be preserved depends at least to some extent upon the choices of the people. It would "be severed or dissolved" by any of the four vices he lists. It is scarcely possible that Hamilton would promote one of these vices insofar as he realizes it undermines "that sacred knot which binds the people of America together."

The term "avaricious" appears four times in *The Federalist*. As was the case with "avarice," the term only appears in papers written by Hamilton. In addition, every time "avaricious" appears in the work, the term is given an unambiguously negative connotation. In *Federalist* No. 71, Hamilton observes that "[t]hey [the people] know from experience, that they sometimes err; and the wonder is, that they so seldom err as they do; beset as they continually are by . . . the avaricious, [and] the desperate; . . . " (482). Similarly, in *Federalist* No. 72, Hamilton remarks that "[a]n avaricious man, who might happen to fill the [executive] offices, . . . might not scruple to have recourse to the most corrupt expedients to make the harvest as abundant as it was transitory" (489). Hamilton also points out in this essay that the avaricious man is sometimes so dominated by avarice that it "would be likely to get the victory over his caution, his vanity, or his ambition" (489). Finally, in *Federalist* No. 75, Hamilton expresses concern that "[a]n avaricious man might betray the interests of the state" to gain wealth (505).

Neither Plattner nor Pontuso mention Hamilton's use of the term "avaricious." If Hamilton intended to "promote . . . avarice," one wonders why he saw fit to cast the avaricious man in such a denigrating light. A reading of *The Federalist* which accounts

---

[7] *The Federalist* was written by Alexander Hamilton, James Madison and John Jay under the pseudonym Publius. According to Douglass Adair, Hamilton wrote 51 papers, Madison 29 and Jay 5. "The Authorship of the Disputed Federalist Papers," in *Fame and the Founding Fathers: Essays by Douglass Adair*, edited by Trevor Colbourn. (New York: W.W. Norton, 1974), pp. 27-74.

for each of the work's references to the terms "avarice" and "avaricious" casts doubt upon the assertion that Hamilton's praise of the political utility of commerce promote avarice. Rather, Hamilton thought that the commercial way of life would foster commercial virtues and, all things considered, thereby improve the characters of most Americans.

Plattner refers to only one of the dozen times the term "avarice" appears in Hamilton's *Federalist* essays. He quotes extensively from *Federalist* No. 12, where Hamilton writes:

> The prosperity of commerce is now perceived and acknowledged by all enlightened statesmen to be the most useful as well as the most productive source of national wealth, and has accordingly become a primary object of their political cares. By multiplying the means of gratification, by promoting the introduction and circulation of the precious metals, those darling objects of human avarice and enterprise, it serves to vivify all the channels of industry and to make them flow with greater activity and copiousness. The assiduous merchant, the laborious husbandman, the active mechanic, and the industrious manufacturer—all orders of men look forward with eager expectation and growing alacrity to the pleasing reward of their toils. (73-74).

Nowhere in the passage above does Hamilton encourage the promotion of avarice. To be sure, he refers to "the precious metals" as "those darling objects of human avarice and enterprise" (73). However, Hamilton is here noting a statement of fact, he is not advancing a judgment about that fact. In this particular instance, he neither commends nor condemns the fact. If this were the only mention of avarice in *The Federalist*, it would not be wholly implausible to conclude that Hamilton's use of the term is shrouded in some degree of ambiguity. However, as there are ten references to avarice with negative connotations, along with four references denigrating to the avaricious man, it is unwarranted to view *The Federalist* and the Constitution as avarice-promoting works. Such a view is not only inconsistent with a careful reading of these texts but it may also have politically harmful effects insofar as it has the tendency of undermining the attachment of decent American citizens to the principles of their political regime.

If America's founding principles promote avarice, then it would seem that the extent to which devout Christians may support the American political regime would have to be diminished. Christ exhorts us to "Watch and be on your guard against avarice of any kind, for life does not consist of possessions, even when someone has more than he needs" (*Luke* 12:15). St. Paul writes that "the love of money [not money itself] is the root of all evil" (1 *Timothy* 6:10). Plattner points out that avarice "traditionally has been considered a vice," which seems to imply that it is no longer seen in this way (8). This implication, however, receives no support from either Christianity or the American political regime. "Avarice" remains one of the seven deadly sins and, along with the term "avaricious," is condemned fourteen times in *The Federalist*.

In response to the comments made above, one might point to *Federalist* No. 31, where Hamilton refers to "the usual sharp-sightedness of avarice" (193). However, while Hamilton here attributes the quality of sharp-sightedness to a vice, he by no means implies that avarice is worth promoting. To think that he so implies would be similar to thinking that in exhorting us to "be as cunning as snakes" Christ wanted us to be snakes (*Matthew* 10:16). This view is mistaken because it fails to acknowledge that Christ also wanted us to be "as innocent as doves." Just as one may be cunning without being a snake, so too one may seek sharp-sightedness but abhor avarice.[8]

The assertion that Hamilton promotes avarice goes too far in one direction and Naomi Emery's claim that Hamilton scorned commercial pursuits leans too far in the other. She writes:

What resentments [fueled by Hamilton's father leaving the family when Alexander was ten] filled her [Hamilton's mother] or her children are conjectural, but they may have resulted in Alexander's later scorn for purely commercial pursuits, in his sense of merchants to be used in the interests of the state. Years later in an outburst to his friend John Laurens he wrote, 'You know I hate [the] money making men.'"[9]

Hamilton's comment in this letter to Laurens is striking because it is one of a very few instances of which scholars are aware in which Hamilton speaks disparagingly about "money making men." In light of the importance Emery attaches to the observation, the context in which it was made is worth recounting.[10]

Silas Deane was chosen in March, 1776, to represent the United Colonies in Europe. One of his responsibilities in this capacity was to secure military supplies from France. After Dean single-handedly carried out this work for almost half a year, Benjamin Franklin and Arthur Lee were selected, along with Dean, to a committee entrusted with the responsibility of securing the supplies. After treaties were signed with France in February, 1778, Deane was notified that he had been recalled by Congress, chiefly

---

[8] In *Federalist* #72, Hamilton considers the possibility that in certain circumstances, the "avaricious man's . . . avarice might be a guard upon his avarice" (489). As elsewhere in the *Federalist*, avarice is here presented as something to be guarded against.

[9] Naomi Emery, *Alexander Hamilton: An Intimate Portrait*, (New York: G.P. Putnam's Sons, 1982), p. 18. The last line of the excerpt is quoted from a letter from Hamilton to John Laurens, May 22, 1779, *Papers of Alexander Hamilton* [hereafter referred to as *PAH*], Harold C. Syrett, ed. and Jacob E. Cooke, assoc. ed. (New York: Colombia University Press), vol. 2, p. 53. The word "the" does not appear between "hate" and "money" in Hamilton's letter, so Emery probably inserted it into the quotation.

[10] The historical context presented here draws heavily from Syrett's *Papers of Alexander Hamilton*, vol. 2, p. 54.

because Lee leveled the charge that France had already given military supplies to the United States and Deane intended to divert to himself any money appropriated by Congress for the purchase of the supplies. According to Harold C. Syrett, "Deane's accounts were never settled during his lifetime, and by the end of the Revolution he was an exile."[11]

In the letter to Laurens, Hamilton writes: "I hate money making men—I am no partisan of Deane—But Lee ought not to be supported." Hamilton then argues that it would be imprudent to credit Lee's accusations, in part because Vergennes, the Minister of France, distrusted Lee, as did the Court of Spain. In light of these facts, when Hamilton writes that he "hate[s} the money making men," he means that he does not sanction the dishonest behavior of which Deane had been accused.[12] Also, the letter to Laurens was written during the Revolutionary War, from one military officer to another. Forrest McDonald's description of some of the practices in the colonies at this time helps us to better understand why patriotic officers might have been disgusted with the behavior of some of their fellow Americans:

> Meanwhile, Americans on all levels, not just in Congress, were disregarding honor, and even decency in their actions. Merchants were profiteering through price-gouging and manipulation of markets; they preyed upon the very troops defending them . . . In New England state politicians played loose with the war effort in order to facilitate private speculations.[13]

Far from Hamilton's scorning merchants, as Emery would have us believe, Hamilton regards them as the "natural representatives" in the new American political regime.[14] Emery asserts that Hamilton saw "merchants as tools to be used in the interests of the state" but she nowhere tries to substantiate this assertion nor does she even attempt to explain how merchants might be used in this way. The primary reason Hamilton presents for opposing "[e]xhorbitant duties on imported articles" is that such duties "oppress the

---

[11] *Ibid.,* p. 53.

[12] *Ibid.* Unlike Hamilton, John Laurens's father Henry, a South Carolina delegate to Congress, gave credence to Lee's charges against Deane.

[13] Forrest McDonald, *Alexander Hamilton: A Biography* (New York: W.W. Norton & Company, 1982), pp. 19-20.

[14] *Federalist* No. 35, p. 220. Not all the founders shared this view. Thomas Jefferson, for example, entertained an entirely different opinion of merchants than that presented in the *Federalist*: "The cultivators of the earth are the most virtuous citizens and possess most of *amor patriae*. Merchants are the least virtuous, and possess the least of the *amor patriae*." (quoted from "Answers to Demeunier's First Queries, January 24, 1786," in *Papers of Thomas Jefferson*, vol. 10, p. 16).

merchant," especially "when the markets happen to be overstocked" (216). If Emery's claim that Hamilton saw merchants as tools "to be used in the interests of the state" were accurate, we would not expect Hamilton to care if merchants were oppressed. An oppressed person is used merely as a means to an end, and I argue below that it is apparent from passages in the *Federalist* that Hamilton opposed oppressing merchants.

"Merchant" appears eleven times in *The Federalist*, and ten of these usages appear in essays written by Hamilton. The term is nowhere in the document given a negative connotation and most citizens would be pleased to have the commercial virtues Hamilton attributes to the merchant applied to themselves. In *Federalist* No. 11, he recommends conditions that would make "the operations of the merchant . . . less liable to any considerable obstruction, or stagnation," thereby implying that the merchant's operations are good for the merchant and/or the country (71). He writes in *Federalist* No. 12 that "[t]he assiduous merchant, the laborious husbandman, the active mechanic, and the industrious manufacturer, all orders of men look forward with eager expectation and growing alacrity to this pleasing reward of their toils" (74).[15]

"Merchant" appears seven times in Hamilton's *Federalist* No. 35. He mentions that "discerning citizens," many of whom "are immediately connected with the operations of commerce . . . know that the merchant is their natural patron and friend" (219). Such citizens "are aware that however great the confidence they may justly feel in their own good sense, their interests can be more effectually promoted by the merchant than by themselves" (219). Hamilton then asks: "Will not the merchant understand and be disposed to cultivate as far as may be proper the interests of the mechanic and manufacturing arts to which his commerce is so nearly allied?" (221). We would not expect a man who scorned commercial pursuits to so eloquently describe how merchants help "discerning citizens."

As was the case with "merchant," the term "merchants" also appears eleven times in *The Federalist*, and all but one of these references appear in papers written by Hamilton. With two exceptions, which concern English merchants rather than their American counterparts, Hamilton associates only praiseworthy characteristics with merchants.[16] He refers in *Federalist* No. 11 to "[t]hat unequalled [sic] spirit of enterprise, which signalises

---

[15] One who is assiduous is "[c]onstant in application to the business in hand, persevering, sedulous, unwearyingly diligent." *The Compact Edition of the Oxford English Dictionary* (Glasgow: Oxford University Press, 1971), vol. 1, p. 127.

[16] In the only reference to merchants not made by Hamilton that appears in the work, in *Federalist* No. 4, John Jay praises "the enterprize [sic] and address of our merchants" (19). The only disparaging comments made about merchants in the Federalist are contained in No. 6, where Hamilton argues that the War of Jenkins' Ear "sprang from the attempts of the English merchants to prosecute an illicit trade with the Spanish main" and that "[t]he complaints of the [English] merchants kindled a violent flame throughout" Europe that led to war (34).

[sic] the genius of the American Merchants and Navigators, and which is in itself an inexhaustible mine of national wealth" (69). Hamilton also points out in *Federalist* No. 35 "that the influence and weight and superior acquirements of the merchants render them more equal [than mechanics and manufacturers] to a contest with any spirit which might happen to infuse itself into the public councils unfriendly to the manufacturing and trading interests" (219).

The Modern Commercial Republic Ameliorates Some of Antiquity's Harsh Inhumanities

Hamilton advocated the pursuit of commerce but discouraged avarice. His ideal merchant is "assiduous," infected with the "spirit of enterprise" and is the "natural patron and friend" of "discerning citizens," without being avaricious (74, 69, 219). We also noted earlier that "[m]any," not all, of these "discerning citizens" "are immediately connected with the operations of commerce" (219). Insofar as Hamilton's merchant is the "natural patron and friend" of "discerning citizens," we would expect this merchant and anyone worthy of the name "discerning citizen" to realize that people are America's best asset and therefore to choose the population growth associated with a culture of life and to eschew the infanticides, abortions, forced miscarriages and homosexual actions in the culture of death. The first three sins kill (in a worldly sense) lives already created while homosexual actions simulate procreative actions without the possibility of procreation. The victims of the first three sins were made in the image and likeness of God and will live forever. Those who engage in homosexual actions are also made in God's image and likeness but their homosexual actions do not create life.

Hamilton and his wife helped God bring nine children into the world and he rejected infanticide:

> When Hamilton contemplated certain harsh features of antiquity, he recoiled in horror. Concerning the Spartan practice of exposing infants who were deformed, sickly, or weak, his notes on Plutarch remark: 'A horrid practice, mentioned with no mark of disapprobation.' As remarkable to Hamilton as the horrid practice of infanticide was the lack of disapproval of this Spartan practice by the ancient non-Spartan [Plutarch] who wrote about it.[17]

In promoting the modern commercial republic, Hamilton rejected the teachings of ancient thinkers such as Aristotle, Plato and Plutarch. They viewed the pursuit of commerce and civic virtue as mutually exclusive because the latter requires a considerable degree of

---

[17] Quoted from Harvey Flaumenhaft, *The Effective Republic: Administration and Constitution in the Thought of Alexander Hamilton* (Durham: Duke University Press, 1992), p. 29.

self-abnegation while the former is usually driven by, and unleashes selfish desires.[18] The ancient thinkers looked down on commerce to such an extent that Aristotle excluded merchants from what he considered the best regime.[19]

As we have seen, Hamilton, contra the ancient thinkers, considered merchants to be the "natural representatives" of the new American political regime.[20] This view of merchants is most comprehensively articulated and defended by Montesquieu. In *Federalist* No. 9, Hamilton refers to Montesquieu as "that great man," (p. 52) and in *Federalist* No. 78 he writes of "the celebrated Montesquieu" (p. 523). Montesquieu argued that the more humane and civilized way of life fostered by commerce is superior to the harsh features of antiquity. We noted earlier that Hamilton found it remarkable that Plutarch did not mark his disapproval of "the horrid practice of infanticide." The following observations from the *Politics* suggest that although Aristotle did not sanction infanticide, as Hamilton understood Plutarch to do, Aristotle advocated forced miscarriages, in certain situations:

Concerning exposure and rearing of offspring when they are born, let there be a law that no deformed [child] should be raised, but that none should be exposed after they are born on account of number of offspring, where the arrangement of customs forbids [procreation beyond a certain number]. A number should indeed be defined for procreation, but in cases of births in consequence of intercourse contrary to these, abortion should be induced before perception and life arises (what is holy and what is not will be defined by reference to perception and life)."[21]

Similarly, Plato's Socrates observes that in his "perfectly just city," the babies of women over forty years of age and men over fifty-five would be either aborted or victims of infanticide:

---

[18] Plato, *The Laws*. Thomas L. Pangle, trans. (New York: Basic Books, 1980), 739e11-740a6, 741b3-6, 741c6-11, 741e1-8, 742c6 and 743e2-4. Plato, *The Republic of Plato*. Allan Bloom, trans. (New York: Basic Books, 1968), 416d4-417b80. Aristotle, *The Politics*. Carnes Lord, trans. (Chicago: The University of Chicago Press, 1984), 1255b31-40, 1258a33-40 and 1280a20-1281a5.

[19] Aristotle's *Politics*, 1328b37-29a2.

[20] *Federalist* No. 35, p. 220.

[21] Aristotle's *Politics*, 1335b20-26. Inasmuch as Aristotle considers decisive the point at which "perception and life arises," it is possible that if he knew that life begins at conception, he would oppose abortion. There appears to have been an ambiguity in the ancient evidence in establishing when human personhood begins.

Now I suppose that when the women and men are beyond the age of procreation, we will, of course, leave them free to have intercourse with whomsoever they wish . . . and all this only after they have been told to be especially careful never to let even a single foetus see the light of day, if one should be conceived, and, if one should force its way, to deal with it on the understanding that there's to be no rearing for such a child [461b9-c8].

In addition to the endorsement of infanticide by these Greek thinkers, it should be noted that Aristotle also apparently did not disapprove of homosexuality. Montesquieu writes: "The vile means employed by the Cretans to prevent having too many children [i.e., homosexual actions] is reported by Aristotle, and I have felt modestly frightened when I wanted to report it."[22] As Plutarch mentions the infanticides carried out by the Spartans "with no mark of disapprobation," Aristotle refers to the homosexual acts of the Cretans without disapproving of them. As Hamilton is horrified that Plutarch would mention infanticides in such a blasé manner, Montesquieu is "modestly frightened" by the vile actions of the Cretans, so he only alludes to them, directing us to the explicit report in Aristotle. "Strange though it may seem," maintains historian Paul Rahe, "the Greeks regarded the homoerotic passion linking a man with a boy as the cornerstone of political liberty."[23]

Montesquieu points out a crucial difference between the ancients and the moderns: "just as the Greek political men always tell us that the republic is tormented by having a large number of citizens, today political men tell us only of the means proper for increasing it [the number of citizens]."[24] In Montesquieu's view, the fear of Aristotle and other Greeks that the republic might have too many citizens led them to endorse population control:

> The Greek political men were thus particularly attached to regulating the number of citizens. Plato fixes it at five thousand forty, and he wants propagation to be checked or encouraged according to need, by honors, by shame, and by the warnings of the old men; he even wants the number of marriages to be regulated in such a way that the people replace themselves without overburdening the republic.
>
> If the law of the country, says Aristotle, prohibits the exposing of infants, the number of children each man is to beget has to be limited. To someone who has more

---

[22] *The Spirit of the Laws*, p. 438, cf. Aristotle's *Politics* 1272a24-26.

[23] *Republics Ancient and Modern* (Chapel Hill: The University of North Carolina Press, 1992), p. 133. See also pp. 71, 131 and Aristotle's *Politics*, 1265a38-b12, 1267b21-1268a12, 1330b21-31 and 1335b22-23.

[24] *The Spirit of the Laws*, p. 453.

children than the number specified by the law, he counsels causing the woman to miscarry before the fetus has life.[25]

In contrast, the modern commercial republic, according to Montesquieu, has a greater number of life-affirming characteristics than did the ancient martial republic. This partly explains why political men alive at the time Montesquieu wrote *The Spirit of the Laws,* in the mid 18th century, talked "only of the means proper for increasing" the number of citizens. "Modern, commercial political life," in Thomas Pangle's view, "will have room for every human being."[26] This is not necessarily to say that the modern commercial republic provides room for every human being for all the right reasons. Still, a diversified economy provides a healthy environment for the people to cultivate diverse talents and the full capacities of their minds. As we have seen in the excerpts advocating forced miscarriage in Aristotle's *Politics*, and in the endorsement of infanticide and abortion found in Plato's *Republic,* there was not room for every human being in the ancient martial republic. "Therefore, one should not be surprised," remarks Montesquieu, if our [modern commercial] mores are less fierce than they were formerly. Commerce has spread knowledge of the mores of all nations everywhere; they have been compared to each other, and good things have resulted from this."[27]

The modern commercial republic welcomes population growth because people produce, transport and consume goods, which fuels prosperity and economic growth. Hamilton noted that compared to Europe, the United States, at the time he lived, had a "scarcity of hands" and a "dearness of labor."[28] As one of the primary architects of the American commercial republic, Hamilton welcomed population growth as good in itself and as a means by which to remedy this shortage of workers. He called for "the United States to open every possible [avenue to] emigration from abroad" in order to "extend[] the population, and with it the useful and productive labor of the country."[29] Commerce

---

[25] *Ibid.*, p. 438. Montesquieu cites Plato's *Laws*, 737e, Plato's *Republic*, 460a and Aristotle's *Politics*, 1335b21-23 and 1335b23-25.

[26] *Montesquieu's Philosophy of Liberalism* (Chicago: The University of Chicago Press, 1973), p. 246.

[27] *The Spirit of the Laws*, p. 338. Montesquieu and Hamilton each endorsed the commercial republic, and the latter agreed more than he disagreed with the former on the benefits of commerce, but it should be noted that Hamilton was not as sanguine as was Montesquieu that commerce would lead to fewer wars among nations. (Cf. *Federalist*, No. 6, p. 33).

[28] *PAH, vol.* 10, pp. 269-270.

[29] *Ibid.*, pp. 252-56.

is like fertile land, according to Pangle, (quoting Montesquieu), in that it "gives, with ease, softness and a certain love for the conservation of life."[30]

Hamilton never acquired much by way of personal wealth, though with his considerable talents and impressive work ethic, he almost certainly could have, had he wanted to. He was largely indifferent to personal, not to say national wealth, because he was more moved by the public-spirited part of his soul to become a statesman of a great nation than he was by a desire for comfortable self-preservation. His intelligence, background and connections gave him a unique perspective from which to reflect upon the virtues and vices of the rich and the poor. He grew up poor in the West Indies but he came to know many wealthy people in the United States. In a statement addressed to the New York ratifying convention, he argued that the rich and the poor have different vices:

> Experience has by no means justified us in the supposition that there is more virtue in one class of men than in another. Look through the rich and poor of the community . . . Where does virtue predominate? *The difference indeed consists, not in the quantity, but kind of vices, which are incident to the various classes;* and here the advantage of character belongs to the wealthy. Their vices are probably more favorable to the prosperity of the state than those of the indigent and partake less of moral depravity.[31]

The characteristic vice of the rich is avarice and that of the poor is sloth. As was noted earlier, the claim that Hamilton promoted avarice is unwarranted. Yet he realized that in any political regime some people would act avariciously. Hamilton asserted that the vices of the rich "are probably" more conducive to the prosperity of the state than are those of the poor. He asserted with more confidence that the vices of the rich are less morally depraved than those of the poor and that the wealthy tend to be better than the poor in terms of character. Insofar as avarice and sloth are both deadly sins, they are probably equally pernicious to the soul but from the perspective of the country's good, which is statesman's lens, avarice may be, all things considered, more politically salutary than is sloth. If that is true, then the modern commercial republic and those virtues associated with the legitimate gain seeking that it fosters, along with the particular vices it might inadvertently give rise to, may be politically preferable to any practical alternatives.

Therefore, to the extent that the political thought of Montesquieu and Hamilton promotes the modern commercial republic, it is more conducive to population growth and the culture of life than is the teaching of the ancients. This is not to suggest that the

---

[30] *Montesquieu's Philosophy of Liberalism*, p. 204; quoting from *The Spirit of the Laws*, p. 287.

[31] Jonathan Elliot (ed.), *The Debates in the Several State Conventions on the Adoption of the Federal Constitution* (5 vols.; Philadelphia: J.B. Lippincott Co., 1836), vol. 2, p. 257 (emphasis added).

modern commercial republic is anywhere near flawless. There is much truth in the comparison of today's young urban professional with Midas in that each is so affluent that whatever he touches turns to gold. Many "yuppies" are not having children perhaps because they are too selfish to raise them. And it is outrageous that in our advanced modern commercial republic, the organs of aborted babies are bought and sold as part of a moneymaking business. Partial birth abortion, recently declared illegal in the United States, involves delivering intact babies for the convenience and profit of abortionists. Whether this atrocity is mostly attributable to commerce or to perversions such as moral relativism is not clear, however. The excessive desire for material gain is particularly dangerous because there are few, if any, natural limits on how much money the avaricious man can accumulate.[32] In comparison, there are obvious natural limits to the extent to which the gluttonous man can gorge himself. Hamilton attempted to avoid the problems associated with the excessive desire for material gain by discouraging avarice.

Some of Hamilton's thoughts regarding the commercial republic call to mind the Church's teaching about sanctification through our work. The pursuit of commerce might even be ennobling if it is carried out within reasonable bounds, if it gives people an opportunity to do their jobs well, put their talents to good use, develop their abilities, and offer their achievements to God. Hamilton's thought points in this direction in three ways. First, he wrote that "a habit of labour in the people is . . . essential to the health and vigor of their minds and bodies."[33] We bring glory to God when we use our capacities for good. It would seem disproportionate for people with healthy and vigorous minds to buy into the culture of death.

Second, Hamilton appears to have had a glimpse of a sense in which God calls us to be co-creators. As Flaumenhaft points out:

[W]riting of the need for funding to make the public debt solid and stable, one important effect being to make it 'useful as Capital,' Hamilton showed how even an 'edifice' of 'business,' a structure of interested enterprise that one would not think to call noble, may present a 'spectacle' so 'wonderful' as to evoke, by its vast liveliness, a kind of disinterested delight.[34]

---

[32] Stephen T. Worland, "The Benevolence of the Baker," *The Review of Politics*, Spring, 1996, p. 358.

[33] *PAH*, vol. 2, p. 167.

[34] *The Effective Republic*, p. 17. Quoting from Hamilton's "Defense of the Funding System," July 1795, *Papers of Alexander Hamilton*, vol. 19, pp. 66, 69-70.

In the words of the *Catechism of the Catholic Church*, "[b]y means of his labor man participates in the work of creation."[35]

Third, as noted earlier, Hamilton observed that "the genius of the American Merchants and Navigators" is their "unequalled [sic] spirit of enterprise." The modern commercial republic provides opportunities for those who are gifted in that way to give that spirit an outlet. "When all the different kinds of industry obtain in a community," according to Hamilton, "each individual can find his proper element, and can call into activity the whole vigour of his nature."[36] God has blessed different people with different gifts and it is desirable that they have opportunities to exercise these gifts, whether they lead to action or contemplation.

---

[35] *Catechism of the Catholic Church* (Missouri: Liguori Publications, 1994), p. 590, **2460**.

[36] Ibid., vol. 10, pp. 252-56.

Immersed in a Culture of Science: Cautionary Tales and Reflections

William R. Marty[*]

Every age has its final authority. Once philosophy reigned, then theology. Now, if it is not the inner light of personal desire and personal autonomy, it is science. For most people, and certainly for most people in the major institutions of this society, an argument is understood to be settled when someone can say of the disputed matter, "science says." Science is the "trump card" of disputation in our age and culture. And there is reason for this. Science has helped produce a cornucopia of benefits with its increasing mastery of nature. The advance, indeed, has been breathtakingly rapid. As a graduate student, I lived in the basement apartment in the home of a gracious lady, even then in her seventies. She could remember, she told me, when the first automobile she had ever seen came to her little town in North Carolina. She was a teenager. She was invited to ride in it. She was, she remembered, almost immeasurably pleased and proud. And yet, before that lady died, in her nineties, Americans had rocketed to the moon, and returned. Think of that. In one long life to see, as a teenager, a very early and simple automobile, and before you die, to see televised images of men walking on the moon. Probably there was never a lifetime in human history that saw such dramatic change, and so much of it for the better, materially speaking.

So science earned its authority in the mind of the culture. And we were mostly taught, and believed, that science, unlike philosophy, which argues endlessly, but never seems to gain agreement, or theology, with its endlessly disagreeing and rival schools, could and did settle things. It had the "scientific method." It produced results which could be replicated, tested, validated. It gave us certainty. And so, when a matter is disputed, and someone can say, with authority, "science says," then the matter has been settled. There are no grounds left on which to continue the dispute, or so we understand.

Indeed, increasingly we are asked to change even the teachings of the church to accommodate the latest pronouncements of science. The miracles of the Gospels, and the Resurrection, were early called into question, traditional understandings of moral questions followed, homosexuality being a case in point. Still, the argument for accommodation in such cases would be stronger if those who had invoked the authority

---

[*] William R. Marty is professor of political science at the University of Memphis. He serves as associate editor of the *Journal of Interdisciplinary Studies* (*JIS*), an interdisciplinary forum for exploration of the human condition in the light of Christian understanding. He is a board member and sometime coordinator of the Christianity in the Academy Conference. His research principally investigates why both Christians and secularists so often produce policies of political, social and economic folly, but also why aspects of Christian understanding enable it, when not forgotten, to produce a practical wisdom about worldly things surpassing the capacity of both the secular enlightenment and post-modernity.

of science had consistently given us good advice. But they have not. Quite the contrary, over the last two centuries the authority of science has been put confidently, forcefully, and repeatedly in the service of mistaken and often pernicious ideas and movements. We all know and are taught the sins of religion against science. We have for centuries done penance for Galileo. But it is surely time to give some attention to the sins of science, and its frequent and costly failures as a reliable guide in human affairs. Consider the record of the last two centuries.

Begin with Samuel Morton, an American scientist with a great international reputation. Morton made his reputation by measuring cranial capacities. He found, he thought, racial differences, and concluded that whites were more intelligent than Indians, Indians than blacks. Among whites, gentiles were more intelligent than Jews (Broad & Wade 1983:194). These results, coinciding nicely with the prejudices of his time, were reprinted throughout the century as irrefutable evidence of the different capacities of the races (Broad & Wade, citing Stephen Gould 1981: 195). Alexander Stephens, Vice-President of the Confederacy, invoked this research to prove the inferiority and "natural aptitude" for slavery of blacks. He used it, as well, to refute the principles of the Declaration of Independence (Jaffa 1988: 129-30). Ironically, errors discrediting the findings were apparent in the published data themselves, but *these errors went unnoticed for more than a century* (Broad & Wade, citing Gould 1981: 194-95). Ah, scientific rigor!

Later in the century, in France, Paul Broca, for whom a part of the brain is named, weighed in. He found brains to weigh more "in men than in women, in eminent men than in men of mediocre talent, in superior races than in inferior races...." When the brains of five eminent professors were found to be only average in weight, Broca took this as evidence, not that his correlation of brain weight and intelligence might be faulty, but that the reputations of these professors should be reassessed (Broad & Wade 1983: 197). Ah, interpretation!

Brain size and weight gave way, in the last century, to intelligence tests. H. H. Goddard discovered, he thought, that "there are great groups of men, laborers, who are but little above the child...." and he concluded that "the feeble-minded should not be allowed to reproduce" (Broad & Wade 1983: 198). Lewis Termon, the Stanford psychologist who produced the revised Stanford-Binet test, agreed. He hoped intelligence testing "will ultimately result in curtailing the reproduction of feeble-mindedness..." (Broad & Wade 1983: 199).

And then there was Robert Yerkes of Harvard and Yale, President of the American Psychological Association, who concluded from Army tests–despite strong internal evidence to the contrary–that the average American adult male was little above a moron, that North Europeans were more intelligent than South Europeans, and whites than blacks. These findings led to discussion of the viability of democracy, and may have influenced laws restricting immigration from Southern Europe (Broad & Wade 1983:

200-202), as well as laws passed in more than half the states in the 1920s mandating sterilization for various categories of the "unfit" (see Neuhaus 1988: 17).

Despite the best scientific advice, not many were sterilized. But the urge to weed out the unfit endures. Nobel Prize-winners Francis Crick and James Watson, co-discoverers of DNA's structure, have urged that "newborn infants should be subjected to rigorous examination and permitted to live only if they are found fit" (Neuhaus 1988: 22). After all those centuries of Christians battling infanticide, Nobel Prize-winning scientists would bring it back.

But the counsels of science have often been harsh. Social Darwinists, once well-regarded in the best universities, told us, as science, that human progress requires unimpeded market competition, and that any compassion for the losers will allow the unfit to survive, destroying human progress (Grimes 1960: 302-309)–a use of scientific authority to defend the most ruthless version of capitalism.

Marxists, conversely, were absolutely confident that they had a science of society and history, and, following it, they built and defended murderous tyrannies. Tens of millions died at their hands (*The Listener* 1979: 271; Courtois, Werth, Panne, PaczKowski, Bartosek, and Margolin 1999), and hundreds of millions lost their freedoms. The infamous Spanish Inquisition, for which the church has properly been rebuked, killed perhaps ten people a month at its height.

"Scientific socialism," a generation into the revolution in Russia, executed more than 40,000 a month (Solzhenitsyn 1975: 9). But Russia is huge. In little Cambodia, with only 7 to 10 million people, 1 to 3 ½ million died in 3 ½ years under Pol Pot's Marxist tyranny (Hawk 1982: 20-21; *Economist* 1971: 61). Science can be a stern taskmaster.

Nor should we forget the Fascists, who acted on the principles of Social Darwinism, using war instead of markets to weed out unfit nations and peoples. In its Nazi instead of its Italian variant, the most famous universities of Europe taught racial science, and the existence of a master race. In its application, this science led to the attempt to exterminate whole peoples–the Jews and the Gypsies–and to literally enslave others. Only military defeat intervened, but not before millions were rounded up and sent off to the exterminations camps.

The list could go on. There is hardly a movement or idea that has not been able to invoke the authority of science. Scientists of the political left told us that conservatives had defective personality structures (McClosky 1958: 27-45) or "authoritarian" personalities (Adorno, et al.: 1950). They didn't notice that the world was full of murderous left-wing authoritarians. Ah, political and psychological science! A continuation of this tradition, indeed a summary of it, is to be found in "Political Conservatism as Motivated Social Cognition" (Jost, Glaser, Druglanski and Sulloway 2003). Sigmund Freud told us that we must repress the *id* if civilation is to survive (Freud 1961); but later psychologists told us that we must get rid of our inhibitions, especially our sexual inhibitions, to be loving and kind and good (see Vitz 1977 and Kilpatrick 1983). Ah, psychiatry and psychology! The American Psychiatric Association told us until 1974, as science, that homosexuality is a disorder; it tells us now, as science, that it is not (Cort 1987: 20). Ah, psychiatry! Margaret Mead taught a generation about sexual mores; now we have reason to wonder. Ah, anthropology! And so it goes, concerning the effects of televised sex and violence, pornography, working mothers, not-traditional families, the consequences of welfare programs, capital punishment, the comparative influence of inheritance and environment....

Consider the record. In the last two centuries, the authority of science has been used, by scientists and others, to defend the innate inferiority of women, blacks, Indians, Jews, laboring class males, and the poor. Its authority has been used to justify slavery–in both the 19th and 20th centuries–and the elimination of the unfit by sterilization, infanticide, and by killing the aged, the incompetent, and the infirm (Neuhaus 1988: 21-22). It has been used to defend a merciless survival of the fittest in economics and international relations. It has been used, for long periods, to defend a pitiless capitalism, a mass-murdering socialism, and a genocidal Nazism. And along the way it has been used to undermine Christian concern for the poor, Christian marriage, and Christian sexual morality.

There are clearly limits to scientific objectivity, reliability and authority. Why? As Thomas Kuhn has explained: "Philosophers of science have repeatedly demonstrated that more than one theoretical construction can always be placed upon a given collection of data" (Kuhn 1970: 76). And when data has more than one possible interpretation, and humans bring assumptions, agendas, biases, and blind spots with them to their research, as they do, and, being human, on occasion even bend the data and its interpretation to their purposes (Broad & Wade 1982), then the "findings of science" on controversial questions will often be dangerously, even catastrophically mistaken. And that is why we should be extremely cautious lest the invocation of science in current controversies, religious and other, should cause us to exchange a birthright of truth for a mess of pottage.

References

Adorno, T. W., Else Frenkel-Brunswik, Daniel J. Levinson, and R. Nevitt Sanford. 1950. *The Authoritarian Personality.* New York: Harper & Row.

Broad, William, and Nicholas Wade. 1983. *Betrayers of the Truth.* New York: Simon & Schuster.

Cort, John C. 1987. "Christ and the Neighbor." *New Oxford Review* 54 (September): 20-21.

Courtois, Stephane, Nicolas Werth, Jean-Louis Panne, Andrzej Paczkowski, Karel Bartosek, and Jean-Louis Margolin. 1999. *The Black Book of Communism: Crimes, Terror, Repression.* Cambridge, MA: Harvard University Press.

Economist. 1979. "China's Awkward Little War." February 17: 61.

Freud, Sigmund. 1961. Trans. and ed., James Strachey. *Civilization and Its Discontents.* New York: W. W. Norton & Co.

Gould, Stephen J. 1981. *The Mismeasure of Man.* New York: W. W. Norton & Co.

Grimes, Alan Pendleton. 1960. *American Political Thought.* Rev. ed. New York: Holt, Rinehart and Winston.

Hawk, David. 1982. "The Killing of Cambodia." *New Republic.* November 15: 17-21.

Jaffa, Harry V. 1988. "Humanizing Certitudes and Impoverishing Doubts: A Critique of *The Closing of the American Mind* by Allan Bloom." *Interpretation* 16 (Fall): 111-138.

Jost, John T., Jack Glaser, Arie W. Kruglanski and Frank J. Sulloway. 2003. "Political Conservatism as Motivated Social Cognition." *Psychological Bulletin* 129 (3): 339-375.

Kilpatrick, William Kirk. 1983. *Psychological Seduction: The Failure of Modern Psychology.* New York: Nelson.

Kuhn, Thomas S. 1970. *The Structure of Scientific Revolutions.* 2nd ed. Chicago: University of Chicago Press.

The Listener, London. 1979. "Solzhenitsyn: The Way Ahead." February 22: 270-72.

McClosky, Herbert. 1958. "Conservatism and Personality." *American Political Science Review* 52: 27-45.

Neuhaus, Richard John. 1988. "The Return of Eugenics." *Commentary* 85 (April): 15-27.

Solzhenitsyn, Alexandr I. 1975. *The Voice of Freedom*. Washington, D.C.: AFL-CIO.

Vitz, Paul C. 1977. *Psychology as Religion: The Cult of Self-Worship*. Grand Rapids, MI: Eerdmans.

"Who Is My Neighbor?"
Christian Conduct in a Dangerous World

Proceedings of the 2002 Christianity in the Academy Conference

Edited by

William R. Marty

Bruce W. Speck

Carolinas Press
Southern Pines, North Carolina

Contents

"Soft" and "Hard" Just War Theory: A Proposal and Analysis 1
Keynote Address by David P. Gushee

The Unveiled Mask 9
Steven B. Fonville

Language and Power: A Case Study of the Manipulation of Language in Theological Education 13
Sean E. Asbell

Nominalism: Enemy of the Individual 25
Diane G. Lemmon

"Who is their God?": Reflections on the Civil Rights Era 41
William R. Marty

Religion: Stepchild of the First Amendment: Free Speech, as Long as It Is Not about Tradition Christianity (a University of Memphis Case Study) 53
Candace C. Justice

Whiskey Priests, Japanese Canadians, and World War IV: Christian Behavior in an Always Dangerous World 57
Bill Jenkins

The Patriotic Christian—An Oxymoron? 65
Bruce W. Speck

C. S. Lewis on the "Public Mind" of Our Neighbor 71
W. E. Knickerbocker, Jr.

Inclusive Exclusivism 79
Larry Lacy

C. S. Lewis and the Problem of Christian Behavior toward Others 87
Harry Lee Poe

Religious Toleration and Dangerous Fanaticism: The Natural Limits to Religious Liberty in a Liberal Democratic Society 95
Pamela Werrback Proietti

'Soft' and 'Hard' Just War Theory: A Proposal and Analysis

David P. Gushee[*]

Introduction

Every time our nation's leaders sound the alarm, claiming the need for military action, Christian theologians, ethicists, and others break out what they/we call "the just war theory" and seek to apply it to the situation at hand. The horrific terrorist attacks of September 11, and subsequent U.S. military response, are just the latest occasion of this consistent practice. Yet my files bulge with writings offering just war evaluations of U.S. military engagements in Iraq, Bosnia, Somalia, Kosovo, Panama, Grenada, Haiti, and so on. And the tradition extends back well into American–and of course western–history.

In my ten years or so as a Christian ethicist, I have grown increasingly dissatisfied with both scholarly and popular uses of just war theory in the American setting. There are many sources of this dissatisfaction, but here I want to focus on one: an apparently irreconcilable ideological split between the American Christian "left" and "right" concerning the application of just war criteria to US military engagements. The split works like this: politically and theologically conservative Christians, both Catholic and Protestant, tend to find in the just war theory grounds for support of all (or nearly all) US military actions. Politically and theologically liberal Christians tend to find in the just war theory grounds for opposition to all (or nearly all) US military actions. Even the response to the terrorist attacks of September 11 has revealed this tendency, though in somewhat more muted form than is usually the case.

The most pessimistic reading of this evidence would be that the just war theory, at least in its current form and application, has decayed into nothing more than a tool that can be used at will by theological/political partisans to reinforce their pre-established convictions via the illusion of supposedly "objective" confirmation through application of just war criteria. If this were true, the only honest course for Christians genuinely seeking truth would be to throw out the just war theory and replace it with something that could avoid such ideological misapplication.

---

[*] David P. Gushee is Graves Professor of Moral Philosophy and Senior Fellow of the Carl F. H. Henry Center for Christian Leadership at Union University, Jackson, Tennessee. Previously he served three years on the staff of Evangelicals for Social Action and another three on the faculty of Southern Baptist Theological Seminary. *Christianity Today* listed him in 1996 as one of the 50 "Up and Coming" evangelical leaders under the age of 40. He is an ordained minister. He has written or edited eight books, including the groundbreaking *The Righteous Gentiles of the Holocaust*, with another forthcoming in 2005, and dozens of articles, book chapters, and reviews in the areas of social ethics, public policy, and Christian Higher Education. He created and leads an undergraduate Christian Ethics degree program at Union University.

My actual proposal here is less radical than this. My thesis is that in contemporary American Christian usage, *there exist two just war theories, or at least two strikingly divergent patterns in interpretation of this ancient tradition of Christian reflection.* Borrowing from a heuristic device often used in philosophy, I want to call these two patterns "soft" and "hard" just war theory. This indicates that both approaches belong to the same family (that is, they both are a kind of just war theory), but they are significantly different not just in their conclusions but in their intellectual substructure. In this paper, I want to contrast hard and soft just war theory, probe the origins of their differences, and offer some suggestions for further reflection.

To illustrate my thesis, I want to compare the approach to just war theory taken by *The Challenge of Peace*, a document offered at the height of the Cold War (1983) by the US Catholic bishops, and Keith Pavlischek, a leading conservative lay Catholic ethicist who serves as a fellow at the Center for Public Justice in Washington.

A note of personal disclosure before proceeding: as an ethicist-in-training, I cut my teeth on what I am now calling soft just war theory. *The Challenge of Peace* was a much-admired reading in a seminary class with Glen Stassen. Later, as a young scholar, I worked in a soft JWT/pacifist organization (Evangelicals for Social Action). There I met and worked with Keith Pavlischek and watched him struggle against the soft just war theory of an organization whose perspective he came to reject. The struggle within just war theory that I articulate here is in a real sense a struggle within my own soul, rooted in my own personal pilgrimage.

Soft Just War Theory

Soft just war theory is characterized by a strongly articulated horror of war; a strong presumption for peace and against war; a tendency to be skeptical of US government claims about the need for military action; an inclination instead to trust the efficacy of international treaties, agencies, and perspectives; a stringent application of just war criteria, both in entry into war and conduct of war; and a sense of common ground with Christian pacifists despite obvious differences.

The Challenge of Peace, for example, begins its treatment of just war theory with a discussion of "the nature of peace" (21). Peace is described as a reality that humans must construct out of such ingredients as truth, justice, freedom, and love; yet it is also a divine gift. Peace, for the bishops, is clearly normative. It is God's will for humanity, our origin and our destiny, and our task in the time given us on this planet.

Quoting earlier papal and conciliar documents, *The Challenge of Peace* moves on to a stark condemnation of the savagery and horror of war, especially modern war and its bitter fruit, such as genocide. The bishops cite approvingly a Vatican II declaration in favor of the outlawing of war "by international consent," recognizing that this requires the strengthening of international law and public authority well beyond current realities.

The right of governments to defend themselves is granted by the bishops only within the context of this lack of adequate international governance. Given this (to them) lamentable reality, however, and in the context of a strong presumption against war, the bishops do grant governments a right and obligation to defend peace against aggression. While individuals may renounce the right to self-defense, governments may not do so without violating their mandate.

However, after granting this point, the bishops come around again to emphasize the importance of nonviolent means of national defense and conflict resolution as most in keeping with "the call of Jesus" (25). The horrors of war, especially war involving weapons of mass destruction, are again emphasized.

"The presumption that binds all Christians," according to the bishops, is that "the possibility of taking even one human life is something we should consider in fear and trembling" (26). Just war "teaching" is actually an effort to prevent war. Only if "extraordinarily strong reasons" exist "for overriding the presumption in favor of peace and against war" may war be considered. Even then, just war theory's primary function is to "seek to restrict and reduce [war's] horrors."

The classic *jus ad bellum* just war criteria are then reviewed and expounded; just cause, competent authority, comparative justice, right intention, last resort, probability of success, and proportionality. The discussion of competent authority notes bitter divisions in American life over whether certain US military actions have met this test given the lack of a formal declaration of war at times. The bishops' reflection on comparative justice emphasizes limiting both the ferocity of war and any kind of "absolute justice" moral absolutism on our part; it also notes the role of propaganda and the "ease with which nations and individuals either assume or delude themselves into believing that God or right is clearly on their side" (29).

The treatment of last resort notes and laments the difficulty of applying this requirement given the lack of "sufficient internationally recognized authority" to mediate disputes, and calls for support for the United Nations–quoting Pope Paul VI to the effect that the UN is the "last hope for peace" on earth (30). Discussion of proportionality emphasizes the grave costs of war, not just in blood and treasure but in its spiritual dimension, and notes that proportionality must be considered at all stages of a war–footnoting the fact that this same body of bishops publicly rejected the Vietnam War in 1971 due to its failure to meet this test.

Further discussion of the *jus in bello* criteria of proportionality and discrimination (noncombatant immunity) includes a striking condemnation of the horrors of technologically advanced weapons of war, such as nuclear, biological, and chemical weapons, claiming that the nature of war in the modern era is fundamentally changed. Thus modern war, especially any war involving a nuclear-armed superpower, is especially dangerous and resolutely to be avoided. The section on just war theory closes with a warm affirmation of the value of the pacifist witness within the Catholic church, claiming that it shares with just war theory "a common presumption against the use of force as a means of settling disputes" (37).

My familiarity with the literature of just war theory, both Catholic and Protestant, leads to the conclusion that the essential cluster of themes and emphases found in *The Challenge of Peace* is likewise found in soft just war theory of all types. Indeed, this document itself played a significant role in shaping what I think should now be called soft just war theory.

Hard Just War Theory

But now let us turn our attention to its rival. Hard just war theory is characterized by a strongly articulated disdain for injustice and disorder; an assumption that war is a necessary and inevitable aspect of human affairs in a fallen world; a tendency to trust the US government and its claims of a need for military action when it makes such claims; an inclination to distrust international treaties, agencies, and perspectives; a less stringent or differently oriented application of some just war criteria; and no sense of common ground with Christian pacifists.

In an October 2001 paper entitled "Just War Theory and Terrorism: Applying the Ancient Doctrine to the Current Conundrum," Keith Pavlischek laments what he labels as the "irresponsib[le]", "blame America first" perspective of many religious leaders and others after September 11. In response, he calls for rigorous retrieval of classic just war theory. While Pavlischek's essay was not intended as a comprehensive theoretical treatment of just war theory, it is possible to find within its pages the elements of hard just war theory as I am defining it.

Pavlischek claims that the foundational presumption of just war theory is the government's mandate to pursue justice, order, and peace. Government is ordained by God to prevent the victimization of the innocent, the violation of public order, and the disruption of peace. It is granted a monopoly on coercive, even lethal force in order to accomplish this mandate. In a fallen world, such force will be required both in domestic and international relations. This use of force is to be restrained and law-governed, to be sure, but it is a necessity–not an evil, but a good and proper exercise of "God's governance in a fallen world." Thus, classic just war theory, according to Pavlischek, "do[es] not begin with a presumption against force or violence, but rather with a presumption for justice" (15) and a recognition that until history ends force will be an aspect of that work for justice.

At no point in Pavlischek's essay does he indicate a concern about the trustworthiness of the US government (or any other) in its application of just war criteria or general use of force. In a related essay, Pavlischek (and co-author Jim Skillen) acknowledge that governments do "often exhibit structures and policies and practices of injustice." But that essay goes on to claim that all who hold divinely mandated authority (parents, pastors, elders, etc.) do sometimes misuse their authority because all of us are sinners. Thus the fact that governments cannot always be trusted with their authority has no impact whatsover on whether Christians should generally support US military action, just as the fact that parents sometimes exhibit unloving actions toward their children has no impact on whether Christians should generally support the exercise of parental authority.

Unlike *The Challenge of Peace*, Pavlischek's hard just war theory reflects no yearning for the establishment of an international governing authority that can ensure justice, peace, and order in a manner transcending the actions of individual states. The relevant "political community" or "competent authority" for Pavlischek is the individual nation-state. *The Challenge of Peace* recognized that for now nation-states are the highest form of political community but emphasized their limited ability to resolve conflicts peaceably and thus turned considerable attention to the UN and other international actors. Indeed, Vatican II-era Catholic documents clearly call for the formation of some kind of world government. Pavlischek appears not simply to mistrust international actors but theoretically to believe that the God-ordained monopoly on coercive force resides with individual states. Indeed, he considers the transition from private wars to public wars waged (and thus limited) by the nation-state to be a significant human accomplishment, and does not appear to seek the establishment of political community at a higher level.

In working through the just war criteria, Pavlischek offers some strikingly different interpretations than those offered by the bishops in *The Challenge of Peace*. Under just cause, for example, he includes retributive justice; that is, punishment for evil (2); the bishops raised questions as to whether this had ever been a legitimate cause for war and rejected it as a just cause for modern war. Pavlischek disagrees.

In Pavlischek's discussion of just war theory, he quotes Augustine, Aquinas, Luther, and Calvin extensively to the effect that God places coercive power in the hands of political authorities and authorizes them to use it for the common weal as they see fit. Whereas *The Challenge of Peace* offered an extensive discussion of conscientious objection to the unjust application of government power, Pavlischek does not address the point in the essays I have reviewed. Government leaders, duly authorized by God to exercise public authority, are the focus of his analysis. Just war theory is especially useful for statecraft and military planning by such authorities, Pavlischek argues. The role of just war theory as a tool for conscientious individual or ecclesial reflection is also noted, but appears to have lower priority.

Finally, Pavlischek has no use for pacifism. Where the bishops linked just war and pacifism as "distinct but interdependent methods of evaluating warfare" (37), Pavlischek argues that pacifists are profoundly unbiblical when they claim that governments should not threaten and use force, or when they argue that "the use of force is evil, perhaps a necessary evil, but still an evil" (21). Indeed, the bulk of his paper claims that pacifism and a kind of crypto-pacifism have corroded the sturdy recognition of the need for lethal force on the part of governments that once grounded just war theory, and that this threatens to weaken both national and ecclesial resolve to fight terrorism today as it needs to be fought.

Four Critical Questions

I will not seek to resolve the conflict between soft and hard just war theory in this paper. I will have accomplished my fundamental purpose if my basic thesis is regarded as established, or at least indicated: that *there exist two just war theories, or at least two strikingly divergent patterns in interpretation of this ancient tradition of Christian reflection, and that they are significantly different not just in their conclusions but in their intellectual substructure.* I believe that the contrast between soft and hard just war theory in the Catholic community could be demonstrated with even greater ease on the Protestant side where, sadly, intellectual traditions on the issue of war and peace tend to be less disciplined than among Catholic scholars.

Still, this discussion leaves the inevitable question in the air: who is right? I believe that this is a question that can be answered in four ways; or better, that demands four different approaches to its resolution.

1. *Intellectual genealogy*. Which approach to just war theory is more in keeping with the thought of its historic proponents, such as Augustine, Aquinas, Luther, and Calvin? Pavlischek is convinced that his approach wins this argument. Yet the soft just war theory of the Catholic bishops certainly lays claim to the same intellectual inheritance. My own sense is that hard just war theory does win this argument; but I am not sure what this proves, for I do not believe that the intellectual tradition of the just war theory carries any intrinsic authority. Perhaps historic Christian just war theory needs to be updated or altered. Perhaps it needs to remain unchanged. Genealogy does not settle the argument.

2. *Contemporary fruitfulness*. Which approach to just war theory is more likely to bear the fruit of justice, peace, and order today? That is, which is more likely to enable citizens and policymakers to advance God's will on this planet under contemporary conditions? This is undoubtedly a pragmatic test, but given that just war theory is not revealed willy-nilly in Scripture it is not inappropriate to ask the question. Just war theory in this sense constitutes the use of reason applied to the materials of Scripture in the context of contemporary life. How we construe just war theory must bear good fruit or that construal must be altered. In this case, I find that hard just war theory can make Christians too likely to support unjust wars, while soft just war theory can weaken our resolve to fight just ones. Which is the greater problem today?

3. *National discernment*. Which approach to just war theory is more likely to help *American* Christian citizens and policymakers to discern their particular responsibilities? The gravest flaw of all recent discussions of just war theory in this nation has been their ahistorical and acontextual quality. When *we Americans* talk about war and its justice, we're not Swedes, Costa Ricans, or Malaysians, we're Americans–the most powerful nation on earth, with the largest military--the single nation in the world today most likely to threaten and use military force. Which version of just war theory best helps us to remember both the opportunities and the dangers of our extraordinary international power? Which helps us to have an *appropriately critical* stance toward the claims of our own government? Here I tend to give the nod to soft just war theory, with its horror of

war itself, its relativizing of national loyalties, and its attention to the powerless ones whose homes lie in the path of our bombs, however justly intended or delivered.

4. *Biblical fidelity*. Which approach to just war theory is more faithful to the scriptural witness? This, of course, is the ultimate question, at least for those who seek to ground their theological and ethical convictions on the rock of biblical authority. Of course, if the question were easy to settle, there wouldn't be soft and hard just war theory, not to mention pacifism, just peacemaking, and holy war approaches. The sheer range and diversity of the biblical witness on this issue is staggering. Interpretation of texts ranging from the exterminationist motif in Joshua to "turn the other cheek" in Matthew is an art form indeed.

But we can at least say this. This particular art form is one we must exert every effort to develop, for the stance of American Christians on the issue of war is of signal importance not just to America, and not just to Christians, but to the entire world, and to God's kingdom project on a planet staggering under the load of *both* injustice *and* war.

The Unveiled Mask

Steven B. Fonville[*]

Dear Grandson,

    I write this short story to you because of something you found in our living room tin of photographs when you were only seven or eight years old. Photographs, faded and frayed, sometimes reflect sweet memories, but often are evidence of horrible mistakes. The picture you found was enclosed then in a heavy envelope with a simple question scribbled on the back: "Exe.?" The photograph was a picture of a hooded man seemingly frozen on the steps to a stage surrounded by people. At seven you asked me, "Was it Halloween?" I could only dream it had been, but the truth is that it was an all too real part of my life, a part of my life so powerful once that only a life given for me could cause me to see the darkness of its error. Listen to the story:

    The haze stationed itself around us as if to hide what was obvious to our mind. The smell of days old unfettered death precisely fixed our environment and its branding effect was hedged only by the unknown which would appear inevitably and I feared terribly soon. Isolated in war; comfort came only from the cavity of mud and dust carved from the carnage of battle. Alone ahead of the line when forced back from advance by enemy fire, I found myself here, in the trench. Only yards away were the enemy I hoped not to kill or be killed by, but the threat of death would not wane. Our company was so threadbare that no engagement was probable of our own initiative. Before, our last advance word was that a French battalion might reinforce us, but every minute that passed crept into what could be life spans. Hope failed and only faith remained. Fear enhanced every tiny sound and punctured states of mind numbing still with the thumping of my heart. At times I gazed up into the early morning haze looking for God, for help, for escape, for Him.

    Sounds of heavy feet thudded in my ears as if the cavity were my flesh. Where was it coming from, my soul stuttered? I gripped my rifle tightly enough to feel the wide grain on the stock and the cool of the trigger that quickly warmed as my own being was lacerated at the thought again of killing. I peeked quickly, but cautiously, to the horizon ahead of me; from left to right I ran my eyes and back again. I breathed. No enemy. No death. Relief. But the cascade of catharsis was clotted by the crumble of dry clods behind me and by the time I realized what was happening an avalanche of dirt surrounded my feet and sent a charge up my spine I was sure could only be detonated by on-coming death. I spun and began to lunge with panic-tightened muscles, but the recognition of the French uniform relaxed my defense. But the sustenance that should have been, was replaced by shock. Where the face should be were the rounded lens of what appeared to

---

[*] Steven B. Fonville lives in Humboldt, Tennessee, with his wife and son. He is a senior student at Memphis Theological Seminary and serves as a supply pastor in The United Methodist Church. He also owns a landscaping business.

be a specter—A specter not of the night, but of the shadows of my soul. In the lensed reflection of the gas mask, the ghastly memories revisited. The grain of wood, the cool of metal, my thumping heart--all was too clear. My eyes tried to see friend or foe in who lay behind, but haze could not hide me, my own dread eyes in mask were all I could see. Rough rope swinging, hinge squeaking, man descending, hazy gray growing dark.

As I stare at the figure before me, seeing what was behind me, my stupor was broken when, unmasked, his eyes met mine. His gaze was cold yet not unfriendly and his stature spoke of previous strenuous work. I motioned to my canteen, knowing no French other than some phrase that reminded me of a word a doctor used to describe the top of my mouth when by chance I had an infected tooth. I surely did not want to offend my new ally knowing our lives would be inevitably intertwined. To my surprise he stated, "Let me." He then rummaged through his pack as dust flew from what must have been years of this war. He finally retrieved a flask of alcohol. He began to twist the small top and look up at me as if to gesture when the container fell almost in a frozen spiral to the dust. He immediately seized the flask in disgust thinking that some of his prize would be lost in the sweat of other's death and my prayers. But a small grin appeared as he noticed no loss of wine so he lifted it very huskily to his cracked lips and took a sucking gulp through the dusty spout he left unwiped. His eyes lowered to meet mine and he gestured the flask toward me. I shook my head slowly, "No." He wiped off the lip of the bottle and again gestured to me. "Thanks, but I don't drink." He rolled his eyes and tucked the drink away in his belongings and began to concentrate his focus on the slowly clearing horizon. He scanned wisely what might as well have been nothing, but with all care he scanned as if a wild cat waiting for the slightest movement of his prey. Soon he looked again toward me and asked in a heavy accent, "What do you do?" "You mean here, in the military, or at home," I questioned. "In your home," he answered somewhat warmly. I ran his words through my mind as if his English was foreign to me in a foreign land. I glanced from his eyes to find haven for the soon to be lie, and that dreadful mask hung around his neck and beckoned me to truth. But I could not tell nor would I tell. I had lied since day one, no Frank nor any other could force me to it. I must say something, fiction is half-truth. "I work for the state." "What state?" he inquired. Quickly I quipped, "My home state, Tennessee, and you?" To my surprise he mumbled, and stared away as if the haze might decipher his dialect. "Excuse me," I replied. Then again his eyes met mine with a gaze clouded with storms not of this world, "I manage properties of the deceased." "I've found some companionship then, you too work for the state," I replied, somewhat bewildered. But with a simple shake of his head he denied the claim. "A banker then, a lawyer?" No affirmative response was given. So in jest, I said, "You must be a thief." Finally, he uttered, "No, I kill and then I steal." Trying to lighten the tone, I stated, "Perhaps, but taking a helmet or ammunition from a fallen enemy is a fact of war." With a guttural blast he half shouted, "No, I have killed, not the enemy but those who sleep in their fortunes, just to hear their final gasp. Yankee, I am a murderer!"

My mortal enemy was not entrenched against me but with me. Fear tingled, adrenaline rushed. If he knew who I was, what I was, I too would be killed. Or perhaps he would fear me. Perhaps he would fear me! I could kill him, I thought, what would be the difference, I had…I had done it before. The bayonet would make no sound; his groan would only be mistaken for the wounded. He deserved it. No one would hold me accountable, no one would know. As my eyes narrowed with mind in plot, I looked to find a man bent as if aged by a century's worry. His eyes were mired in his chest, "I could do it now," I thought. But a spark of the rising sun glimmered off his chest, reflected from that mask directly into my eyes. Blinded, I closed my eyes and wood creaked again under my feet, step by step. In my mind I stood as the soldier I had not yet been, and the mask I had once worn rubbed against my hidden face. All seemed focused again through the small eyeholes, screams of "Let him swing," "I hope you find friends in Hell, for we won't miss you," echoed again. But I did not flinch. Finally when the nod was given I again grasped the wide grained handle, with its cool metal knob, and with a swift jerk, to death another convict descended. Again I jerked the lever, and a convict descended. Again and again. Finally I cried out, "No, no I won't do it again."

"Yankee, Yankee?" questioned my French confessor. Finally his syllables broke my silence. "You won't do what?" he questioned in confused tones. "I said I am a murderer, not you," the French man uttered as if to offer some strange consolation. I looked at him, and then to the slowly parting haze that was seemingly melted away by the warmth of the peeking sun. I confessed, "I know what you said, but I have killed too, for the same reason you did, for wealth. I worked for the state. I was the executioner. I carried out the justice I so firmly believed in." His eyes never wavered, he simply asked, "Why?" "Why?" I replied. "Why? Because people like you must be punished. You deserve what you get. You have broken the highest of all moral codes. In your taking of another's life you forfeit your own life, your own rights. What value could your life have? Why? Isn't the answer obvious, isn't it simple?" One might think this would have enraged the demon within, but instead of sullen slights, he seemed to peer into my very soul, so transfixed were his eyes on mine that the clear blue of the morning sky reflected without hint of haze. He replied, slowly, "My whole life I have never had value." What did he mean? Was he agreeing with me? Was he arguing with me? Never had value? How despicable a thing to say. Silence fell like crescendo, leaving in its wake a great void, a great void that meant everything. Oh God, no value? Surely I could not curse any soul with such a thought. I must recant. I turned to him with sun now in full beam, making the haze of night appear as if from dungeon now released. I turned to try to salvage the life I had taken from him, but what words would I use? I pondered exactly what phrase to use, what tone might convey worth. I needed poetry with no rhyme, music with no meter. Finally some logic began to come forth. I could convince him now even if I believed it ever so slightly. I began to utter his name, when a tide of sound rolled over us, boot soles, and flashing metal swept by us like an arch of lightening. Shots rang and smoke billowed, mortars rained around us. We were pinned between enemy and ally. If we advanced on the enemy it would appear that we were the enemy firing into the direction of our own besieged ranks. Whistling rounds from both sides secured our inability. Clod-filled showers descended upon our heads and the odd vacillating whistle of the enemy's hammer-like grenades and ensuing "boom" gave melody to the death march that had begun. We must fight, I thought. I grabbed for my ally's collar to lead him out of what had been our haze-filled den of confession, when he shoved his shoulder into my chest, knocking me to what would have been prostrate had the wall of the mortar designed fox-hole not caught me. As I struggled to make sense of what had happened I saw an enemy soldier lying above our heads with hand dangling in our hole. I focused then to see my friend scrambling on hands and knees as if to catch a falling child, then motionless lay, as if trying to press his way into the blood stained soil. I shook my head and began to try to move toward him to help him when a muffled thud jolted his body and curled it into a fetal position. I lunged toward him and grasped his hand as I fell to my knees. He squeezed my hand with the might surely never known to his frame before and his eyes rolled slowly up to me. I must tell him his value; I must give him hope. As his hand weakened I began to panic, I leaned without thought and said all I knew to say, all I could hope would be said to me, "I love you." His grip tightened once more, and he blinked slowly. I wept. I fell in anguish on my back fearing not death but the deaths of my life. As the silence overcame the turmoil and the sun fully illuminated our trench, I realized the blood of this man gave value to my life.

Surely, my dear grandson, no person can ever forfeit their value to society and to God, but they may never redeem it if we do not show them their worth.

Language and Power
A Case Study of the Manipulation of Language in Theological Education

Sean E. Asbell[*]

On a very warm Wednesday in the summer of 1999, my wife Tina and I arrived in Memphis. We had an 11:00 appointment with the Dean of Admissions at a seminary here. At half past eleven, we made the turn from East Park onto Union. "There it is." I said. "Is that it?" Tina asked. "That's it. Memphis Theological Seminary." "Oh." She said, "I thought it would be bigger than that."

At first glance, MTS is . . . modest. Many Memphians don't even know it's there. The campus occupies only a few scant acres of Midtown Memphis real estate—just a dot on the map. But MTS is the seminary of the Cumberland Presbyterian Church, educating our students in theology, as well as students from over 30 different denominations.

On the world's stage, the Cumberland Presbyterian Church is . . . modest. The largest church in Memphis could hold a third of our denomination. In many ways, we are a microcosm of the Protestant Church. We wrestle with the same theological and social issues as the larger denominations, but when the more pressing matters reach our body, we smart a little more than most. The smaller parts of the body are more sensitive to pain.

A topic of much debate in my generation of seminarians is the use of language. We talk a lot about words. This debate isn't new. In the 15th Century, this issue was pressing enough that John Calvin found it necessary to issue the following caveat in his *Institutes*:

> I am not, indeed, such a stickler as to battle doggedly over mere words. For I note that the ancients, who otherwise speak very reverently concerning these matters, agree neither among themselves nor even at all times individually with themselves. . . . But [Calvin writes] I have long since and repeatedly been experiencing that all who persistently quarrel over words nurse a secret poison. As a consequence, it is more expedient to challenge them deliberately than to speak more obscurely to please them. (McNeill: 126-28)

This paper is about words. It is my intent to tell the story of how the phenomenon referred to by some as "inclusive language" has progressed through MTS, and the General Assembly of the Cumberland Presbyterian Church. It is not my intent to be the stickler that Calvin says he is not. (God help me if I become more of a stickler than John

---

[*] Sean E. Asbell is from Kentucky and lives in Memphis, Tennessee, with his wife and two sons. He is a senior student at Memphis Theological Seminary and plans to do additional graduate study in philosophy and theology.

Calvin.) It is my hope that this story will shed some light on what I believe to be the secret poison behind the language game.

MTS adopted an "Inclusive Language Policy" that first appeared in the 1986-87 *Student Handbook*. The policy statement received little attention until the 1991-92 academic year, when an adjunct professor and pastor of the Cumberland Presbyterian Church began to hear students apologize for sometimes using the term "Father," in reference to God (Irby: 134). After consulting with the administration and a few Board members, this professor was astonished to hear that professors had the right to require students to conform to the language policy, even though the student could not adopt such language as his or her own (Irby: 135).

The following is the portion of the policy that this professor was questioning. It appeared in the 1992-93 MTS *Student Handbook* under the heading "Inclusive Language Policy":

> Further, while the Christian tradition has used masculine terms to refer to God, we have never wished to say that God is masculine or that God possesses masculine traits to the exclusion of the feminine. We therefore recommend that in speech and writing about God an effort be made to avoid the use of masculine terms exclusively and to use inclusive terms. Less androcentric language about God will be a significant Christian witness to our oneness in Christ. (24-25)

In the January, 1993 meeting of the Board of Trustees, the professor mentioned read a statement in response to the above policy. The following is a part of that statement:

> I am of the opinion that no seminary board of trustees, faculty, or president has the authority to dictate, mandate, or suggest, by policy, [that] there is only one adequate, right, or appropriate way by which one must refer to God. Nor do we have the authority to dictate what one must believe about God. . . . [A professor may guide, instruct, enlighten, et cetera] but never by coercion, intimidation, or policy force any particular belief upon a student. To do so is to limit academic freedom. (Irby: 135, 136)

A few months after reading this statement, the professor mentioned presented his resignation to the Board of Trustees of MTS, and the "inclusive language" controversy began to reach the congregations of the Cumberland Presbyterian Church. It became a topic of much discussion in editorial articles of the denomination's magazines. As is often the case, instead of serving to clarify the issue and discern the will of God, the ensuing (media-driven) debate diverged onto the use of inclusive language in reference to persons (which was not an issue at MTS). Despite very good efforts of many excellent contributors, the issue of concern soon became hopelessly sunk in a quagmire of semantic confusion.[1]

---

[1] See Suggested References at the end of this paper.

The point this professor was making in his statement (if I understand him correctly) is that by mandating the use of feminine or gender-neutral terms in speech and writing about God, MTS was requiring that some students speak and write about God in a manner that is inconsistent with their beliefs about God—if they are to speak or write about God at all. Furthermore, if a student is not allowed the academic freedom to refer to God in a way that is consistent with his or her beliefs, then theological education is severely hampered, if not rendered useless.

The point I am making is that I believe this and all like policies set a very dangerous precedent of using language not to educate students, but to manipulate them—to control them by insidious means to suit a predetermined agenda. When does education become manipulation? Here, I turn to the writings of 20th Century linguistic philosopher Ludwig Wittgenstein as an archetype of what I consider to be the underlying philosophy guiding this (and other) policies of contemporary Western theological education.

Ludwig Josef Johann Wittgenstein was born on April 26, 1889 in Vienna, Austria to Christian parents of Jewish descent (Richter, 1). Wittgenstein himself was baptized a Roman Catholic, "but was neither a practicing nor a believing Catholic" (Richter, 1). "By his own philosophical work and through his influence on several generations of other thinkers, Wittgenstein transformed the nature of [linguistic] philosophical activity in the English-speaking world" . . . not once but twice in the 20th Century (Kemerling, 1). From two different approaches, he argued that philosophical disagreements can be avoided by the application of an appropriate methodology—a methodology that focuses on the analysis of language. (Kemerling, 1)

Language, according to Wittgenstein, had no fixed meaning, but was rather a game played by members of a community, according to rules set forth by the members of the community. Garth Kemerling, in an article entitled, "Ludwig Wittgenstein: Analysis of Language," writes the following about what Wittgenstein called "language games":

> On this conception of the philosophical enterprise, the vagueness of ordinary [language] usage is not a problem to be eliminated but rather the source of linguistic riches. It is misleading even to attempt to fix the meaning of particular expressions by linking them referentially to things in the world. The meaning of a word or phrase or proposition is nothing other than the set of (informal) rules governing the use of the expression in actual life. (3)

In philosophical terms, some refer to Wittgenstein as an anti-realist—one who is not concerned with the existence of universal, objective, metaphysical reality. "Metaphysics and ethics, he supposed, transcend the limits of human language" (Kemerling). Denying any universal appeals to "rightness" or "wrongness," Wittgenstein argued that language within a particular community was governed by a set of "rules" determined solely by the community. Kemerling (quoting Wittgenstein) continues:

Like the rules of a game, Wittgenstein argued, these rules for the use of ordinary language are neither right nor wrong, neither true nor false: they are merely useful for the particular applications in which we apply them. The members of any community—cost accountants, college students, or rap musicians, for example—develop ways of speaking that serve their needs as a group, and these constitute the language-game.... Human beings at large constitute a greater community within which similar, though more widely-shared, language-games are played. (3)

The most revealing (and disturbing) aspect of the Wittgensteinian, anti-realist approach to language is the way in which the "rules" of the "language game" are determined. Duncan J. Richter, in an article entitled "Ludwig Wittgenstein (1889-1951)" writes (quoting another author):

It all depends on how the rule or series is interpreted. Any rule for interpretation will itself be subject to a variety of interpretations, and so on. What counts as following a rule correctly, then, is not determined somehow by the rule itself but by what the relevant linguistic community accepts as following the rule. So whether two plus two equals four depends not on some abstract, extra-human rule of addition, but on what we, and especially the people we appoint as experts, accept. Truth conditions are replaced by assertability conditions. To put it crudely, what counts is not what is true or right (in some sense independent of the community of language users), but what you can get away with or get others to accept. (9, italics mine)

This, I believe, is the point at hand: If this approach to linguistic philosophy is guiding contemporary theological education (and I believe it is, at least in some quarters) then the question moves from, "Does our language about God reflect our metaphysical understanding of God?" to "Does the god of our language reflect the ethical concerns of our community?" Furthermore, if language is really a "game" (as the Wittgensteinian, anti-realist approach suggests) then a community need not concern itself with the "rightness" or "wrongness" of the "rules" of the game, but only with the delineation of (and enforcement of) the "rules." As Richter suggests, questions of truth are replaced by degrees of assertability. In other words, those within the community are no longer concerned about what is right or wrong, but with what they can get away with. After all, it's only a game; in a game, the strongest competitor wins. This is when education becomes manipulation.

In 1994, the "language game" of MTS reached the floor of the General Assembly of the Cumberland Presbyterian Church. The body deliberated, and acted. The following is a portion of the recommendation adopted by the body and addressed to the Board of MTS:

While affirming the extremely valuable ministry being carried out by MTS . . . [this body] respectfully submits that it would be in the best interest of the peace and harmony of the church, as well as the overall best interest of MTS if the board of trustees would reconsider the institution's present "Inclusive Language Policy." It is the considered opinion of [this body] that the policy is no longer capable of intending the author's stated intention, namely, helping the members of the community to be more sensitive to others and their views, to be more inclusive in their behavior and thought, and to help deepen and enrich the theological understanding of all members of the community. However well intended the drafters of the policy were, the present policy is now perceived by a significant number of students and church members to be more of a negative statement opposing certain language for God rather than a positive statement which enables one to expand and enlarge her or his thinking and language about God. It is perceived by a significant number of church members and among present and past seminary students to be by its nature exclusive. That interpretation of the policy has now taken on a life of its own and has become reality for a significant number of people in the church. Consequently reconsideration of the policy with a view toward amending it in critical ways, revising it or formulating a new policy would be wise in the judgment of [this body] (*Minutes* of the 1994 General Assembly of the Cumberland Presbyterian Church: 263).

The Board of Trustees immediately revised the policy, temporarily substituting in its stead a "Statement on Language" used in reference to persons. The Board then began drafting another statement on language used in reference to God. After some tinkering, the Board's revised and final draft came before the floor of the 2001 General Assembly (2001 *Minutes* of the General Assembly of the Cumberland Presbyterian Church: 374). The body recommended further changes, and the Board complied. The current statement is found under the heading of "Community Life" in the 2001-2002 *Student Handbook*. The following is the "Language" paragraph of that statement:

Believing that God creates and redeems humanity by "word" and "word made flesh," the MTS community takes seriously the agency of language within the classroom and the sanctuary. The use of inclusive language in writing and speaking expresses respect for all persons. It promotes reconciliation and harmony while affirming every member of the human family as no less than a child of God. The practice of using diverse and inclusive names, pronouns, and metaphors with reference to God in classroom discussion, worship, and in written assignments honors the expanding theological perspectives of participants in the MTS community while recognizing that the fullness of God is beyond all human naming. (18)

It would give me great pleasure to set all hearts at ease and tell how this statement has truly fostered an atmosphere of academic freedom, but that is not the case. In some classes at MTS, academic freedom was never infringed upon. But during the opening week of this semester, students in some classes were handed a list of "suitable" terms for God. On that list were terms such as: heart that inspires within us a vision of justice and love; eternal father and mother god; the mind that unifies all creation.[2] Glaringly absent from that list were the traditional terms of Father, Son, and Holy Spirit.

---

[2] I have a copy of this list in my possession, as do most students of MTS.

If I may, please allow me to draw three observations from a student's perspective on the nature of the language game. First, I have witnessed an aversion within my seminary community to engage in genuine theological debate over this issue. We have never, to my knowledge, addressed this issue in an open forum. We have never presented papers on this topic. We have never heard rebuttals on this topic. To my knowledge, we have never openly discussed this topic at all. Instead, we have met both formally and informally (sometimes behind closed doors) in Board and committee meetings and attempted to mandate by policy a certain ethical behavior—a behavior that requires of us specific metaphysical and epistemological assumptions that we haven't even begun to discuss. To the student, the question has never been: Do you agree or disagree with using feminine or gender-neutral terms in reference to God? To the student, the question has instead been: Will you comply with this policy? Some of us have answered with a resounding "No." And I'm ashamed to say that we've never been asked why. This issue began in the subtle (and sometimes not-so-subtle) power dynamics of closed-door meetings, and it is still confined there. It has yet to escalate into an open and honest debate.

Second, I have witnessed a tension that exists between the chapel and the library of my seminary community. Institutions like MTS are unique in that we must answer to two bodies: our accrediting body and our church body. Our relationship with our accrediting body is symbolized in many ways by our library, which is often full and always expanding. On the other hand, our relationship with our church body is symbolized in many ways by our chapel, which isn't getting as much use these days. In many ways (this case being no exception), we have manipulated our relationship with our accrediting body with the intent of exerting undue influence on our relationship with our church body, in order to enforce a predetermined ethical behavior within our seminary community.[3] This ongoing manipulation has adversely affected our relationship with our church body. It has created an atmosphere of distrust, which has been detrimental to the communal worship of our seminary community.

Third, I have witnessed first-year students unwittingly accept the terms of a terrible compromise (often for the sake of harmony, or in the name of hospitality)—a compromise that in fact denies them the use of the traditional language of the church. I believe the intent of at least some of the drafters of this policy was to recommend that students avoid using masculine terms (both in reference to persons and in reference to God) in such a way that excludes people. I believe this intent was then twisted by some to the point that students were told in some classes that masculine terms (used in reference to persons and in reference to God) always exclude people. Then, what

---

[3] When defending this policy, we have often said to our church body, "We have no choice, our accrediting body has mandated this policy." When, in fact, our accrediting body hasn't mandated this policy at all. They have simply held us to a policy that we have delineated ourselves. Then, we have turned to our church body and said, "We have no choice, they are demanding that we do this." See the "Self Study for Reaffirmation of Accreditation" in works cited.

appeared to be a good compromise was presented to students in these classes: Don't use names or pronouns in reference to God at all. When this compromise was struck, I believe the desired intent of the professor(s) was fulfilled. Traditional language was denied. And to ease the troubled minds of first-year students groping for substitutionary terms to compensate for their apparently archaic and supposedly daft vocabularies, they were handed a list of "suitable substitutes" that were more acceptable to the sensitivities of their seminary community. At this point, I believe many students were "duped" into sacrificing the traditional language of the church in the name of inclusivity, when in fact the traditional language of the church was the only language being excluded from the life of the community.

On a more positive note, the "Community Life" statement in the 2001-2002 *Student Handbook* now includes a paragraph entitled "Academic Freedom," which reads as follows:

As the Holy Spirit forms MTS into a community of faith that shares in Jesus' ministry of love and justice to the world, participants experience growth through the process of theological education. The seminary respects the uniqueness of each person's intellectual and spiritual growth in discipleship and affirms the freedom of individual conscience in dialogue with the wisdom of Christian tradition. Therefore, every professor and student at MTS shall have the freedom of thought, discussion, and action which is required in individual and communal pursuit of truth. The exercise of academic freedom also entails respect for the purposes of the seminary and the responsibility to support its objectives. (18)

I am proud of my seminary community for taking this much-needed step in what I believe to be the right direction. In adopting this statement, we have acknowledged that we have indeed infringed upon student's academic freedom in prior policies, and it is our intention to do so no longer. But this issue has certainly not been laid to rest. A precedent has been established that I am afraid will be revisited not only to further this issue, but others as well.[4]

In conclusion, one might argue that this is the way in which the "language game" is played—that there's nothing wrong with it—that the seminary has every right to lay down the "rules" of the game by assertive (or any other) means, that the students have a responsibility to respond by assertive (or any other) means to change the "rules," that the

---

[4] The "Self Study for Reaffirmation of Accreditation" includes a recommendation (made by the seminary) that the seminary strike a portion of the "Statement on Morality" in the *Student Handbook*—a statement that declares, "the practice of homosexuality will not be advocated at MTS" (see p. 33, 34). This statement (as it now stands in the handbook) is in full accord with the beliefs of the Cumberland Presbyterian Church, of which MTS is a part (see the *Minutes of the 1996 General Assembly of the Cumberland Presbyterian Church*, p. 314). This recommendation was adopted by the seminary without due consideration of the beliefs of the Cumberland Presbyterian Church.

church must govern by assertive (or any other) means to enforce the "rules," and in the meantime, theological education will take place. One might argue that this is the only fair, equitable way in which the "rules" are to be determined. Even if this were true (and I don't believe it is) the students (especially first-year students) are in no position to compete in a "game" like this. In the classroom setting, the balance of power is significantly shifted in the professor's favor (as should be the case if education is to take place). Therefore, the professor of Christian education has the responsibility to use their power with the Christian education of the students in mind. The Christian educator ought not to play "language games" with their student's education.

I want to close with the words of a brilliant (albeit certainly not Christian) educator. In Hell, at the annual dinner of the Tempter's Training College for young devils, the guest of honor, Screwtape, raised his glass to his fellow . . . Gentledevils of education. His prophetic toast resonates a little too clearly with the practices of some contemporary educators:

> [He says, our patients] do not understand either the source or the real character of the prohibitions they are breaking. Their consciousness hardly exists apart from the social atmosphere that surrounds them. And of course we have contrived that their very language should be all smudge and blur. . . . The job of their Tempters was first, of course, to harden the choices of the Hellward roads into a habit by steady repetition. But then (and this was all-important) to turn the habit into a principle—a principle the creature is prepared to defend. After that, all will go well. Conformity to the social environment, at first merely instinctive or even mechanical . . . now becomes an unacknowledged creed . . . of Togetherness. . . . Mere ignorance of the law they break now turns into a vague theory about it . . . a theory expressed by calling it conventional "morality." Thus gradually there comes to exist at the center of the creature a hard, tight, settled core of resolution to go on being what it is, and even to resist [those] that might tend to alter it. It is a very small core. . . . But it will serve our turn. Here at last is a real and deliberate, though not fully articulate, rejection of what the Enemy calls Grace. . . . All said and done, my friends, it will be an ill day for us if what most humans mean by "religion" ever vanishes from the Earth. It can still send us the truly delicious sins. The fine flower of unholiness can grow only in the close neighborhood of the Holy. Nowhere do we tempt so successfully as on the very steps of the altar. (Lewis: 119-128)

References

McNeill, John T. (ed.) *Calvin: Institutes of the Christian Religion.* Philadelphia: Westminster, MCMLX.

Cumberland Presbyterian Church. *Minutes of the 1994 General Assembly of the Cumberland Presbyterian Church.* Memphis: The Historical Foundation of the Cumberland Presbyterian Church and the Cumberland Presbyterian Church in America, 1994.

Cumberland Presbyterian Church. *Minutes of the 1996 General Assembly of the Cumberland Presbyterian Church.* Memphis: The Historical Foundation of the Cumberland Presbyterian Church and the Cumberland Presbyterian Church in America, 1996.

Cumberland Presbyterian Church. *Minutes of the 2001 General Assembly of the Cumberland Presbyterian Church.* Memphis: The Historical Foundation of the Cumberland Presbyterian Church and the Cumberland Presbyterian Church in America, 2001.

Irby, Joe Ben. *This They Believed: A Brief History of Doctrine in the Cumberland Presbyterian Church.* Distributed by the Cumberland Presbyterian Resource Center, 1978 Union Avenue, Memphis, Tennessee 38014, 1997.

Kemerling, Garth. "Ludwig Wittgenstein: Analysis of Language." *Philosophy Pages . . . from Garth Kemerling*: http//www.philosophypages.com/ph/witt.htm 1997-2002.

Kemerling, Garth. "Ludwig Wittgenstein (1889-1951)." *Philosophy Pages . . . from Garth Kemerling*: http//www.philosophypages.com/ph/witt.htm 1997-2002.

Lewis, C.S. *The Screwtape Letters.* New York: Touchstone, 1959.

Memphis Theological Seminary. *A Report of the Institutional Self-Study for Reaffirmation of Accreditation: Prepared for the Association of Theological Schools in the United States and Canada and the Southern Association of Colleges and Schools.* Memphis Theological Seminary library, 1998.

Richter, Donald J. "Ludwig Wittgenstein (1889-1951)." *The Internet Encyclopedia of Philosophy*: http://www.utm.edu.research/iep/w/wittgens.htm 2001.

1992-93 Student Handbook. Memphis Theological Seminary, 1992.

1994-95 Student Handbook. Memphis Theological Seminary, 1994.

2001-2002 Student Handbook. Memphis Theological Seminary, 2001.

Suggested References

Allison, C. Fitzsimmons. *The Cruelty of Heresy: An Affirmation of Christian Orthodoxy.* Harrisburg: Morehouse Publishers, 1994.

Brown, Paul B. *In and For the World: Bringing the Contemporary Into Christian Worship.* Minneapolis: Augsburg Fortress, 1992.

Campbell, Thomas D. "The Confession of Faith and Inclusive Language." *The Cumberland Presbyterian* 166.2 (February 1994): 19-20.

Cumberland Presbyterian Church. *The 1984 Confession of Faith of the Cumberland Presbyterian Church.* Memphis Theological Seminary library, 1984.

Hester, David J. "Inclusive Language Policy." *The Cumberland Presbyterian* 165.5 (May 1993): 31.

Jeremias, Joachim. *The Central Message of the New Testament.* New York: Charles Scribner's Sons, 1965.

Kidd, B.J. *A History of the Church to A.D. 461.* 3 vols. Oxford: Clarendon Press, 1922.

Knickerbocker, W. E. *Nicene/Chalcedonian Reflection and Inclusive Language for God in Post-Modern Western Culture.* Prepared for the March 30th 2001 "Christianity in the Academy Conference". University of Memphis, 2001.

Miller, John W. "Rays of Fatherhood Shining Forth-Why We Call God Father: Biblical and Cultural Considerations." *Touchstone* 14.1 (January/February 2001), 40-46.

Murrow, Hubert W. "Of Languages and Images of God." *The Missionary Messenger* 65.3

Thompson, Tommy. "The Other Side of Gender-Inclusive Language." *The Cumberland Presbyterian* 165.9 (September 1993): 24-24.

Thompson, Tommy. "Not So For Me!" *The Cumberland Presbyterian* 166.2 (April 1994): 13, 29. (March 1994): 18-20.

The Permanent Committee on Theology and Social Concerns of the Cumberland Presbyterian Church. *Words Are Just Words—What's All the Fuss About?: A Cumberland Presbyterian Look at How We Use Language.* Memphis: The Resource Center of the Cumberland Presbyterian Church, undated.

Reardon, Patrick Henry. "Father, Glorify Thy Name," *Reclaiming the Great Tradition: Evangelicals, Catholics, and Orthodox in Dialogue.* ed. James S. Custinger. Sowers Grove IL: Inervarsity Press, 1997.

Rolnick, Philip A. "Fatherhood and the Name of God." *Names* 40.4 (December 1992).

Nominalism: Enemy of the Individual

Diane G. Lemmon[*]

With the rise of nominalism in the later Middle Ages and its current emphasis in contemporary society, both secular and within the church, the worth and capacity for the growth of the individual have been significantly diminished, resulting in effects on relationships within the society as a whole. After a clarification of the terms "universals" and "nominalism," the relationship of the universals with the communal nature of the church will be examined. As humanity is seen in transition in the Middle Ages and afterwards, the destructive effects of nominalism on the society and the individual will then be examined. A conclusion will end with an expression of hope.

Clarification of Terms
Universals

In philosophy, there is a concern with the reality and relationships of the universal forms and the particular things of the sensible world. The particulars include things such as a man, ideas such as love, and understandings such as colors.

Plato was the champion of the universal. His view of the relationship between the universals and the particulars was that the universal, or the idea, was the stable and true reality. Anything in this sensible world was a particular part of a universal, and was actually only a shadow or representation of the universal. The particulars were unstable. The sensible world was given attributes from the universal (idea), but was incomplete. The universals were the foundation and origin of this sensible world in his doctrine of metaphysics (De Wulf). In a clear statement of Plato's theories:

> The unities which underlie the changes and the singular aspects of things, beds, or men, or acts of bravery, are not constructions of our minds. They have a being which is independent of our knowledge of them (Carre` 34).

As mathematicians and scientists have sought understanding and investigated diverse phenomena, they continually discover connections and "universal relations underlying and connecting the mass of facts with which experience is confronted" (Carre` 34). A follower of Plato and believer in the realism of universals would simply see this as a testimony of the greater idea, the universal that exists in true reality. "It is assumed that everything possesses a fixed and definite essence" (which would be the universal) (35).

Aristotle dealt with the universals in a different manner. The sensible world was not a shadow of the universal but was reality itself. Reality was found in individual

---

[*] Diane G. Lemmon lives in Pope, Mississippi, with her husband and children. She is a senior student at Memphis Theological Seminary, and she and her husband serve as supply pastors in The United Methodist Church.

substance. The universals, in a sense, were shadows of the particulars. The universals were "products of our subjective consideration" (De Wulf). Nominalism continued to develop and the next step was taken.

Nominalism

In the Middle Ages, this thought line of the universals continued until the resurgence of Aristotle. "Corporations were prior to individuals, as the universal was prior to its particulars" (Carre` 38). However, a challenge began to arise.

As the reality of the larger idea, or universal, was questioned, Aristotle's emphasis on the particular began to strengthen. Abelard followed this line of thinking in the early 1100's. He believed we in our own understanding related commonalities to things, "while the individual alone exists," (De Wulf) thus eliminating the reality of the universal. St. Francis of Assisi was devoted to "Jesus of Nazareth, the individual (opening) a new perspective on the unique particularity of the person" (Dupree` 38). His religious genius began a challenge of the tradition of the universal, however unintentional. Bonaventure (1221-74) upheld the universals but placed them in the "incarnated Word as in their divine archetype . . . with) Christ, the synthesis of all ideas" (38). A shift was slowly occurring to the singular.

John Duns Scotus, the Franciscan monk, developed the "primacy of the individual into a wholly new philosophy" (38). "(He) argued that the universal is not the whole of the essence of an individual but part of its essence"(Carre` 108). Individuality and knowledge of the individual were becoming dominant.

As this shift continued, Ockham saw how the new emphasis on the individual wouldn't fit either Plato or Aristotle. He abandoned the relationship of the universal and the particular. He stated that "the universal....is not actually different from the individual. It is present in particular things in a contracted form. Humanity is present in Socrates in a specific way." (Carre` 108) He broke from both Plato and Aristotle as he stated that reality is found through the senses with our contact with physical substances (Dupre` 39). Ockman saw the universal as illogical and unnecessary.

> But they exist neither in an independent realm outside the mind as Plato was believed to have held, nor even inside the singular reality as Aristotle had taught. Our only access to the real consists in an intuition normally conveyed through the senses (Dupree` 39).

As nominalism took shape, reason, as concerning the particulars of the sensible world, became dominant above the metaphysics of the universal.

The abstract universal was viewed as a sign with no real value since it was seen as not existing outside of the mind. There was no connection between the particulars since the universals were simply ideas formed in the mind. Sensation guided life (Carre` 122). The individual was placed totally in isolation of any larger form or idea. As the scientific revolution grows, the study of the particulars of nature complements, and was complemented, by nominalism.

Universals and the Church

However, the universals continue in philosophical thought. The church upholds the universals where the communal nature of the body and early Christian dogma and theology is practiced. It merits a look at how the early practices of the church related to the universals, even into the Middle Ages.

The early church fathers brought Christianity in touch with philosophy, mainly Neoplatonism which was a direct offshoot of Plato's philosophies. The Neoplatonic concepts of reality complemented the Christian view of God as being perfect and the ideal form of man (Carre` 5). The belief in a higher form, the universal, explained Christian belief in the divine attributes as being communicated to man from God, through Jesus Christ.

Indeed, the idea of God's immanent presence in creation soon drove Christian theologians….to Neoplatonic philosophy….The soul recognizes the divine image in itself and in the cosmos and returns both to their archetype (Dupre` 31).

The communal nature of the early church fit neatly with the Neoplatonic emphasis of the corporate rather than the individual. The heritage of the close bond of brotherhood the disciples had shared was carefully maintained and nurtured in the early church. There was a new love in the world, and this is "the bond of union in the early church" (Knox 61). The shared experiences of the body of believers strengthened and enlivened the ties. The developing faith that was common to the believers had Christ as its clear focus (64).

There was no deliberate attempt to lower the ideals of the individual or to dull the voice of his conscience, but his conscience had to be educated in the sphere of larger social obligations and greater practical effectiveness for the welfare of the group (Case 205-6).

The Pauline organization of the church is a clear example of this strong community. It emphasized the welfare of the group without sacrificing the well-being of the individual. Paul's model of the church body is the clearest and best recorded vision of the communal nature of the early church movement.

Although divisions are evident and addressed throughout the New Testament writings, this was understood to be undesirable. In his letter to the Roman church, Paul appeals for them to see the group as "one body" with the individuals contributing diverse gifts that are to be used for the building up of the body, the group of believers. Again, the individual is an important part of the larger body, but it is a part, not to be isolated. "The strong are to be patient with the weak… They are not to please themselves, but each is to 'please his neighbor for his good, to edify him'" (Knox 89). In the letter to the Philippian church, there is an emphasis on one spirit, one mind for the church. They are reminded that this honors the selfless sacrifice of Christ (89).

Discipline is needed within the body to maintain unity. This is not a discipline for being "different," but a reminder to remain faithful to the unity of the group. Diversities are applauded and encouraged. Divisiveness and harm to the unity of the community are met squarely, with the possibility of exclusion for those who will not respect the community or the leaders. The leaders are seen as laborers, without class distinction (Knox 90). They are to work for the unity and preservation of the corporate body, not for their own concerns.

This sense of unity stretches beyond the single church and reaches to all the churches of the Christian movement. Paul refers to both the churches of God and the churches of the saints in I Corinthians. He appeals to the group to match the generosity of another church in II Corinthians. Monetary gifts were often corporate, being from several different churches. As he reaches out to evangelize the Gentiles, an even larger catholic church is seen (Knox 90-95).

In other New Testament writings, there is a constant call, concern, and description of the unity of the church. The gospels each contain indications of the consolidation of the believers. The fourth gospel especially dwells on the bond of love and unity of the believers with their God and each other.

The pastoral letters are dominated by this concern of order and unity. "First Peter sees the church as a 'holy nation, God's own people'" (Knox 113). All three Johannine letters emphasize the bond of union as love. Later church fathers, such as Ignatius and Polycarp, write of unity and order. Their vision is that of a growing catholic body of believers (113-114).

Thus the early church, although not free from struggles, places a high value on a community of love, bound by a common faith and Lord. Individuality is not squelched in this environment, but is necessary and encouraged. Competition with the intent to harm or better oneself at another's expense is frowned on as the strong are to use their energies to not only tolerate but to aid the weaker members.

This group of believers grew within a society that was inundated with belief in the universal. It thrived as the belief of a greater form, the conviction of things unseen. It fed the movement's belief in a God Who existed in a reality that was not seen by the senses, which truly lived in the realism of the Neoplatonists.

Another movement that exemplifies the communal aspect of the treasured individual appeared later. Consideration of this movement, called the Benedictine monastic movement, is important as it appeared and continued in a time that belief in the universal was beginning to falter and erode. It is also a balanced interaction of the group and the individual, largely reminiscent of the early church.

As the monastic life rose and began to organize, St. Benedict searched for a rule to give to those in his monasteries on first Subiaco and then at Monte Cassino. In his time, there were no orders and he formed a group somewhat unintentionally (Butler 28). However, as he established his vision of a family that remained stable and faithful, he participated in a Christian view of community. Cardinal Gasquet in his *Sketch of Monastic History* states the following:

> The monastic life "is nothing more than the Christian life of the Gospels' counsels conceived in its full simplicity and perfection...it adapts itself to the workings of grace in each individual soul, and gains its end when it has brought that individual soul to the highest perfection of which its natural and supernatural gifts render it capable" (Butler 29).

St. Benedict achieved this through an emphasis on common prayer offices and service to the community with gentle relationships among the monks.

The divine office is a distinguishing mark of the Benedictine form in its frequency. There are seven corporate offices. Individual prayer is expected and encouraged but the seven offices mark their day. There is communal power in these times not only by merit of the participation but in the reasoning. At the end of Chapter 13, the Superior is required to speak the Lord's Prayer at the morning and evening offices. This is done for all to hear for the purpose of circumventing the "thorns of scandal" as they pronounce together the phrase, "Forgive us as we forgive." Thus, each one has spoken words of grace and forgiveness twice daily with each other and their leader. At other times, the conduct of the monks is encouraged and suggested by the words spoken at the office.

Active service to the community is another mark of the Benedictine family. Due to the vow of stability (a promise to never leave) taken at the entrance of the life of the monk into the monastery, a unique family is formed. The monk is bound to spiritual ideals *and* to a human family. Again Cardinal Gasquet states:

> "The monastery is erected into a family to which the monk binds himself forever; acting only through it, sharing in all the joys and sorrows of its members, giving and receiving that help, comfort, and strength which came from mutual counsel, and the free intercourse of thought and desires, and watched over by a superior who is the father of his family" (Butler 201).

Benedict also allows for the human follies common to relationships. As sleeping arrangements are described in chapter 22, younger ones are to sleep between the older. Those who awaken easily in the morning are to encourage and help those who don't. In the night office, grace is given again for those arriving late. They are allowed until after the reading of the third psalm before being considered late.

There are also careful prescriptions of the problems and disagreements that inevitably occur. Instead of removing an offender, the Rule includes a carefully detailed methodology for bearing with the failings of one another while the abbot seeks resolution. Removal is a loss of family, and this is to be avoided (Butler 209).

This strong communal aspect of the Benedictine monastery gives it the strength needed to last. "There is no phenomenon more wonderful than the persistence of the spirit of a community through long ages..." (Butler 214). No matter what problems surround the family, the flame survives. In the "goods bestowed on us by God, they can more easily be preserved and the external attacks of the Enemy more easily warded off; the conquest of habits of sin is easier 'if he fears the shame of incurring censure from many acting together'" (Tunink 49). The responsibility of each monk is to serve and be devoted to the needs of the community. "Zeal in fraternal service flows from faith in Christ" (86). Again we return to the ideal of the communal Christian life, as shared by the early church.

Society in Transition
As society continues and the Middle Ages struggle with collapsing governments, individual wars, and plagues, there is also a shift in the philosophies. The belief in universals begins to wane as nominalism emerges, and humankind moves towards the advent of scientific investigation and the rise of the individual. The Reformation and the Renaissance approach and extol the glories of the individual over the traditions and restraints of the church at large.

When the Roman Empire breathed its last strained breaths, the world in Europe began to change significantly. The movement of the barbarians prevailed as the crumbling empire fell. The empire was stagnant and weak and easily overrun by the vigorous peoples. The European continent changed from a happily populated and ordered world to a still and desperate wasteland. The many invasions of the barbarian tribes decimated the glory of Rome, leaving people afraid and alone (Fremantle 14).

The old Roman system was too complicated for the barbarians to perpetuate. They used the ancient system of villages without a ruler. However, another system soon began to emerge. Feudalism appeared, being the natural result of combining the Teutonic villages of the new residents and the Roman elements (Coulton 3).

The feudal system emerged as a way of providing safety for the people. In Roman patronage, there had been voluntary ties of vassalage. At this time, lords with land and enough power to fend off the violence became the centers of life. Safety was promised in return for a pledge of service. The great manors appeared and became a system within themselves. The manor was the agricultural counterpart of the feudal lords. The large manorial home was surrounded and supported by the work of many servants and serfs. Agriculture and livestock were cared for, and shared, sometimes sparingly, with the workers. Within this system, the serfs were given homes and food, as well as the protection of a local feudal lord (Coulton 5).

Leaders rose and fell as the barbarians struggled to rule their new lands. The Franks perfected the military feudal system and the agricultural manor. As their strong influence spread, so did the power of these systems.

As the feudal system became more deeply entrenched, loyalties began to shift. Men bonded themselves and their families to these local chieftains, and society solidified in a fragmented sense, to simply survive. The feudal system provided structure and safety (Fremantle 15).

The church had also remained as a surviving system as the barbarians destroyed the "civilized" world. As the two systems existed side by side, there was an interesting interaction between them.

In the early Middle Ages, community had flourished as people needed each other, and society endorsed a higher and greater good. The church spread quickly as missionaries were sent throughout the continent to the barbarian conquerors while loyalties would remain with the larger concept of the church.

The Christian movement had grown from being a small sect within the Roman society to the state religion of the empire. The church had maintained a strength and continuity due to the partial restraint by the barbarians in dealing with their institutions and the superstitious nature of the barbarians. The Roman bishops were an efficient system that could also weather the storm of the invasions. As experienced administrators, they offered the leadership and stability needed in the chaos.

The church had also initiated the ceremonies of the Roman Empire. Standing as a civilized power in a chaotic time of invasion and bloodshed, and due to its endurance and authority, the church had also amassed great monies. Bishops and priests were not usually destroyed as were civil governments. By 700, the Roman church was all that was left of the Roman Empire. St. Augustine's "City of God" had helped the church remain somewhat autonomous in thought and respect from civil roles, but not in reality and actions. In this time of the absence of civil authorities, the church became just that (Coulton 8). Since it was the state religion of the highly respected Roman Empire, it had more credibility than other systems (11). This pressure of being the civil authority would be a poison for future trouble.

As monasteries were often spared in the bloodshed, they flourished and became a secure place to live, offering civilization in a dark time. During this time, St. Benedict's work flourished in the monasteries (Fremantle 31-33).

The church had preserved education (Fremantle 12). Education and books were kept safe in the monasteries and great churches which the feudal lords helped to build. The church held the people capable of leading civilization (Coulton 31). The church held the power of excommunication, so the great lords wooed it with cathedrals and lands for monasteries (13). The church held the social and political power as every child was baptized and heresy was punished by death. The illiterate parishioner spoke his will on his deathbed to the priest, often involving land (39-40). The church, even as it began to suffer from the corruption of its power, was the center of village life. It offered spiritual protection to a superstitious people as the lord of the area offered physical safety (44).

Medieval civilization was at its height. Under Innocent III, the papacy saw a time of power and authority. Italy was developing, and the Holy Roman Empire appeared. The cathedrals were ornate with universities attached. The friars were active. Other monastic orders were organized, especially the mendicant. With manors intact, the feudal system was at its strongest. Society was safe and happy. Towns were new and flourishing. All the systems were healthy and active. But the play for power would soon dominate the society. The marriage of the systems would quickly grow into conflict.

In the early centuries, the church and state had existed peacefully. As the power of the papacy grew and the feudal lords became kings of great lands, it became an uneasy relationship. In what had started as a mutually beneficial relationship, the activities and ambitions of both began to conflict (Fremantle 36).

As the feudal lords battled, the successful lords increased their power. The feudal system became one of monarchy as the lands consolidated. The papacy played a large part in the coronation of the kings as the national spirit grew, but the exact nature of their role was never clear. As a good example of this tense relationship, the coronation of Charlemagne has long been debated as to the actual role of the pope (Fremantle 37).

As the Charlemagne Empire crumbled, Frankish feudal lords emerged. Bishops and abbots throughout the continent found themselves within the demanding feudal system. Land was used as a powerful hold in investiture of the church and monastery. (Fremantle 37).

The church fell to corruption and greed as the great lords incorporated it. The papacy suffered from the fighting of clans as three popes claimed the position (38). Clergy of little training and education often became subject to the local lord and his desires. The church at large was beset with internal quarrels and ambitions. It all too often acquiesced to the power of the feudal lords, and became a part of the problem. The local parish priest was given difficult decisions of loyalty. The pope was often too distant and/or ineffective to be influential as the local lord's demands took primary importance. After all, he provided sustenance for life and safety. Monastic life struggled with the same difficulties as it was in a seemingly "middle man" position in the "big corporation" of the papacy. "The papacy had to be rescued from the mire, monastery life had to be reformed, and the secular clergy had to be rid of such evils as lay investitures, simony, clerical marriage, concubinage, and general sexual laxity" (Fremantle 39). Reforms came, but no one was cleansed of politics.

The Crusades marked a time of the society coming together in a common goal, no matter how questionable. This served as a brief bond of unity and common purpose for the continent. The Crusades, however, began also to drain the feudal system of its knights and lords, as well as monies used in ransoms for the traveling lords (Ross 33). Due to the influence of the Crusades and other changes at the time, the merchant and middle class began to develop independently of the collapsing feudal system, learning spread through the universities among a people no longer consumed with mere survival, and Aristotle was re-discovered in the West.

Disease stalked all, with no respect for status, military might, or papal position. The Black Death ravaged the continent. Whole towns were left standing empty. Animals wandered and died in the streets and ditches from the disease, for lack of serfs to tend them. Lesser lords would lower the rents and services, to retain the few men who were left to tend the castle and manor (Ross 220-221). As the disease took its toll, another power arose with disastrous results for all.

The philosophy of the individual blossomed and began to spread. The problems of a corrupt church had never been completely remedied. The crisis of the plague had caused a severe mistrust in the church's power and theology. The rediscovery of Aristotle began to replace the position of Platonism in theology. Ockham and Scotus appeared as scholastic theology was replaced with nominalism. Scholasticism had held to the universals, even though it had doubted its position. But as nominalism began with its total rejection of the universals, the seed for a deeper spiritual crisis was sown.

Theologians had been writing and attempting to systemize the faith for centuries. Anselm, Aquinas, and Bonaventure struggled to use and reconcile philosophy in these pursuits. Scholasticism was rising, and the role of knowledge in relation to faith was disputed. Theologians and academicians eagerly pursued these questions of faith and knowledge, as they debated which one was primary.

A look at Anselm and Thomas Aquinas effectively shows the debate. This also reflects the struggle of Platonic thought and the rise of the Aristotelian method.

Anselm followed in the Augustine tradition in that faith precedes and leads to understanding. He used this in his arguments, which helped lead the way to scholasticism, a name of the method of thought that evolved in early medieval times. This term describes the shift of theology from the monastery to the schools, as well as naming a specific method of reasoning by using questions (Gonzalez 312).

Anselm's ontological argument was a play of things in reality and things in understanding. He showed a Platonic influence as he described God as "'something than which nothing greater can be thought'" (Rogers). His successive arguments were as follows: God, to be God, must exist in both reality and understanding. God, to be God, must have necessary existence *and* contingent existence (Rogers). He was assuming the Platonic concept.

As Thomas Aquinas explores the question, he went to Aristotle. He used the emphasis that Aristotle put on the sensory world, and the idea of natural reason, which was apart from faith or illumination. He did not allow faith to be dominated by reason, but stated that it could be used to reach God. He did believe the intellect was primary but allowed that God could be reached also by faith. He took the "sin" out of the intellect. In Platonic thought, intellect and the sensible world had been labeled as bad, or inferior (Rogers). "Thomas synthesized Aristotle with the traditional thinking of the church and produced a massive systematic theology" (Rogers). He turned Aristotle from "a threat into an instrument in the hands of faith" (Gonzalez 319). In this way, he hit a middle road that few, if any, would ever return to.

The emphasis of reason over faith continued as theologians pursued this new path. The points of understanding as perceived from the sensible world were applied to faith. As scholasticism became more and more complex, there was an eventual reaction. The universals were completely abandoned as the particulars of this world dominated faith, and nominalism was born. As nominalism came into being with Scotus and Ockham, philosophy and theology began to be assigned separate places. The fragmenting of faith and theology from the rest of life was complete, and the things human and sensible reign.

Theology went through many changes as the tradition of Platonism was lost. A paradigm shift soon took place as the Reformation began. The lifeblood of the Reformation was the position of the individual before God. Although Luther protested he was not a nominalist, he inherited the theological nominalism of the later middle ages (Dupre 203). He avidly attacked the positions of Ockham and other nominalist writers (204). However, the society continued seeking the power of the individual, and the emphasis of the individual's faith in God flourished.

The Destructive Effects of Nominalism

These changes resulted in destructive effects. Society was no longer a place of cooperation and support, but an interaction of rights and privileges of various individual concerns. The church segmented into many groups of different beliefs and views, with the resulting clashes and struggles.

The individual was given the responsibility to establish identity within a changing society. The position of the individual was affected continually as society continued to shift.

Within the Society
The changes were destructive to society. The European world had gone through a dark and chaotic time. Society had drawn close, and communities flourished. Now, as daily life eased, the communal aspect of life was disappearing. Nominalism was permeating society on many levels.

There was a strong surge of nationalism as the feudal system fell. Language, loyalties, and customs became the framework as nations grew and solidified. As these powers grew, the rulers often came into conflict with papacy and its claim to power within the society. As the Reformation broke out, with the ensuing formation of the church England and the Catholic Reformation, a voice called for moderation. Erasmus of Rotterdam spoke of moderation as each side claimed his support. He was a humanist who looked to the Platonists. "He would complain, 'I detest dissension because it goes both against the teachings of Christ and against a secret inclination of nature'"(Gonzalez 13). But society continued to fragment.

The church itself became dangerously tainted with the nominalism that ruled the society. As the Protestant Reformation matured, the resulting groups continually divided and sub-divided. There was no longer a catholic church or a great community of believers. Labels and points of doctrine reigned supreme. The rights and call of the individual and his/her individual relationship with God was the battle cry as doctrine and methodologies were hotly debated. Suppression, oppression, and violent persecution ensued but failed to prevent the process.

In this fragmented society, each group claimed importance. In the continual situation where the individual reigns and is the ultimate value, community disappears. Inherently each person has certain rights. As the nominalistic influence emphasizes the particulars, the individual stands above community. Rights become confused with privileges, and often take precedence.

The ensuing and continual struggle then becomes one of each individual or part of society (as distinguished by a common characteristic) in a contest of whose "rights" become more important. There is a constant "one-upmanship" of one part over another part. The community has become defenseless against the individual. "It is time, in the West, to defend not so much human rights as human obligations" (Solzhenitsyn 21).

The invasive and destructive forces diminishing the experience and possibility of any sense of community surround us. The dynamics of pluralism have shattered the sense of mutuality associated with a common place (seen in the concept of "parish") or common task (as seen in the concept of voluntary society) to evoke or create some sense of mutuality and interdependence (Foster 56).

As the dynamics of the society itself is shaped, the individual is also touched. In a society where the individual is valued above all, it would seem logical that this would be a favorable situation. But the destructive effects are frightening.

On the Individual
The individual becomes lost in a group without community. As parts of the group compete for the prime spot, the individual is placed in a difficult and stressful position. Power and identity become critical, and remain unresolved issues.

In this society, as the individual's civil rights are emphasized, people become parts of artificially formed groups. Instead of being ruled by a higher power that is perfect and strong, the individual must find a position within a group of some type. Without the hierarchy of an Absolute Power, the group exists and finds life in and of itself. Without the hierarchy of a higher power, the individual is involved in a constant power struggle. Energy spent on maintenance of this position is energy not spent on growth.

The life and the very existence of the group depend on a static trait or quality possessed or perceived to be owned by each individual part. This places decided restrictions upon the individual. As each small group seeks the attention of the larger group to attend its "rights," the individual must find a place and an identity. Instead of relying on its own unique characteristics to contribute to the community, it adopts a distinguishing mark that is noticeable in either a positive or negative manner, so it can receive recognition and a place within a smaller group. That limits the individual, actually robbing it of its natural individuality. It has to find a commonality with a small group within the larger one to gain power. Existence becomes a play for power instead of simply living and thriving as a treasured individual. Whatever else that is unique in the individual--for humanity is immensely diverse in make-up--may need to be sacrificed to capitalize on the element that maintains its power level in the group. That attribute can become a fixed "brand" on the individual, again limiting its ability to grow and mature. Thus, a person with a handicap cannot become anything but handicapped without losing position in the society.

However, the models seen in the early church and the Benedictine monastic movement provide for the individual within community, rather than a group. The Pauline vision provides structure and allows for growth. The Benedictine model gives freedom under a higher power, the abbot, and acceptance for both weakness and individual strengths.

In the Pauline vision of community, each individual's gifts are needed. To lose individuality is to harm the community. There is not the play for power, but a careful network of diverse and necessary parts. Instead of fighting for recognition and position, there are complementary relationships with all the other parts. There is also room for growth. If a position changes in the community, other parts can shift and work together to complement the change. In a group of widely diverse and complex individuals, there is much room for transition. Thus, a handicapped person can become much more without losing safety or prestige in the group, recognized for his/her many other traits.

In the Benedictine community, the presence of a strong but kind leader is an important feature. Within the hierarchy, where the leader is seen as servant and father figure, the individual is protected, and the struggle for power is unneeded.

A weaker member is not penalized for being such in the Rule. Dignity is given to each member for living within their capabilities, with honor and compassion given for failures and lack of abilities. In a group where individuals are given position by being prominent, weakness is dangerous: Failure is a death sentence, whatever it is perceived to be. In a group where weakness is seen as acceptable and not harmful, the individual has safety.

In contemporary society, as the individual is involved with a struggle for power and safety, fatigue begins to grow. Weakness and fear become dominant in daily life, with a growing militant attitude. As power or authority becomes associated with oppression, then all hierarchy is seen as threatening. Fear and mistrust of servanthood is fostered and the individual is further isolated in this society of scattered particulars.

In contemporary times, there seems to be such a growing fatigue by individuals in this threatening society. An overwhelming sense of apathy has pervaded our American culture. Mistrust of authority in most forms, as well as scorn for servanthood characterizes our post-modern world. This makes a world dangerous and cold where the interaction of individuals is measured and cautious. As the individual struggles to hide its weaknesses, to maintain a position of power and acceptability, it spends immense energy on the recognition of its "rights". There comes a point of overload. A sense of apathy is likely to develop. Purpose is lost as the individual is devalued by the loss of its place in community.

> It lies behind the high rate of mental illness and the soaring number of suicide attempts among adolescents... It undercuts the productivity of men and women who fear for the future of their jobs. These symptoms, however, point to a deeper fear--the loss of a viable future (Foster 112).

The legacy of the rise of the individual as a result of the nominalistic emphasis in Western culture has left humanity with much to worry about.

Conclusion and Hope

With the rise of nominalism in the later Middle Ages and its current emphasis in contemporary society, both secular and within the church, the worth and capacity for the growth of the individual has been significantly diminished, resulting in effects on relationships within the society as a whole. The preeminence of the individual above community is a hopeless and dangerous vision.

Christianity with its communal emphasis offers hope for our contemporary society. As the primitive church worked together to establish and honor community, humanity was much safer. In this environment, the question, "Who is my neighbor?" was unnecessary. Currently, it is haunting and difficult.

In order to preserve the individual and provide a place of growth and health for each person, the ancient vision of community must be recalled. The reality of a larger world and system, in which the perfect forms of what we struggle to establish here truly exist, offers stability. In contemporary society, where the particulars dominate with a rejection of the greater good, humanity flounders and slowly dies of apathy and fear. What we are doing now is not working. Community governed by the Higher Power seems the best alternative. It has worked in the past, in spite of human failures.

I propose that we work to cleanse the contemporary Christian community of nominalistic philosophy and its insidious influence. This would affect the culture in large ways, as the church has always wielded great influence for better or worse. It would open the doors of growth and health for the society. In turn, community offers hope to the individual, making this world one of warmth and safety, rather than fear and danger.

References

Butler, Dom Cuthbert. *Benedictine Monachism.* New York: Barnes & Noble, Inc., 1924.

Carre', Meyrick H. *Realists and Nominalists.* Oxford: Oxford University Press, 1946.

Case, Shirley Jackson. *The Social Triumph of the Ancient Church.* New York: Harper & Brothers, 1933.

Coulton, G.C. *The Medieval Scene.* New York: Cambridge Press, 1959.

De Wulf, M. *"Nominalism, Realism, Conceptualism." The Catholic Encyclopedia, Volume XI.* (1999): 3 March 2002. <http://www.newadvent.org/ cathen/ 11090c.htm >.

Dupre', Louis. *Passage to Modernity: An Essay in the Hermeneutics of Nature and Culture.* New Haven: Yale University Press, 1933.

Foster, Charles R. *Educating Congregations.* Nashville: Abingdon Press, 1994.

Fremantle, Anne. *Age of Faith.* New York: Time Incorporated, 1965.

Gonzalez, Justo L. *The Story of Christianity: Volume I.* San Francisco: Harper Collins, 1985.

Gonzalez, Justo L. *The Story of Christianity: Volume II.* San Francisco: Harper Collins, 1985.

Knox, John. *The Early Church and the Coming Great Church.* New York: Abingdon Press, 1960.

Rogers, Jack B. *Introduction to Philosophy.* San Francisco: Harper & Row, 1981.

Ross, James Bruce, ed. at al. *The Portable Medieval Reader.* New York: Penguin Books, 1949.

Solzhenitsyn, Aleksandr I. *A World Split Apart.* New York: Harper and Row, 1978.

Tunink, Wilfrid, O.S.B. *Vision of Peace.* New York: Farrar, Straus, & Company, 1963.

"Who is their God?": Reflections on the Civil Rights Era

William R. Marty[*]

> "Over and over I have found myself asking: "What kind of people worship here? Who is their God?"
>
> Martin Luther King, Jr.,
> "Letter from Birmingham Jail,"
> April 16, 1963

> "There are laws greater than the laws of Memphis and Tennessee, and these are the laws of God."
>
> Rabbi James A. Wax, speaking for about
> 300 clergy to Memphis Mayor Henry Loeb,
> April 5, 1968

Introduction

The questions of Dr. King and the statement by Rabbi Wax provide a framework for the examination of the initial failures, and then the historically quick successes, of white Christians and others in the era of the Civil Rights movement. But those questions and statements pose further questions, for the very foundations on which the civil rights successes were built are now severely eroded and under furious intellectual, political, and legal attack, which threatens to leave us without the tools and weapons with which Dr. King and others waged their largely successful struggle to revise the practice of American democracy. That, at least, is the argument of this essay.

"What kind of people worship here? Who is their God?" Why did Dr. King have to ask himself these questions? Why did they come back to him, again and again? The answer is a sobering one to Christians. The questions kept coming back because Dr. King lived in a region, and a nation, where most people professed themselves Christian, but few acted, on race matters, as though they were. Consider the words of the Apostle Paul. In Christ, he said, "There is neither Jew nor Greek, there is neither slave nor free,

---

[*] William R. Marty is professor of political science at the University of Memphis. He serves as associate editor of the *Journal of Interdisciplinary Studies* (*JIS*), an interdisciplinary forum for exploration of the human condition in the light of Christian understanding. He is a board member and sometime coordinator of the Christianity in the Academy Conference. His research principally investigates why both Christians and secularists so often produce policies of political, social and economic folly, but also why aspects of Christian understanding enable it, when not forgotten, to produce a practical wisdom about worldly things surpassing the capacity of both the secular enlightenment and post-modernity.

there is neither male nor female; for you are all one in Christ Jesus" (Galatians 3:28). That is the faith. Yet white Christians, who profess that faith, had accommodated themselves easily, comfortably even, to a system of segregation and discrimination that held others, fellow Christians in the main, both unjustly down and humiliatingly apart. What kind of people can do this? Who is their God? Dr. King was specific in his disappointments: "Where were their voices," he asked, "when the lips of Governor Barnett dripped with the words of interposition and nullification? Where were they when Governor Wallace gave a clarion call for defiance and hatred?" (King 1964: 91). The answer, for most, was that they were standing silently by, doing little or nothing. White Christians mostly did not hurry to stand up for their faith, their fellow believers, or elementary justice. "What kind of people worship here? Who is their God?"

Accounting for the Failure

What accounts for the initial failure of so many Christians to respond to the unjust plight of their fellows during the civil rights protests of the nineteen fifties and sixties? One answer would be that these Christians were sinners. And indeed they were. None, since the Fall, come to God but by the divine mercy. But sin, if it touches all, explains little, for at other times and places individuals and even multitudes of Christians behaved bravely, facing even death itself for the faith or their fellows. So the question becomes, why so little response from these Christians, at this time?

One possible answer to the fecklessness of these Christians is that they were not, in any deep sense, Christians at all. Their lives, that is, were hardly touched by the religion they professed. In practice, they were more American, or Southern, or white, or secular than Christian. We all have a range of identities–husband, father, attorney, American, Southerner, Cardinal fan, or any of a number of things, and they touch us at different times, at different levels of our being, and they sometimes conflict. It was the 'fifties, after all, that Will Herberg was describing when he noticed, paradoxically, both evidence of a religious revival and a continuing secularization of ideas. Here is his explanation:

> The secularism dominating the American consciousness is not an overt philosophy: it is an underlying, often unconscious, orientation of life and thought. Because it is so pervasive and omnipresent, it is hard to put one's finger on it. Yet perhaps something of what it implies may be suggested by a startling contrast. When Ignazio Silone, the Italian writer and Socialist, was asked what he felt to be the "most important date in universal history" he replied unhesitatingly: "The twenty-fifth of December in the year zero." But when nearly thirty outstanding Americans were asked not long ago to rate the hundred most significant events in history, first place was given to Columbus' discovery of America, while Christ, His birth or crucifixion, came fourteenth, tied with the discovery of X rays and the Wright brothers' first planned flight (Herberg 1960: 1-2).

Herberg comments that Silone, however unorthodox he was, took Christianity seriously in a way that the Americans did not, and he observed that: "The secularism that pervades the American consciousness is essentially of this kind: it is thinking and living in terms of a framework of reality and value remote from the religious beliefs simultaneously professed" (Herberg 1960: 2). In some ways, in the America of that era, Christianity was a pool very broad, but for most, only ankle-deep. As Herberg put it: "the religion that actually prevails among Americans ... has lost much of its authentic Christian (or Jewish) content" (Herberg 1960: 3).

Second, and here again Herberg provides a key, to profess religion in the America of the 'fifties was often less a matter of commitment, as a person of faith, to God, than a matter of establishing one's identity. For it was not enough to be an American, one had to be some kind of an American, and there were, then, according to Herberg, three acceptable kinds:

Not to be a Catholic, a Protestant, or a Jew...is, for increasing numbers of American people, not to be anything, not to have a <u>name</u>: and we are all, as Riesman points out, "Afraid of chaotic situations in which [we] do not know [our] own names, [our] 'brand' names...." To have a name and an identity, one must belong somewhere; and more and more one "belongs" in America by belonging to a religious community, which tells one <u>what</u> he is (Herberg 1060: 40).

Robert Booth Fowler of the University of Wisconsin has put forward a related thesis. He has argued that America is a very competitive, individualistic society. But people cannot sustain a life in such a harsh environment, lacking in community and mutual support, so many people flee that harsh weekday workaday world on weekends, in church. It is in church that they find a community that will give them the emotional support that they cannot get in the world of business, and do not get from their neighbors, whom they may not know, or from their extended family, from whom they are probably separated, at least by distance (see Fowler 1989). These people, seeking emotional support, are not interested in theology, for theology divides people, and what they want from the church is community, or even a sense of family, which may otherwise be missing in their lives. Religious revival (as during the 'fifties) and increasing secularism can go hand-in-hand, then. The harsher the secular environment of competitive, individualistic capitalism, the greater the need for a refuge of community, and the church increasingly served that purpose, but that was a purpose that had little to do with changing one's life to bring it into conformity with the deeper understandings of the faith.

The theses elaborated by Herberg and Fowler would indicate that serious attempts to understand or live one's faith may be much rarer than church attendance might lead one to suppose. Benton Johnson, Dean R. Hoge, and Donald A. Luidens' recent study of baby boomers among Presbyterians casts light on this, and on the boomers' parents. In questioning these baby boomers, they discovered that they were "hard put to offer theological reasons why anyone should remain a Presbyterian, or even a Christian" since "they seldom discuss religious matters even with their family and closest friends" and "they had only the vaguest idea what their own parents–or more commonly their fathers– believed" indicating that "silence on matters of faith is not new in many Presbyterian families." They concluded: "It seems likely that a significant portion of mainline

Protestant parents of the 1950s did not have a deep commitment to the tenets of orthodox Christianity" (Johnson, et. al. 1993: 16).

To identify oneself in the 'fifties or 'sixties as a Christian, then, was not necessarily a *religious* statement at all. And to expect a genuinely religious response of such a Christian–who was often only seeking identity or community, not God, and was in any case likely to be ignorant of the faith, as well as indifferent to its deeper meaning and demands–was to ask of him what he might not have to give. (That this may be just as true today, for many, is obvious.)

In addition, the Christianity of the 'fifties and 'sixties was handicapped by a series of structural and theological obstacles to serious engagement with the problems of race in America. One was the division of the races: for the most part, white and black Christians attended different churches, so that there was little contact, as Christians, between the two. This had obvious ramifications for the civil rights struggle, for institutional and personal contacts were limited, which meant that white Christians did not have to confront, on any immediate level, the conflict between their Christian doctrine and their cultural practices.

A second, and related, division had occurred within the white churches at the time of the Civil War. Northern and southern branches of the same church typically divided, and afterward went their separate ways, politically, theologically, and socially. This too led to less confrontation with prejudice and discrimination in race relations, for those who, by geography and culture, were less likely to accept Jim Crow were now members of separated branches of the same church. Again, contact broke down. This may in fact have had considerable importance. It has been noted in an article on the outspoken Southern rabbis of the civil rights era that: "Most of the Southern rabbis who spoke out against the segregation were born and educated outside the South, some in the North but many others in Eastern Europe. Southern Jim Crow laws and attitudes startled them." As Hollace Ava Weiner put it: "As outsiders, they saw the South differently than most of their white clergy colleagues" [who had usually grown up and been educated in the South] (Waters 1995: A12). Separation of the Northern and Southern churches meant that there would be fewer "outsiders" in the South to be startled by Southern practices and bring Southern Christians into confrontation with their culture.

Fragmentation of the Christian community may have had another interesting consequence. The large number of different Christian denominations, all competing, in a sense, for market share (a capitalist idiom for a capitalist nation), meant that the churches were in a poor position to go seriously against the culture in which they were immersed. In a stronger church, this would have made less difference, but in the churches as they were, shallow, at best, in their spirituality, at least among many of the laity, this may have made a substantial difference. There was, how should one put it, no demand for a prophetic stance on the relation of the races among Southern white Christian lay people.

For clergy who might have taken a prophetic stance, and a few did, there were two additional obstacles, one structural, one theological. The structural obstacle was the congregational church organization that typified many of the churches strong in the South. This meant that individual congregations "called" their ministers, and, if they became unhappy with them, they could oust them as well. Like the politician, then, it was hard for these ministers to get far out front of their congregations–and still stay in office. Hierarchically organized churches in which bishops had firm control of where their priests or ministers served had more ability to stand somewhat apart from the people in the pews, and this occasionally showed itself. In Memphis, for example, the aftermath of the *Brown* case, calling for integration of the public schools, illustrated the difference. The Catholic bishop, in control of a system of already existing parochial schools, decreed that Catholic parents with children already in the parochial schools could keep them there, but parents with children then in the public schools could not switch them to parochial schools–he did not intend that parochial schools be used as an escape from integration. It was a stance that was, if not heroic, at least principled. Among churches differently organized, there developed a sudden, if not heretofore noticed, demand for religious education, and a number of private religious schools sprang up–to gain the scornful appellation of "segregationist academies." Congregationalism in church organization, for all its early usefulness in establishing the principles and practices of representative government in church and state, did not prove useful in dealing with the race problem.

Southern laity and clergy were likely to be housed in congregational churches, deeply embedded in the local culture. They were likely to share a certain theology, too, often called fundamentalist or evangelical, in which the individual's personal relationship to God was stressed (unlike the more liberal or progressive mainline churches of the North, which tended to stress the "Social Gospel"), and in which intervention in politics, or social matters, was then regarded as deeply suspect. These Southern evangelicals were more likely to stress the transcendent element of religion than those in the mainline churches of the North, but they were crippled in their witness to the world on matters such as race by a theology which stressed individual sin and repentance, rather than sinful social structures and the need for reform of those sinful structures through political action (see Reichley 1985, esp. 311, but also 203-219 and 311-331).

In the end, one can find many reasons why the Christians of the 'fifties and 'sixties led Dr. King to ask, again and again, "What kind of people worship here? Who is their God?" Still, if Christians were initially dull and tardy in their response, many finally did respond, and that response was essential to the successes the civil rights movement did achieve.

Christian and Jewish Response

It is important to note the situation that confronted African Americans at the beginning of the Civil Rights era. The Civil War had brought an end to slavery, but Reconstruction, whatever its promise, ended as part of a tacit political settlement of the disputed election of 1876. The terms devised by the Republicans and Democrats were that the Republican was to become President, but the Federal Government was to end its occupation of the South, thereby largely withdrawing its protection of Southern blacks. This sad affair was the beginning of the climate in which there began that long development of the Jim Crow system of segregation and discrimination that came to dominate the South, and in fact, part of the rest of the nation. Blacks, having barely tasted the liberating institutions of democracy, were once again excluded from the democratic processes designed to protect people, and the KKK and others soon organized to exclude African Americans once again, by lynching and terror if needed, as others stood by in the Democratic South.

It was difficult for black Americans to confront this restored oppression. Denied the vote, denied the effective support of even Northern whites, confronted by overwhelming force including the use of terror without any recourse to law and courts, facing a whole system of laws and customs built up to exclude black Americans, there did not seem to be a way forward. Marcus Garvey suggested "Back to Africa," but this was neither practical nor was it wanted, and he was, in any case, soon brought down. A more promising path was chosen by the NAACP and its sister legal organization, an interracial effort to achieve a "color-blind" society by education and litigation. This in fact had some success–albeit agonizingly slowly. The NAACP legal arm achieved a long string of victories in the courts, but each was fought, then resisted in implementation, and it did begin to look like the South was going to make good on its defiant boast of "a hundred years of litigation."

This was the situation confronting Dr. King and the incipient movement of nonviolent protest. Beginning, at the level of national consciousness, in the Montgomery Bus Boycott of 1955-56 (James Farmer and CORE had acted in Chicago as early as 1942), Dr. King and the nonviolent protest movement quickly captured and held the national attention. Though it seemed agonizingly slow and difficult to those involved in the struggle, historically speaking this movement–working in tandem with the legal and political arms that were greatly expedited by it–brought about a remarkably fast collapse of the legal and moral structure of Jim Crow that the South had built up over the period of a century, and which had seemed firmly entrenched. The public accommodations act of 1964, the voting rights act of 1965, and the open housing act of 1968 stand as monuments to this swift revolution of law and status. And just as important, the moral legitimacy of the old system was destroyed. No public figure or movement of respectability could, after this period, publicly make arguments for discrimination against black Americans.

How can one explain this historically rapid change? It is most illuminating to focus on the career of Dr. King, the greatest leader of nonviolent protest for civil rights, and arguably one of the great public figures in the history of the republic, for he certainly did more to move the nation forward on civil rights for African Americans than anyone since Lincoln, and the historical mistreatment of black and other excluded Americans has been perhaps the greatest failure of American democracy.

The first thing to note about Dr. King is that he was a Christian minister, raised in a family of Christian ministers on both sides, educated at Morehouse in Atlanta, Crozer Theological Seminary in Chester, Pennsylvania, and in theology at Boston University, where he received his doctorate in 1955. In Montgomery, he was elected president of the Montgomery Improvement Association (MIA) and became its leading spokesman in the bus boycott movement there. The MIA was a group of ministers, meeting in their churches, appealing to their church members. He then formed a larger organization, the Southern Christian Leadership Conference (SCLC), which was the primary organizational vessel of his leadership of the nonviolent protest movement.

The next thing to note is that Dr. King understood his theory of nonviolent protest to derive, in its principles, from Christianity. As Dr. King said:

> From the beginning a basic philosophy guided the movement. This guiding principle has since been referred to variously as nonviolent resistance, noncooperation, and passive resistance. But in the first days of the protest none of these expressions was mentioned; the phrase most often heard was "Christian love." It was the Sermon on the Mount, rather than a doctrine of passive resistance, that initially inspired the Negroes of Montgomery....It was Jesus of Nazareth that stirred the Negroes to protest with the creative weapon of Love (King 1958: 84).

Dr. King had been deeply influenced by Mohandas Gandhi, but he expressed the relationship in this way: "Nonviolent resistance had emerged as the technique of the movement, while love stood as the regulating ideal. In other words, Christ furnished the spirit and motivation, while Gandhi furnished the method" (Ibid., p. 85).

Indeed, if we look at the points that Dr. King stressed again and again in his campaigns, we find them suffused with Christian themes: reconciliation and forgiveness as the goals, the call to love the enemy, to remember that we are all sinners and must be forgiven, the need for faith, and hope in the future, the importance of redemptive suffering, his understanding of the needed love as *agape*, a creative understanding of the opponent, not a liking for what he does, and the nature of his defense of civil disobedience in "Letter from a Birmingham Jail," which is filled with appeals to Divine Law, examples from the Bible, as well as the understanding that the natural law is from God and trumps any merely human law. While King appealed to our democratic tradition and to natural right, he interpreted them in terms of his faith, as he had Gandhi's understandings, and it was by this bridge that he hoped to bridge race lines, and finally did.

Dr. King, then, worked for human rights as a Christian, in the light of Christian understandings, and he cooperated with others who were, in the main, Christians, while mobilizing many of his army of nonviolent protesters in Christian churches, preaching nonviolent protest as Christian love in action, the practical application of the Sermon on the Mount. (Black Christians had always had a strong pull toward the justice themes of the Bible, and a strong drawing toward a God who had freed his people from bondage in

Egypt, and led them to the "Promised Land." In this Egypt, black Americans looked to that past with hope, and looked for their own Moses to lead them out of bondage. One can usefully view Dr. King's career, and his final speech, in this light.)

Finally, it is useful to reprise Dr. King's strategy for making nonviolent protest work. It was his understanding that the comfortable do not give up their privileges voluntarily, merely from persuasion. His strategy, then, was to build such a crisis that the republic would have to choose: either give up the cancer of a racial caste system or stand exposed before the world as hypocrites, only pretending to value law, human equality, and the principles of Christianity and democracy. His tactic was to employ the tool of nonviolent protest in such a way that he made of our cities a stage before all the world, a stage upon which was played out a modern morality play confronting the republic with the choice of good or evil. And his genius was to combine coercion and persuasion–the first so that the republic had to finally face up to the problem; the second so that it (and we) had every chance humanly possible to choose the just resolution to the crisis.

Dr. King's achievement was to turn an appeal to morality into an effective political weapon that divided whites so that racist white power would be balanced, then overterned, by the combined power of other whites and blacks as expressed through the interventions of the overwhelmingly white courts, Congress and Executive. Thus we associate Dr. King with the 1964 and 1965 Civil Rights Acts, with presidential and judicial interventions, and with the consequent opening of public accommodations and enforcement of voting rights–events associated with the major events in Dr. King's career: the Montgomery bus boycott, the Birmingham campaign, the Selma campaign, and the March on Washington.

Dr. King led an oppressed people excluded from the political institutions designed to prevent that oppression and aimed, not at hatred and revenge, though nothing is easier than to hate, and nothing is more destructive (look at the sad travail of Northern Ireland, or Palestine and Israel, where those who believe in hatred and terror have been followed, and whose people have bled and bled and bled), and he preached, instead, love, justice, forgiveness, and reconciliation. And, more to the point, Dr. King's efforts were, to a remarkable degree, effective. Many people did respond to his appeals. And Washington D. C. was flooded with Christian clergy and Jewish rabbis. Even in 1963, Joseph Rauh, longtime civil rights activist, present at a Senate Judiciary Committee hearing, made this observation in wonder: "Standing outside the Committee Room was the most beautiful sight I had ever seen–twenty Episcopalian priests, fully garbed, all young beautiful WASPS. I used to think that the only two people out in front for civil rights were a Negro and a Jew–[Clarence] Mitchell [Washington lobbyist for the National Association for the Advancement of Colored People] and myself. But this was something we had never seen before. I knew then we really were in business" (Reichley 1985: 247). Soon Washington swarmed with clergy and laity committed to the passage of the civil rights bills. Soon Congress responded. The lonely battle was over, and allies in abundance had finally come.

"What kind of people worship here? Who is their God?" When King coerced them to confront themselves, and their consciences, many of those people proved themselves Christian in fact, and not merely in name. And one must note that the words delivered by Rabbi Wax to Mayor Henry Loeb, in Memphis, "There are laws greater than the laws of Memphis and Tennessee, and these are the laws of God," were words delivered for about 300 local black and white clergy in a very southern city. There was enough Christianity, and Judaism, left to produce a significant, nation-changing response.

The Future

The civil rights movement was effective, in part, because there were commonly held beliefs and principles to which one could appeal over the gulf of race and privilege. This is worth pondering because the grounds on which those effective appeals were made are increasingly mocked or disbelieved, and the religious ones are increasingly driven from the public square. This is of vital importance because a large pluralistic and diverse republic must have a foundation for appealing across group lines, and the ones we had in the Civil Rights era are now under increasing attack with nothing in sight to put in their place. Thus an appeal to the founding principles of the Declaration of Independence is undermined by the increasing disbelief among intellectual and opinion leaders in any kind of objective moral truths; the same is true of the increasing secularization of the academy and intellectual elites, for whom an appeal to religious principle is now regarded as in bad taste, if not altogether dangerous and bigoted. Thus the most foul and offensive attacks on religion are defended in the name of artistic expression and the First Amendment, while the treatment of any other groups in such a manner would produce a firestorm of outrage. Postmodernism attacks all foundationalism (without, perforce, stripping its adherents of their own fervent political views and their willingness to impose them on others). But if there are no objective moral truths to be found by reason and revelation, one is hard-pressed to understand how a nation can be a nation, or maintain harmony among groups. If there is no moral truth, then it is hard to see why one advantaged group should give up its privileges for a disadvantaged group.

By the same token, the fervent movement to make sure that religion is removed from the public sphere, and that it not be considered legitimate grounds for public policy-making, deprives us of one of the appeals that can cross group lines, and lift us above our selfish interests. It would have deprived us historically of that fervor for justice that fueled the abolitionist movement here and in Britain, movements that ended slavery here and the international slave trade by the intervention of the British navy. Moreover, it would have denied us the offices of Dr. King as leader of the Civil Rights movement, a movement that did much to finally make this democracy legitimate, and that had enormous moral impact around the world. It would have denied us much of the rest of the leadership, and the followers and supporters of that movement, and drained effective political support in the time of crisis.

Moreover, the increasing "secularization" of religion whereby the religious right takes its cues from the secular right, and the religious left from the secular left, effectively removes genuine religious influence on American life. And we have seen the fanaticism and cruelty of some of the great secular movements in that most bloody of all centuries, the twentieth. Given that, the removal of genuine religion and natural law from public life is no reason for optimism. A great republic requires a moral foundation. At great moments in American history the nation was able to respond usefully to our religious and moral traditions, now under heavy assault. Those bridges to which Dr. King and others appealed are now being stripped away, and it is not at all clear that we have anything with which to replace them. That is cause enough for sober reflection.

References

Fowler, Robert Booth. *Unconventional Partners: Religion and Liberal Culture in the United States.* Grand Rapids, MI: Eerdmans, 1989.

Herberg, Will. *Protestant–Catholic–Jew.* Revised ed. Garden City, New York: Doubleday Anchor, 1960.

Johnson, Benton, Dean R. Hoge, and Donald A. Luidens. "Mainline Churches: The Real Reason for Decline," *First Things.* 31 (Mar. 1993): 13-18.

King, Martin Luther, Jr. *Stride Toward Freedom: The Montgomery Story.* New York: Harper and Brothers, 1958.

_____. "Letter from Birmingham Jail," *Why We Can't Wait.* New York: Signet Books, 1964.

Reichley, A. James. *Religion in American Public Life.* Washington, D.C.: The Brookings Institute, 1985.

Waters, David. "Rabbis Were Key Players in Fight for Civil Rights," *Commercial Appeal* (Memphis), Mar. 26, 1995: A1, A12.

Religion: Stepchild of the First Amendment:
Free Speech, as Long as It Is Not about Traditional Christianity
(a University of Memphis Case Study)

Candace C. Justice[*]

It all began as a routine news judgment call such as those made in every newsroom in the country many times every day. Because of limitations of space and time, it is standard procedure at newspapers, magazines and broadcast news operations to make decisions about what will be covered and how much space or time will be devoted to that subject. It is also common procedure, although not necessarily a daily one, to allow reporters or editors who feel that a certain news event or subject conflicts with his or her personal ethics to recuse themselves from that story and have the story reassigned to someone whose personal ethics or sensibilities are different.

Enter Jonathan Cullum, a graduate student, working as a copy editor at *The Daily Helmsman*, the independent student newspaper at the University of Memphis. A routine news judgment call on March 24, 1999, by Editor-in-Chief Sheila Edmondson, which followed Jonathan Cullum's request to be recused from a news story, resulted in a five-month persecution campaign against Jonathan and the student newspaper by some University administrators, faculty and students and a reporter from the local newspaper, *The Commercial Appeal*. During those five months, Jonathan Cullum was equated with Hitler and the Oklahoma City bomber; his dismissal was demanded, along with a printed apology by the newspaper; funding for the student newspaper was questioned; and demonstrations, boycotts and lawsuits were threatened. Had the incident occurred this spring, Jonathan would no doubt have been compared unfavorably with Osama bin Laden.

What did Jonathan Cullum do to bring down upon himself and his newspaper the wrath of a special interest group and some members of the University establishment? He had the audacity to admit to another student that his Christian beliefs prevented him from personally reporting in the newspaper something he felt was "immoral" and which he believed contributed to the "marginalization" and degradation of women.

On March 24, 1999, Jonathan was handed an announcement from the University of Memphis student group, Women's Action Coalition, known as WAC, about their plan to

---

[*] Candace C. Justice, assistant professor of journalism at The University of Memphis, serves as general manager and faculty adviser for the student newspaper, *The Daily Helmsman*. In 2001, she won the Thomas W. Briggs Foundation Excellence in Teaching Award, the university's highest such award. Before joining The University of Memphis faculty in 1992, she worked for 10 years as a reporter, editor and columnist for the *Memphis Press-Scimitar* and worked 9 years as a freelance writer for *TV Guide*, *Redbook* and other national magazines.

hand out "safe sex kits" on campus. Members of the group planned to dress in bumble bee costumes and hand out condoms and other materials. Jonathan decided he could not in good conscience include the item in the daily campus calendar of events which he put together every day as part of his copy editor duties. Without fanfare, he told his editor-in-chief Sheila Edmondson about his ethical dilemma and offered her the material, if she would like to include it in the calendar.

To quote Jonathan in an e-mail he later wrote in response to complaints from WAC about his actions, "I felt a moral imperative not to contribute to the publicity of what I felt was an immoral event, although it was not necessarily my intention to actively block your group's access to the publicity afforded to other groups…I am a Christian, a Southern Baptist, and I have many objections to the agenda of your group, but it is not my intention to muffle intelligent discussion among adults…I do have legitimate concerns about our culture's marginalization of women…Another moral imperative of a Christian man is to love women as Christ loved the church, which is not to say possessively or forcibly, but selflessly…with sincerity and respect."

Editor Edmondson's response to Jonathan was one of respecting his right to recuse himself from this news story. She said she would add the WAC event to the calendar herself, since it did not violate her personal ethics. However, a few minutes later Sheila was informed by another editor that a reporter had already been assigned to cover the WAC event. Since the event was to be covered in a full story, Sheila decided to omit it from the calendar of events. Subsequently, a full story and a page-one picture of a WAC member in a bee costume handing out condoms ran in the newspaper.

Because of the extensive coverage of the WAC event, the editors and I, their faculty adviser, were surprised when the Women's Action Coalition began a letter-writing campaign accusing Jonathan and the newspaper of discrimination against women and censorship in violation of the First Amendment. The letters called for a "purge of responsible staff members" and the revoking of financial support to the newspaper for at least a semester. The protesters also called the First Amendment Center in Nashville and the Student Press Law Center in Washington, D.C.

Attorneys at both institutions told them in no-uncertain terms that newspaper editors, including student editors at public universities, have the right to make editorial content decisions on any basis they wish, and that it is not censorship when the newspaper declines coverage for any reason. Furthermore, they were told that a state university that withholds funding from a student newspaper in order to control its content is guilty of prior restraint, which *is* a violation of the First Amendment. Therefore, they were more in danger of violating the First Amendment than we were.

The U.S. Constitution and the courts were solidly on our side, so we wrongly assumed the matter would die down in a few days. But it was only the beginning of the furor. During a campus speech by feminist Gloria Steinem, a WAC member stood up and announced that the student newspaper was oppressing minority groups, women in particular. No one mentioned that of the seven editors at our newspaper at that time, five were women. As a journalism professor and faculty adviser to the student newspaper, I received an angry call from the assistant dean of judicial affairs demanding to know what I was going to do about the discrimination against the Women's Action Coalition? Another dean demanded an explanation from my department chair. Most shocking was the reaction of some of our journalism faculty, who normally are ardent defenders of the First Amendment. Three of my colleagues — two women and a man — lashed out in anger at me and the students and demanded the newspaper print an apology to the Action Coalition. The students and I were stunned and hurt by these faculty members' bitter reaction and their failure to support our First Amendment rights.

We stood our ground. No student editor was fired. No apologies were published. No funding was withheld. The last publication day of the semester, editor Sheila Edmondson wrote and published on page one an inspiring and courageous defense of Jonathan and the newspaper.

At this point, there had been some bright spots — the chairman of the journalism department, Dr. Jim Redmond, was our defender and champion throughout the ordeal, and the assistant dean of judicial affairs, Kathy Story, who at first was our accuser, after considering the law and talking with me about newspaper procedure and ethics, became a strong defender of our First Amendment rights.

The spring semester ended, and we assumed the controversy was over. To our great surprise, it was far from over. After not getting the response they had hoped for from the University, the Women's Action Coalition took their cause to *Commercial Appeal* reporter, Sarah Derks, who apparently did not think the student newspaper deserved the same First Amendment rights to determine content that her own newspaper exercises every day. When Derks demanded to know what Dean Story was going to do about the *Helmsman*, Dean Story asked Derks if she favored prior restraint of First Amendment speech. There was no answer from the reporter.

Derks' next move was to ask me for access to *Helmsman* archives from the past year, which I readily granted. She went through every issue counting the number of times Women's Action Coalition was in the calendar of events and the number of times the Baptist Student Center's activities were in the calendar. When she confronted me with her numbers, I explained that the Baptist group, which involves a large group of students, had more activities and therefore got into the calendar more often. I also pointed out that neither the Baptist group, nor any other religious group, had gotten a full story and page one picture about an event as the five-member WAC had with their condom hand-out. She was not satisfied with my answer and continued to pursue the story for weeks until her editor at the *Commercial Appeal* found out about it and killed the story, because it was not newsworthy and was untimely and hypocritical.

In the end, an attorney at the Student Press Law Center in Washington, D.C., put it all into perspective when he said this:

You know, don't you, that if your editor had turned down a calendar item from a Nazi group or some other group like that, there would have been no controversy. In fact, turning down the item would have been considered the morally right decision to make. But because the editor used conservative Christianity as a criteria for his personal decision to step away from the story, he is being persecuted.

Ken Paulson, executive director of the First Amendment Center, said ours was a classic case of all First Amendment rights converging in one controversy. There was the newspaper's right to free press; Jonathan Cullum's rights to religious freedom; the Women's Action Coalition's right to speak out against Jonathan and the newspaper; and the Coalition's right to peaceably assemble if they carried through with their threat to demonstrate outside our building.

This incident, on one hand, could leave First Amendment purists celebrating that the system worked. It could be argued that everyone on both sides exercised their rights and no real harm came to anyone in the end.

On the other hand, in the heat of battle, it did not seem to us that the system was working at all. It felt like a bad dream. It felt very unfair. And it did not feel harmless for the editor and Jonathan and I to spend five months — waste five months, if you will — defending ourselves against those who would deprive us of the First Amendment rights clearly afforded us by the U.S. Constitution.

Although the chairman of the Journalism Department and I were willing to answer accusations in court, if necessary, and attorneys at the Student Press Law Center were prepared to defend us, nobody wanted to waste another year or more on such an exercise. Most of all, those of us at the student newspaper were painfully reminded that having Constitutional rights is one thing, but having them respected by others is not a given. And most painful was the realization that there are those who would defend the First Amendment rights of a variety of causes, religions and institutions, but deny those same rights to orthodox Christians.

Whiskey Priests, Japanese Canadians, and World War IV: Christian Behavior in an Always Dangerous World

Bill Jenkins[*]

In responding to the World Trade Center bombings with questions about Christian behavior in a dangerous world, we can mislead ourselves. The event surprised and shocked us in part because we Americans had become seduced into believing that we were somehow immune to the political and social forces regularly erupting in violence around the world. The symbolic damage of the attack remains the crucial thing, not the body count nor the tons of steel destroyed. In terms of actual human suffering, the attack on 9/11 produced no more human pain and loss than, say, the Ruwandan or Bosnian slaughters of the 1990s. The fearful killing of defenseless American civilians will produce no new theological insights into the meaning of suffering or Christian morality. As devastating as the suicide high-jackings were, the answer to the question of what constitutes Christian behavior in a dangerous world will not vary much from answers given to such previous disasters as the sinking of the Lusitannia, the attack on Pearl Harbor, or, for that matter, the Oklahoma City bombing or the Columbine High School bloodbath.

In a 1998 article on technological change, media analyst Neil Postman makes the following observation which speaks indirectly to this issue: "I doubt the 21st Century will pose for us problems that are more stunning, disorienting, or complex than those we faced in this century, or the 19th, 18th, 17th, or for that matter, many of the centuries before." After quoting snippets from such figures as Socrates, Rabbi Hillel, the prophet Micah, and after pointing to such religious thinkers as Jesus, Mohammed, and Shakespeare, Postman continues: "It is all the same: there is no escaping from ourselves. The human dilemma is as it has always been, and it is a delusion to believe that the technological changes of our era have rendered irrelevant the wisdom of the ages and the sages."

We can see the aftermath of the 9/11 attacks in the heightened attention given to "spiritual issues" as pictures and telecasts of religious services appear in the public media with far greater frequency than before the attack. Experts on Islam in particular and fundamentalism in general rise to visibility, and churches along the entire theological spectrum now offer lectures and sermons on the true nature of Islam, on just war teachings, and on the uses of suffering. But much of the energy fueling these religious responses remains unconnected to the deep tradition that Postman reminds us of. The American outrage that the hatred and violence plaguing other countries should actually touch us is matched with an American hunger for formulaic and quick solutions to the

---

[*] Bill Jenkins is Assistant Professor of English at Crichton College, Memphis, Tennessee. His research interests include the writers Annie Dillard, Willa Cather, and Walker Percy. He is interested in using Trinitarian theology to examine modern culture, especially the ways in which the modern Church interacts with culture.

religious dimensions of our common mortality, which the attack has forced us to see. Christian behavior in a dangerous world, especially when that behavior is located in the Gospel mandate to love all with God's own love, even our enemies, must arise from patient apprenticeship to the habits of mind and worship that honestly face the depths of our common spiritual dislocation.

In another time of impending darkness, the English poet W. H. Auden wrote in his 1939 poem "In Memory of W. B. Yeats" about the violence beginning to rage in Europe:

> In the nightmare of the dark
> All the dogs of Europe bark,
> And the living nations wait,
> Each sequestered in its hate;
>
> Intellectual disgrace
> Stares from each human face,
> And the seas of pity lie
> Locked and frozen in each eye.

These two stanzas delineate the parameters of suffering the world was about to enter, and we must honestly confess that the mayhem unleashed upon us in the recent suicide attacks is not somehow ontologically different from the horrors visited upon the world during WWII. The final three stanzas of the poem express what must be the artist's responsibility to such terror. By encompassing fear and hatred into artifact, the poet points the way to a transcendent response:

> Follow poet, follow right
> To the bottom of the night,
> With your unconstraining voice
> Still persuade us to rejoice;
>
> With the farming of a verse
> Make a vineyard of the curse,
> Sing of human unsuccess
> In a rapture of distress;
>
> In the deserts of the heart
> Let the healing fountain start,
> In the prison of his days
> Teach the freeman how to praise.

This artistic response to human suffering and its implications for Christian practice is what I want to ponder. Three very different texts will help us triangulate our position, but I am not using fiction to dramatize just war theory or to explore theodicies. I want us to listen briefly to *The Power and the Glory*, by Graham Greene, *Obasan*, by Joy Kogawa, and *A Canticle for Leibowitz*, by Walter M. Miller in an attempt to see that the ancient command to love God, neighbor, self, and enemy will always confront us, regardless of the catastrophes that regularly overtake us poor banished children of Eve.

Graham Greene's 1940 novel *The Power and the Glory* is in many ways the quintessential novel about Christian behavior in the dangerous world of the 20th Century. The story is set in revolutionary Mexico during a time of government crackdown on religion. An alcoholic priest tries to carry out his sacerdotal work in secret while the lieutenant of police seeks to capture and execute him. The priest flees from village to village, fighting the temptation to escape to a safer environment, yet he does not present an idealized vision of moral strength that can face martyrdom with equanimity. The priest has fallen in several ways both before and during the dark days of political violence. Previously pampered and indolent, he now wrestles with his alcoholism and the guilt he feels for fathering a girl--and for loving her so intensely. Having grown painfully aware of his flaws, the priest makes his weary way, dispensing the sacraments while bringing danger near to those who hide him.

The lieutenant presents a similarly conflicted individual, the modern radical who would gladly burn down the existing world to bring about a more just one. He kills easily but without sadism, and like the priest he genuinely believes in his own vision even if his attempts to enact it remain stunted by his moral and spiritual deformities. He is "a little dapper figure of hate carrying his secret love" (58), namely a very real desire to improve the lives of the poverty-stricken children whom he awkwardly loves.

This persistent theme dominates the dreary lives of these two desperate people-- love, which surprises them with its force. In one scene, the priest ends up in jail though the police remain unaware of whom they've captured. A "pious woman" demands the priest hear her confession but he challenges her moralistic, class-conscious religiosity with its imperious demands. The pious woman retaliates with hatred, causing the priest to reflect:

> He couldn't see her in the darkness, but there were plenty of faces he could remember from the old days which fitted the voice. When you've visualized a man or woman carefully, you could always begin to feel pity—that was a quality God's image carried with it. When you saw the lines at the corner of the eyes, the shape of the mouth, how the hair grew, it was impossible to hate. Hate was just a failure of the imagination. (131)

In a later parallel scene, the priest tends to the needs of a village that has not seen a priest for months. He "savagely" interrupts one woman's confession, recognizing that she is "another of the pious—like himself." She says "haughtily", "'I love God, father.'" He replies: "'How do you know? Loving God isn't any different from loving a man or a child. It's wanting to be with Him, to be near Him.' He made a hopeless gesture with his hands. 'It's wanting to protect Him from yourself'" (173).

The lieutenant finally catches the priest, and as the priest waits in prison to be executed in the morning, he tries to make his own confession to God. Unable to concentrate on the ritualized language, he thinks of his illegitimate daughter, wishing that the painful love he felt for her extended to all others whose path he has crossed, including the lieutenant himself and the revolting half-caste who turned him in to the police. But he is a man, not Christ himself, constrained by the inevitable limitations flesh is heir to. He goes to his death convinced of his failure. Ironically, the priest's ignoble death does effect change. Having killed the last priest, the lieutenant falls into a depression, and "the dynamic love which used to move his trigger-finger felt flat and dead" (220).

Greene's story tells us of God's love discovered within the horrors generated by the ideological fissures of 20th Century. We rightly value what we could term the novel's Corinthian dialect of strength drawn out of weakness, of love for enemies described without sentimentalization. Radical atheism in its various brutal politicized forms has often marked the boundaries for discerning Christian behavior in the Modern Age. But with Joy Kogawa's 1981 novel *Obasan*, we are reminded of other ways in which the world becomes dangerous for Christians. The novel mostly traces several years during World War II of life in various internment camps for Canadians of Japanese descent. Most of the individuals involved had acclimated well to the social environment of this Western country before the war began. The majority of the Japanese Canadians were Anglican, and they were highly involved in the usual variety of North American culture, such as the Boy Scouts. Yet in the space of a few weeks their lives are reduced to economic and psychological rubble as they lose homes, jobs, and freedom.

The novel charts the slow fall into lower and lower levels of physical hardship of one family in particular. Rather than the obvious polarization between Christian and Atheist in *The Power and the Glory*, here we have a good Christian society apparently planted against the totalitarian nightmare world that Auden foresaw in his poem. Yet this Christian nation suddenly turns on its own, reminding us that the evil that makes the world dangerous does not reside over there, on the other side of the dividing line between good and evil, between us and them. The novel demonstrates the truth that Alexander Solzhenitsyen pointed out: the dividing line of good and evil runs through the heart of each man and woman. Christian behavior does not work itself out free from the environing evil humanity has fallen into, and the dangerous world of *Obasan* is maintained in part by the Christian church. In one scene, the narrator writes, "It was hard to think of Uncle as anyone's enemy. One Sunday when Uncle went to church, the clergyman turned him away from the communion rail. But there was no enemy there" (46).

Kogawa never descends to reinscribing us versus them in the novel, the bad Western white Christianity dominated by men versus the communal, aesthetically sensitive Asian victims of Western oppression. The Japanese Canadians *want* to be Canadian. They practice their Christianity faithfully and are deeply hurt by such things as the United Church parson who wants to kick all the Japs out (120). Father Nakayama, an important character in the novel, does his best to comfort his flock in their time of exile, and he does so by preaching, praying, and singing the Good News of God's love even when circumstances seem to indicate that such a religion obviously fails in a world like this. Near the end of the novel, just after the war ends, a great embarrassment hovers over the Japanese Canadians and the once officially hostile society that called for their isolation. What is Christian behavior in this dangerous world?

> Nakayama-sensei stands and begins to say the Lord's prayer under his breath. "And forgive us our trespasses—forgive us our trespasses," he repeats, sighing deeply, "as we forgive others . . ." He lifts his head, looking upward. "We are powerless to forgive unless we first are forgiven. It is a high calling, my friends—the calling to forgive. But no person, no people is innocent. Therefore we must forgive one another. (287-88)

The little girl who narrates the story begins and ends it as a woman remembering that dark time. In the present tense of the story's telling, the late 1970s, the narrator hesitates to accept the priest's insights. She and her aunt, her Obasan, have joined a political movement seeking redress from the government, and their participation splits the family. In considering the various ways family members have responded to past injustice, the narrator comes to realize, "Somewhere in all these truths lies a failure of love" (final unnumbered page of the novel). We hear the echo of Greene's priest, and while hearing these voices we turn to our current world of sudden, catastrophic death to speak similarly about the ancient teachings the church has been entrusted with.

The first two novels tell variations of stories that have happened far too many times in this century—about lives in interment camps, in concentration camps, in refugee camps, in gulags, in exile, in large scale exterminations. Greene and Kogawa strain to declare without distortion that though an individual might not be ennobled by such suffering, one can resist devolving to the level of hatred of one's persecutors by striving to see clearly and live faithfully while the world turns toxic. The final novel discussed here approaches the issue of Christian behavior in this dangerous world from a much more expansive dimension. The time span covered in the science fiction classic *A Canticle for Leibowitz* (1959) is approximately 1000 years, though the novel begins several centuries after World War III, making the chronological context something like 1500 years all together. Included in this long distance calendar are a new Dark Ages, a New Renaissance, and a new Modern Age, culminating with World War Four and the final removal of all intelligent life on earth, either through destruction or through escape off-planet.

The novel opens with references to the Great Simplification, a time of purging by the survivors of WWIII, when all surviving technicians, scientists, and scholars were executed for having produced the technology of nuclear holocaust. The Catholic Church, though, maintains its loyalty to learning as a pastoral duty. In monastic hideaways barely surviving in places like the Utah desert, monks copy out by hand whatever documents they discover, including circuit drawings, blueprints, and grocery lists. These texts have long lost their original meanings to the monks, but they lovingly preserve them anyway, aware that the detritus of the previous civilization could once again signify if the context can be rediscovered. Thus, the monks preserve a historical sense of past and future, seeing themselves as guardians of a religious vision that demands to be lived out incarnately in time.

In this novel the question of how Christians behave in a dangerous world must confront issues of human identity understood theologically as the Church rebuilds a humane culture. While monks go about their work of preservation, they must also deal with the various barbarians, cannibals, lunatics, and mutated freaks directly threatening the church. Questions about Christian ethics and morality reappear in sometimes literally monstrous dimensions, yet these Christians hear the same summons to worship the Triune God that Greene's and Kogawa's priests also heard in this terrifying century. Ironically, our situation today becomes so anxious that it overbears memory, blanking out once common fears of global holocaust. Certainly as bad as the terrorist attacks on America might become, their effects, even if frequent, would hardly compare with multiple hydrogen bomb warheads wiping out millions and contaminating millions more for centuries to come.

A Canticle for Leibowitz reminds us of the long-term issues involved in Christian behavior in an always dangerous world. The loathsome ideology of the Taliban—embodied as much in the dynamiting of giant Buddhist statues as in the sponsoring of terrorism—is not categorically different from the dozens of other violent regimes that have ransacked humanity throughout the 20th century and before. Human history, in civilized or barbarian guises, is awash with blood. Miller's novel suggests that our spiritual dislocation is so severe that even if WW III had occurred, the fallout, if you will, would not be so terrible that it could never happen again.

At the beginning of the New Renaissance in Part Two of the novel, one monk ponders the Luciferic cycle of scientific discovery and death that seems to be playing out yet again: "How shall you 'know' good and evil, until you shall have sampled a little? Taste and be as Gods. But neither infinite power nor infinite wisdom could bestow godhood upon men. For that there would have to be infinite love as well" (221). Just a few centuries later, in Part Three, as the nuclear bombs begin falling once more, another monk boggles at the evil we do. As Texas goes up in radioactive smoke, the monk expresses his outrage:

> Toad's dung. Hag pus. Gangrene of the soul. Immortal brain rot. . . . And Christ breathed the same carrion air with us; how meek the Majesty of our Almighty God. What an Infinite Sense of Humor—nailed on the cross as a Yiddish Schlemiel by the likes of us. . . . Why do they do it all again? (259)

The novel's final image of a hungry shark patrolling a radioactive ocean implies our predatory qualities which, barring the miraculous, the church will never entirely eradicate. Contrarily, the image also points to the difference between the merely instinctual in animals and the demonic behavior that spiritual beings like humans are capable of. Miller's novel excels in lifting to consciousness the mystery of iniquity--that perduring affliction of soul that the nightly news anchors will scratch their heads over now and in years to come.

In an article on the 1990s spate of high school killings, Larry Allums considers what purpose art may have in helping us understand the supernatural perturbations scarring life on Earth. He writes in "Hamlet and the Grief Counselors" that the way to understand violence is not through the reigning therapeutic categories having to do with secular definitions of well-being but through the evocative and clarifying power of the literary imagination: "mimesis involves a kind of imitation of an action in such a manner that its interior contours and valuations are 'captured' even more faithfully than its exterior surface." Allums claims, for instance, that the *Iliad* and not *Saving Private Ryan* more powerfully teaches the horrors of war because the film relies on the shock given by the exterior visible surface whereas the epic "provides the aesthetic distance necessary for us to be able to keep back and be saved from the savage proximity of the violence portrayed." In contrast, the latest CNN coverage of sundry human disasters can turn us into addicts of the awful. The novelists considered here give substance to Postman's reminder that there is nothing new under the sun, 9/11 notwithstanding, and that imagination and love grow together or fail together.

References

Allums, Larry. "Hamlet and the Grief Counselors."
    <http://www.dallasinstitute.org/Programs/Previous/FALL99/talktext/griefcounc.htm>

Auden, W. H. *Selected Poems*. New Edition. Ed. by Edward Mendelson. New York: Vintage Books, 1989.

Greene, Graham. *The Power and the Glory*. New York: Penguin, 1971.

Kogawa, Joy. *Obasan*. 1982. New York: Anchor Books, 1994.

Miller, Walter M. *A Canticle For Leibowitz*. 1959. New York: Bantam Books, 1997

Postman, Neil. "Five Things We Need to Know About Technological Change." *New Tech 98*. 14 April 2000 <http://www.newtech.org/address10_en.htm>

The Patriotic Christian: An Oxymoron?

Bruce W. Speck[*]

Introduction

This genesis for this paper is what initially appeared to me to be a contradiction between my empathetic emotional response to expressions of American patriotism and my intellectual skepticism about the validity of that empathetic emotional response. As Elvis would say, "I'm caught in a trap." But I refuse to agree with Elvis that "I can't get out." My task, then, is to explore the trap and determine how to analyze my empathetic emotional response vis-à-vis my intellectual skepticism. In attempting that analysis, I will confirm the validity of that empathetic emotional response and defend my intellectual skepticism. If this seemingly impossible task sparks your curiosity, jump on for the ride.

The Validity of Empathetic Emotional Responses to Patriotic Expressions

Perhaps it would be helpful to start with a description of the empathetic emotional response I have experienced to expressions of American patriotism. I will use as my example the singing of the "Star Spangled Banner" at a basketball game. A few months ago, I found myself standing with my hand over my heart at a basketball game listening to a fairly decent rendition of our national anthem. Inexplicably, I found myself moved by the words I heard. My eyes welled with tears, and I was basking in the pride of being an American, even a veteran of the American military establishment. I didn't join my compatriots by shouting lustily at the end of the "Star Spangled Banner"; rather, I tried to regain my composure and to mute with my handkerchief what might have been perceived as an outburst of emotion.

Now the crazy thing about my display of emotion upon hearing the national anthem is that I have grave misgivings about the validity of patriotism. In public forums, I have asked whether patriotic expressions are valid. If I am not stoned for asking such a question, I then ask whether patriotic expressions are valid for all people. That is, is it valid for those in Russia under a communistic regime to have genuine feelings of patriotism about their country and government and to express those feelings openly, even expecting their countrymen to confirm patriotic loyalty? Is it valid for a Chinese citizen to genuinely vow loyalty to the Chinese government and seal an oath of service with the promise of devotion until death? I will not sully my argument by asking whether an Arab can vow fealty to an Arab nation, such as Iraq under the leadership of a dictator. We all know that true, genuine patriotism has to be based on the legitimacy of government, and, therefore, a German patriot under Hitler is an oxymoron. Certainly, American patriotism stands as the premier model of what decent, wholesome patriotism looks like, what ideal patriotism strives for, what legitimate patriotic emotion gazes at in wonder and admiration. Canadians, Brits, some Scandinavians, and perhaps the Dutch have an

---

[*] Bruce W. Speck is Vice President for Academic Affairs and Professor of English at Austin Peay State University in Clarksville, Tennessee.

appreciation of the preeminence of American patriotism as a model for ideal patriotism. However, even some of our supposed allies (and I hesitate to mention the French and Italians, but do so quietly) have yet to understand the value of bowing first to American patriotism before nodding in acquiescence to the call for devotion from their own countries.

A problem of patriotism, it seems to me, is that the citizen of a particular country assumes his or her brand of patriotism is normative, believing that patriotism refers to *my patriotism, my country*. Political allies of my country are fine because their patriotism is akin to mine. After all, allies agree with me and share my values, so their patriotism is legitimate because it appears to mirror my own. Enemies of our patriotism cannot be said to be true patriots because their ideals are contrary to ours. The Japanese during World War II can only be said to be patriots in a fanatical sense of the word. A kama kazi pilot was an extremist of the worst sort, and cannot be classed as a patriot. Insane folk are not candidates for the patriotic hall of fame. Fortunately, most American patriots of note—I include the founding fathers, most Republican presidents, Robert E. Lee, Ulysses S. Grant, Alvin York, General Patton, Audie Murphy, John Wayne, and Mel Gibson—killed other people fair and square and lived to tell about it. They didn't take the posture of human bombs on a suicide mission. They played by the rules in the game of war. No sneak attacks. No false signals for the enemy to misinterpret. No covert action. None of that dirty stuff a true patriot would eschew when defending the hallow ideals of American democracy.

As you can see, I'm exaggerating a little to make the point that the high ideals attached to patriotism are grounded in a pristine notion of conduct that does not comport well with international rivalry. Even the Olympic games, a supposedly open forum for authentic competition based on skill, encourage a combative attitude, an attitude marked by pugilistic threats when nations believe that they have been slighted by judges from rival nations. Skill, perhaps, may not be the *sine qua non* in Olympic competition. In fact, though, patriotism is brought into greatest relief when international rivalry escalates into war. When a country itself is endangered in some way, patriotism is marked by the call to arms on behalf of the aggrieved nation. (Again, the aggressor is not considered a patriot because patriotism takes a defensive posture. Americans, for instance, can take the offensive and be patriots because we are defending America—that is, America's way of life—even in the oil fields of the Middle East.)

If what I've said is correct, why am I gushing when the "Star Spangled Banner" is sung? I had some insight into this problem when I found myself experiencing the same emotion upon hearing the "Hallelujah Chorus." Same trembling in my voice, same heaving in my chest, same tears welling in my eyes. When I saw the similarities between my responses to the "Star Spangled Banner" and the "Hallelujah Chorus," I thought, quite Platonically, "Of course! My emotional commitment to patriotism is but a shadow of my emotional commitment to the Kingdom of God." I can see that the relationship between my two emotional responses may be grounded in a primary identification with the ultimate kingdom. If, as I believe, God is the ultimate point of reference, and people, being made in the image of God, must find their ultimate reference in God, then to trace the impulse for our allegiances back to God, even when those allegiances are idolatrous, makes sense. Thus, even distorted allegiances, attributable to the working of original sin, demonstrate the God-shaped void in our beings.

However, a problem with my analysis is that it gives little room for any genuine expression of patriotism, making any positive emotional response to patriotism no more than either a genuine response to God's Kingdom or a distorted, idolatrous response to God's kingdom. That is, a true patriot can only be a Godly patriot, one who is genuinely a Christian. Others may parrot patriotic feelings and actions, but their patriotism is idolatrous because they do not see God's kingdom—and kingship—as the source of their patriotism. They substitute the shadow for the substance. But such a position vitiates patriotism as loyalty to a particular place, a particular culture, a particular people, in a particular time. Indeed, my analysis, although sympathetic to the need to ground patriotism in theological precepts, appears to radically redefine patriotism. A genuine patriot is equated with being a Christian who experiences patriotic emotions and understands that those emotions are but shadows of the eternal kingdom. The number of people who qualify as patriots is radically reduced under the provisions of the new definition.

Yet the nexus between the eternal and the temporal remains. The dependence of the temporal on the eternal is substantiated by the doctrine of God as the Creator, the Fountainhead of all that exists. "In the beginning was the Word" is not merely mellifluous but also generative, acknowledging that the preexistent Christ, Yahweh, the eternal God, brought into being the material world. As the Genesis account confirms, the world God created was good, so any Platonic attempt to invest the world with value only or primarily because it mirrors the immutable, eternal realm is to denigrate the value of the material world qua material world. But any attempt, such as patriotism, to invest the world—or a slice of the world—with superior value is equally guilty of denigrating the material world *in toto* and of establishing an artificial standard for allegiance to and in the world. My skepticism about patriotism, therefore, remains.

At the same time, a particular reading of the Bible appears to call into question any skepticism about necessity for genuine patriotism. I will articulate the premises of that reading and refute them on my way to showing that skepticism about patriotism is spiritually healthy.

The Relationship between the OT View of Land and the Eschaton

The reading of the Bible that invests great stock in the view that loyalty to a land is an enduring spiritual good derives from Dispensationalism, a widely-held theological perspective, especially among those who identify themselves as evangelicals. According to Dispensational theology, the OT view of land is normative. That is, God designated a particular place—the environs of Palestine—to the Jewish people, and God's designation is irrevocable until the eschaton users in a new heaven and new earth. This view of land is based on a literal reading of the Scriptures. Thus, God's promises related to land, as in the Abrahamic and Davidic covenants, must be fulfilled literally in Palestine. For instance, the yet-to-come Anti-Christ of the book of *Revelation* will desecrate a newly built Jewish temple and inaugurate the great tribulation in which the Jewish nation will be persecuted. Christ will rule the world for a thousand years—from Jerusalem. At the end of that time, Armageddon will be the site of the last battle before the eschaton is fully manifested.

This view of the centrality of Palestine has generated a travel industry that caters to those who seek to trod where Jesus trod, to capture, even in some mystical way, the ongoing significance of THE Land. Dispensationalism also has had a tremendous impact on American political philosophy, promoting American allegiance to the nation of Israel because the Jews are God's people in spiritual exile. To support Israel is to support God's ongoing plan of redemption. To support Israel is to support American interests. To support Israel is a test of American patriotism.

The problems with Dispensational theology are significant, and my task at present is not to identify all the problems and solve them. Rather, my task is to show that the Dispensational view of the land is grounded in a misreading of Scripture, one that promotes an intellectually and spiritually unhealthy view of land that encourages he wrong kind of patriotism.

I say that the Dispensational view of land is incorrect because the Dispensational reading of Scripture is incorrect. Broadly, the typical Dispensationalist equates a literal reading of the Scriptures with literalism. For instance, a Dispensationalist might note that in Christ's final days his rejection by the Jewish people and leaders postponed the realization of the kingdom on earth because the prophetic evidence in the OT foretells of an earthly kingdom in which the Messiah will reign. Because, according to a Dispensational reading of the Bible, Christ must reign on earth and must reign in Palestine and must reign over the Jewish people, His crucifixion delayed the earthly kingdom until the time when the Jews will once again have preeminence on the earth and Christ will reign bodily in Jerusalem.

Such a reading of Scripture surely fails to pay due attention to the typological nature of the OT. Dispensationalists, for instance, in their desire to interpret literally, confirm that temple sacrifices will be reenacted in the millennial kingdom because . . . well because that's what a Dispensational reading of the OT requires. The central teaching of the book of Hebrews—that the final sacrifice has been accomplish and is superior in every way to the cultic animal sacrifices practiced in the OT—seems to be lost in a Dispensational view that privileges a literal view of the OT as an overlay for understanding the NT. That the OT is typological, speaking in language that points forward to the realization of redemption once for all in the humiliation of the Man of Sorrows Who rules and reigns now from the eternal realm, is shunted aside in favor of a literalistic exegesis requiring tortuous and sometimes fantastic exegetical moves. That John on Patmos saw modern military armaments—tanks, missiles, airplanes—really does stretch beyond credulity the prophetic material in *Revelation*.

I assert that the Dispensational view of Scripture fosters a misunderstanding of the relationship between land and God's redemptive purposes, thus identifying God's promises to the OT saints with terra firma, minimizing the typological significance of land as emblematic of the eternal realm and spiritual truths. Indeed, the significance of the land is tied inextricably to covenant obedience. Even the monarchs of ancient Israel, particularly the southern kingdom, could not legitimately demand complete allegiance from the Old Testament saints because those monarchs, for the most part, did not fully subscribe to the OT law. That is, even those who were chosen to represent God to the people had no legitimate claim to their thrones outside of covenantal obligations as identified in the law, particularly the Pentateuch, and even more pointedly in Deuteronomy. The land was unique because God had chosen it for His dwelling and as the dwelling place of His people. But the land was not sacred in and of itself, despite the vials of sand American pilgrims purchase when they visit Palestine as a token of their desire to have a piece of the sacred place. The land was a testing place, and the actions of God's people were to be an expression of their devotion to God for giving them a place to worship Him. The people's allegiance was to be to God, regardless of the land they inhabited, and the curses of the covenant are linked to the land because the land represents God's providential and sovereign choice of dwelling place. After all, would anyone claim that Palestine was superior to Eden? Would anyone seriously claim that God could not have enacted His redemptive drama in ancient Detroit instead of the ancient Middle East? To confuse the covenantal use of land with patriotism and to infuse a particular geographical location with Biblical virtues is to minimize the ontological importance of Law in the OT. Indeed, to wed land and Law in a Dispensational fashion is to undercut the need for a critical appraisal of the OT as a prelude to fulfillment in the NT, fulfillment based on satisfaction of the legal requirements in the covenant.

Conclusion

The doctrine of original sin raises issues about our ability to think with the clarity needed to critique our time and place honestly. As sinners, we tend to accept as natural and normal our place in the sun. Others may be odd, but we are normal. This presumptive normalcy militates against a fresh critique of our allegiances, including our political, geographical, familial, and ecclesiastical allegiances. Presumptive normalcy, therefore, authenticates the patriotism typified by much of American Christianity. As one bumper sticker proclaims, "American by birth. Southern by the grace of God."

Yet a critique of our allegiances from a Biblical viewpoint calls into question the ease with which we glibly yoke Christian commitment and national interests. Is it not inexplicable Biblically why American churches believe that the American flag is an appropriate fixture in the sanctuary? Isn't it curious that American Christians, even today, so readily identify America as a center of redemptive history when secularism is the reigning paradigm in American life?

Any Christian can support any nation that orders its affairs according to Biblical teaching, and, thus, a Christian who has been born in a particular nation and lives in that nation can be patriotic to the extent that the nation is managed according to God's law as codified in the Bible. This means that unquestioning patriotism is an un-Biblical position and that no nation can claim the whole, uncritical allegiance of Christians. Further, high ethical ideals, as symbolized in a country's flag and anthems, can legitimately elicit from Christians genuine, empathetic emotional responses. Genuine emotional response to patriotic expressions is, I think, wedded to the intersection of political and Christian ideals. Those responses, however, should not be misinterpreted—by Christians or others—to mean that the Christian is endorsing particulars not grounded in Biblical law.

C. S. Lewis on the "Public Mind" of Our Neighbor

W. E. Knickerbocker, Jr.[*]

In October, 1946, C. S. Lewis wrote an essay titled "Modern Man and His Categories of Thought." As Walter Hooper tells us, this was done at the request of Bishop Stephen Neill, who was Secretary of the Assembly Commission II, an organization which brought together the two movements, "Life and Work," and "Faith and Order," as a prelude to the formal constitution of the World Council of Churches in 1948 (*Present Concerns*, 10). What Lewis wrote was intended to help Christians develop a strategy for evangelism as the Church presented the Gospel in secular western culture. This essay was not published until 1986 in a volume of essays by Lewis titled *Present Concerns*, edited by Walter Hooper.

The title of this collection of essays was suggested by Jeremy Dyson, President of the Oxford University C. S. Lewis Society, who, after reading some of these essays, said that the concerns expressed by Lewis, who died in 1963, were very present to him in 1986 (*Present Concerns*, 8). The essay, "Modern Man and His Categories of Thought," provides a summary of Lewis's analysis of the "public mind" of western culture which is as relevant today as it was when it was written. In this essay, Lewis speaks of six characteristics of the contemporary western mind which provide insights not only into the public mind of western culture but also into other essays and books written by Lewis.

This paper will outline and examine briefly these six characteristics which, according to Lewis, have radically altered the western public mind since the mid-nineteenth century. The six are: the revolution in education, the emancipation of women, the rise of developmentalism or historicism, the rise of proletarianism, the primary emphasis on practicality, and the skepticism about reason. Also, some of Lewis' suggestions which he believed would aid the Church in the evangelization of contemporary western culture will be mentioned. Let us turn now to the six alterations in the western public mind.

First, there has been a "revolution in the education of the most highly educated classes" in western culture (62). Formerly, western education was based on the Greek and Latin classics. Whether you were a Christian or not, "there was a strong infusion of the better elements of Paganism" (62). Those educated in this way believed that "valuable

---

[*] W.E. Knickerbocker, Jr. is a Roman Catholic layman; a husband, father, and grandfather; and Professor of Church History at Memphis Theological Seminary where he has been teaching Church History and Christian Spirituality for twenty-eight years. He holds the B.A. degree from Washington and Lee University and the B.D. and Ph.D. degrees from Emory University. He and his wife, Sandie, are spiritual directors of "The Household of the Holy Family," a private lay association in formation in the Marianist/Benedictine tradition in the Catholic Church, which encourages Christian family spiritual formation. He is a poet whose published poetry includes the volume: *New Eden: Poems for Living in Community with God's Holy Family*.

truth could still be found in an ancient book. It was natural for them to reverence tradition" (62). Moreover, it meant that whether you were a Christian or not there was a standard of values different from our own against which ours could be judged. The educated had "some sympathetic understanding of *pietas*." (62) However, education today is not based on the Classics. Indeed, the best educated have developed a disdain for the ancient, preferring the most recent book written by people in our own culture. The effect of this has been to cut off from the past the educated person in our western culture. In his essay, "Modern Theology and Biblical Criticism," Lewis gives an example of what this isolation from the past can do. It has caused modern biblical critics to set themselves up as authorities against the beliefs held by the early Church, the Fathers, the Medieval Church, the Reformers, and even the Church of the Nineteenth Century, beliefs which these modern critics discount without even understanding what the historic Church really teaches and why She teaches it (*Christian Reflections*, 152-166). Thus, Lewis in his essay, "On the Reading of Old Books," writes, "The only palliative is to keep the clean sea breeze of the centuries blowing through our minds, and this can be done only by reading old books" (*God in the Dock*, 202). As Lewis says in the same essay, people in the past made mistakes but not the same mistakes we make (202). Thus, while we criticize those who lived before us, we must also allow them to criticize us.

Second, in the last century and a half the minds of people in western culture have been affected by the emancipation of women. Lewis does not consider this emancipation a bad thing in itself, but in his essay he calls attention to what he believes is one deleterious effect it has had, *i.e.* "a lowering of metaphysical energy" (63). According to Lewis, the presence of women in what in past times has been those assemblies where men argued about ideas has meant that frequently the men in such assemblies "*display their plumage.* Any mixed society thus becomes the scene of wit, banter, persiflage, anecdote…rather than prolonged and rigorous discussion on ultimate issues…" (63). Thus, there has been a lowering of interest in and even of the ability to engage in serious argument about metaphysics.

About this contention of Lewis, at least three things can be said. One, Lewis did not mean that women were incapable of such argument. The first woman in his life, his mother, who was also his first tutor, earned a BA degree from Queens University, Belfast, with First Class Honors in Geometry and Algebra, First Class Honors in Logic, and Second Class Honors in Mathematics. On February 2, 1948, at the Oxford Socratic Club, Lewis debated Miss G. E. M. Anscombe, a Roman Catholic philosopher and Research Fellow of Somerville College, Oxford. On the basis of her criticism of Chapter Three of his book on *Miracles*, Lewis revised the chapter for a second edition. Several of Lewis' friends described the debate as an experience which upset Lewis very much (*Breakfast Table*, 163). However, Anscombe said that neither Dr. Havard, a friend of Lewis' who invited Anscombe and Lewis to dinner a few weeks after the debate, nor Professor Jack Bennett thought Lewis was particularly upset by the debate. Anscombe went on to say that her "own recollection is that it was an occasion of sober discussion of certain quite definite criticisms, which Lewis' rethinking and rewriting showed he thought were accurate." She regarded "the odd accounts of the matter by some of his friends—who seem not to have been interested in the actual arguments or subject matter—as an interesting example of the phenomenon called 'projection'" (*Companion and Guide*, 619-620). One of the qualities that attracted Lewis to Joy Davidman, the woman whom he married late in life, was the quality of her mind. After her death, Lewis wrote of her: "Her mind was lithe and quick and muscular as a leopard. Passion, tenderness and pain were all equally unable to disarm it. It scented the first whiff of cant or slush; then sprang, and knocked you over before you knew what was happening. How many bubbles of mind she pricked! I soon learned not to talk rot to her unless I did it for sheer pleasure…" (*A Grief Observed*, 8).

Two, Lewis also seemed to regard another fact in contemporary western culture as a contributing factor to this "lack of metaphysical energy," *i.e.* the rise of the social sciences. For example, a central character in the third of Lewis' science fiction novels, *That Hideous Strength*, is Mark Studdock, a sociologist (17). Lewis describes Mark's education by saying: "It must be remembered that in Mark's mind hardly one rag of noble thought, either Christian or Pagan, had a secure lodging. His education had been neither scientific nor classical—merely 'Modern.' The severities both of abstraction and of high human tradition had passed him by…" (185).

Three, the fact that women are as capable as men of sustained argument about metaphysics does not mean the Lewis failed to understand the profound differences between men and women. In the second of his science fiction novels, *Perelandra*, the central character, Elwin Ransom, is on the planet Perelandra (our Venus) and there, toward the end of his stay, he encounters the guardian angel of Perelandra and the guardian angel of another planet, Malacandra (our Mars). In this encounter, Lewis writes that Ransom is taught "the real meaning of gender….Gender is a reality, and a more fundamental reality than sex. Sex is, in fact, merely the adaptation of organic life of a fundamental polarity which divides all created beings" (200). Malacandra, who is masculine, has a look of "ceaseless vigilance" with "eyes that are impregnated with distance." Perelandra, who is feminine, has eyes that open inward "as if they were the curtained gateway to a world of waves and murmerings and wandering airs, of life that rocked in winds and splashed on mossy stones and descended as the dew and arose sunward in thin-spun delicacy of mist" (200-201).

Lewis concludes his point about the lowering of metaphysical energy in this essay we are considering by saying that women are more likely to have interests that are practical and concrete, *i.e.* the kinds of interests explored by the social sciences, while men are more likely to have interests which lead them to the consideration of metaphysics. In any case, Lewis says that this lowering of metaphysical energy in our contemporary culture "cuts us off from the eternal" even as the disdain for traditional wisdom "cuts us off from the past…" (63).

Third, the minds of people in contemporary western culture have been affected by the rise of "Developmentalism or Historicism" (63). He makes it clear that he distinguishes between "the noble discipline called History and the fatal pseudo-philosophy called Historicism" (63). He said that the chief origin of this is Darwinism, but he had no quarrel with this as a theorem in biology. The problem arose with the extension of this evolutionary idea beyond the realm of biology to the extent that it becomes the key principle of reality. As Lewis writes, "To the modern man it seems simply natural that an ordered cosmos should emerge from chaos, that life should come out of the inanimate, reason out of instinct, civilization out of savagery, virtue out of animalism" (63). The extension of this evolutionary idea is the basis for a modern myth which Lewis writes about in his essay, "The Funeral of a Great Myth." In the development of a theorem of biology into this modern myth, a theory of change is turned into a theory of improvement and then given cosmic dimensions (*Christian Reflections*, 86). In this myth, "To exist means to be moving from the status of 'almost zero' to the status of 'almost infinity'," into a future promising "far better things—perhaps Deity itself…" (*Christian Reflections*, 86). But this modern myth is "wholly inimical to Christianity, for it denies both creation and the Fall. Where, for Christianity, the Best creates the good and the good is corrupted by sin, for Developmentalism the very standard of good is itself in a state of flux" (*Present Concerns*, 64). Thus, in contemporary western culture a modern Creation/Fulfillment Myth challenges the Creation/Fall/Redemption/Consumation Myth of Christianity. Moreover, every myth, according to Lewis, "becomes the father of innumerable truths on the abstract level" ("Myth Became Fact," *God in the Dock*, 66). Thus, when Christians in our western culture have disagreements with others about morality, soteriology, and dogmatic theology, behind these disagreements is a clash of opposing myths which are warring for the minds and hearts of western people.

Fourth, the minds of people in contemporary western culture are also shaped by what Lewis calls Proletarianism, which exists in "various forms ranging from strict Marxism to vague 'democracy'" (64). Lewis acknowledges that in the past the aristocracy has been self-satisfied, but now the proletariat is self-satisfied beyond any past self-satisfaction of the aristocracy. "They are convinced that whatever may be wrong with the world it cannot be themselves….Hence, when the existence of God is discussed, they by no means think of Him as their Judge. On the contrary they are His judges" (64-65). Moreover, they do not think of their duties to God but of God's duties toward them. "And God's duties to them are conceived not in terms of salvation but in purely secular terms—social security, prevention of war, a higher standard of life" (65). The fact that contemporary western people picture God in the dock being judged by them means Christian evangelists can no longer assume that their hearers have any sense of guilt. As J. I. Packer points out, in contemporary western culture desire masquerades as morality (Packer, 160). In his essay, "God in the Dock," Lewis acknowledges that he is far from finding a satisfactory solution to this problem. Perhaps the evangelist might try to awaken the consciences of listeners by talking about conceit, spite, jealousy, kindness, cowardice, meanness, etc. (244). Learning how to translate Christian doctrines into the vernacular should be a necessary exercise for ordinands (243). Finally, Lewis says that his own work has suffered from an "incurable intellectualism." "The simple emotional appeal ('Come to Jesus') is still often successful," though those who lack the gift for making this appeal, including himself, had better not try it (244).

Fifth, this Proletarianism of the contemporary western mind leads to an emphasis on Practicality. Lewis said that in lecturing to popular audiences he found it difficult to make them understand that he believed Christianity's affirmations to be objectively true. They wanted to know if it is comforting, inspiring, or socially useful. Part of the problem is that in the English language in popular speech "believe in" has two meanings. It can mean "to accept as true" or "to approve of" (65). Thus, when a person says "I don't believe in Christianity," the person may not be thinking about truth at all but may be saying "I don't approve of Christianity" in the same way as saying "I don't believe in government by the aristocracy." Usually in the modern mind "I believe" means "I approve of." This results in either an indifference to or a contempt of dogma (65). Thus, if a Christian says, "I believe that the Nicene Creed is a statement of truth," meaning that it is a statement of what is objectively true, or, as Evelyn Underhill says, "an account of that which is," (*The School of Charity*, 5) it may be greeted by the reply that "all religions really mean the same thing" (*Present Concerns*, 65). This syncretism of the modern western mind is a rejection of revelation. It means that we decide how something is to be known. But, as Lewis says in his book, *Miracles*, "An act of knowing must be determined, in a sense, solely by what is known; we must know it to be thus solely because in *is* thus" (22-23). In his essay, "Religion Without Dogma?," Lewis says that if there is a God "then it is so probable as to be almost axiomatic that the initiative lies wholly on His side. If He can be known it will be by self-revelation on His part, not by speculation on ours" (*God in the Dock*, 144). The practical synergism of the modern western mind leads to a god of no dogmas, a god who is a mere shadow. As Lewis writes, "He will not produce that fear of the Lord in which wisdom begins, and, therefore, will not produce that love in which it is consummated" (*God in the Dock*, 142-143).

This leads to Lewis's sixth and final point which is that the contemporary western mind is skeptical about Reason (65). According to Lewis, "Practicality, combined with vague notions of what Freud, or Einstein, said, has produced a general, and quite *unalarmed*, belief that reasoning proves nothing and that all thought is conditioned by irrational processes" (65). For Lewis, reason, conscience, will, faith, and imagination are related in such a way that it is impossible to separate them. Reason allows us to distinguish truth and falsehood, and conscience allows us to distinguish good and evil (right and wrong). Conscience may impress upon us the right or wrong of a particular act or behavior and reason may help us understand why that act or behavior is right or wrong. But, in a fallen world, reason and conscience cannot give the will (heart) the power to follow the right. Initially, reason and conscience may prepare the way for faith in Christ, but they cannot give it. Faith in Christ is an act of the will, an act that is called forth by the myth of Jesus Christ, the myth become fact, working on the imagination. Lewis writes that myth is an "unfocused gleam of divine truth falling on human imagination." The mythology of the Hebrews was "chosen by God to be the vehicle of the earliest sacred truths, the first step in that process which ends in the New Testament where truth has become completely historical….Just as God is none the less God by being Man, so the Myth remains Myth even when it becomes Fact" (*Miracles*,138n). Faith in the truth of the Myth of Jesus Christ directs our reason to focus on God's revelation of Himself as that which we are to reason about, and as we reason about truth we are given grace to follow our conscience, which itself is being formed by the truth given in Christ. Although the Myth of Jesus Christ acts on our imagination, in his essay, "Bluspels and Flalansferes: A Semantic Nightmare," Lewis says that he is not "putting forward the imagination as the organ of truth. We are not talking of truth, but of meaning: meaning which is the antecedent condition of truth and falsehood…. For me, reason is the natural organ of truth; but imagination is the organ of meaning. Imagination, producing new metaphors or revivifying old, is not the cause of truth, but its condition" (*Selected Literary Essays*, 265). Thus, the skepticism about Reason, which is the last characteristic of the modern mind named by Lewis in this essay we are considering, touches also on conscience, will, faith, and imagination.

At the end of his essay, Lewis says that there are some good elements in the modern situation, including "perhaps, more social conscience that there has ever been before…" (66). Moreover, in all of this we must remember that Christianity proclaims the revelation by God of Himself in objective truth, and the human appetite for objective truth may be buried but is not dead (66).

References

James Como (ed.). *C.S. Lewis at the Breakfast Table and Other Reminiscences.* New York: Macmillan, 1979.

Walter Hooper. *C.S. Lewis: Companion and Guide.* San Francisco: Harper Collins, 1996.

C. S. Lewis. *A Grief Observed.* New York: The Seabury Press, 1961.

C. S. Lewis. *Christian Reflections*, ed. Walter Hooper. Grand Rapids: Wm. B. Eerdmans, 1975.

C. S. Lewis. *God in the Dock: Essays on Theology and Ethics*, ed. Walter Hooper. Grand Rapids: Wm. B. Eerdmans, 1974.

C. S. Lewis. *Miracles: A Preliminary Study.* London: Collins, 1960.

C. S. Lewis. *Perelandra.* New York: Macmillan, 1974.

C. S. Lewis. *Present Concerns*, ed. Walter Hooper. New York: Harcourt Brace Javanovich, 1986.

C. S. Lewis. *Selected Literary Essays*, ed. Walter Hooper. Cambridge: Cambridge University Press, 1980.

C. S. Lewis. *Surprised by Joy: The Shape of My Early Life.* New York: Harcourt, Brace, and World, 1955.

C. S. Lewis. *That Hideous Strength: A Modern Fairy Tale for Grown-Ups.* New York: Macmillan, 1975.

J. I. Packer. "On from Orr: Cultural Crisis, Rational Realism, and Incarnational Ontology," *Rediscovering the Great Tradition: Evangelicals, Catholics, and Orthodox in Dialogue*, ed. James S. Cutsinger. Downers grove, IL: InterVarsity Press, 1997.

Evelyn Underhill. *The School of Charity: Meditations on the Christian Creed.* Harrisburg, PA: Morehouse Publishing, 1991.

Inclusive Exclusivism

Larry Lacy[*]

In this paper I will construct the outlines of a Christian theology of the phenomenon of religious pluralism—the fact that there are religions other than Christianity, religions which have millions of sincere, intelligent, admirable adherents. The position I will develop will be a version of what has come to be known as exclusivism, though, as the title indicates, this position will in an important way be inclusivist. I distinguish between *doctrinal* exclusivism and *salvific* exclusivism. By *doctrinal* exclusivism I mean the view that the central doctrines of Christianity are true, and given that they are true, there are central beliefs of other religions (beliefs which are logically incompatible with some of the central doctrines of Christianity) which are false. Here the question is whether holding to doctrinal exclusivism is morally or epistemically arrogant or intolerant. I will not deal with doctrinal exclusivism in this paper; I think Alvin Plantinga has dealt satisfactorily with the issues of doctrinal exclusivism. (See Alvin Plantinga, *Warranted Christian Belief*, 442-47.)

By *salvific* exclusivism I mean the view that some distinctive revelation and/or divine action is a necessary condition of salvation. This is a much more difficult question; the paper will be devoted to this issue.

Christian salvific exclusivism, as I shall understand it, comprises two claims: (i) Christ's atoning death and his resurrection are a necessary condition of salvation, and (ii) no one can fully appropriate this salvation without believing that Christ's atoning death and resurrection make salvation possible. I will not seek to argue that this is the teaching of the Christian faith; rather I shall seek to argue that this does not have the negative implication it is often thought by pluralists to have. Once the objection to doctrinal exclusivism has been answered, the chief problem of Christian salvific exclusivism is that it seems to have the implication that some, by no fault of their own, will fail to attain salvation. (Some, for no fault of their own, never in this life hear the Gospel.) This, however, does not follow from (i) and (ii) above; it follows only by conjoining to these two propositions the following: (iii) In order to attain salvation, a person must *in this life* come to have saving belief. In this section, I will argue that fidelity to scripture does not require that we accept (iii).

Could a God of love at any point pass final condemnation against any of the persons he has created? In order to deal with this question we must be clear about the nature of judgment as depicted in the New Testament. We will begin our investigation with two closely related passages in the Gospel of John. The first is from John, Ch. 3; the second from Ch. 12.

---

[*] Larry Lacy is Emeritus Professor of Philosophy at Rhodes College in Memphis, Tennessee.

16 For God so loved the world that he gave his only Son, that whoever believes in him should not perish but have eternal life. 17 For God sent the Son into the world, not to condemn the world, but that the world might be saved through him. 18 He who believes in him is not condemned; he who does not believe is condemned already, because he has not believed in the name of the only Son of God. 19 And this is the judgment, that the light has come into the world, and men loved darkness rather than light because their deeds were evil. 20 For every one who does evil hates the light, and does not come to the light, lest his deeds be exposed. 21 But he who does what is true comes to the light, that it may be clearly seen that his deeds have been wrought in God (John 3:16-21).

46 I have come as light into the world, that whoever believes in me may not remain in darkness. 47 If any one hears my sayings and does not keep them, I do not judge him; for I did not come to judge the world but to save the world. 48 He who rejects me and does not receive my sayings has a judge; the word that I have spoken will be his judge on the last day (John 12:46-48).

In John 3:17 we are told that "God sent the Son into the world, *not to condemn the world*, but that the world might be saved" (emphasis added). God's desire is to save, not to condemn. In this passage, verse 17 begins with the conjunction "for," thus linking it to verse 16. The reason God sent the Son to save and not to judge is that God loves the world. John 3:16 has justly been called the heart of the gospel. It is worthy of note that the teaching on judgment in John 3:17-21 (and, as we shall see, also in John 12:46-48) is grounded in the heart of the gospel—God's love for a lost world.

We have seen in 3:17 that God's purpose in sending his Son into the world was not to judge but to save. The implication of this is explicitly stated by Jesus in John 12:47. "If any one hears my sayings and does not keep them, I do not judge him; for *I did not come to judge the world* but to save the world" (emphasis added). The reason Jesus gives for not judging those who do not keep his sayings is "for I did not come to judge the world but to save the world" (12:47). This is identical with what was stated earlier in 3:17, "for God sent the Son into the world not to condemn the world, but that the world might be saved through him."

To appreciate the full significance of Jesus' statement that he does not judge those who reject him we must note that in John 5:22 Jesus says, "The Father judges no one, but has given all judgment to the Son" (See also John 5:27). Thus, when Jesus says, "I do not judge him," the implication is that neither the Father nor the Son judges that person.

I can summarize what we have discovered so far about judgment this way: because the Father and the Son love the world, their desire is to save the world and not to judge the world; therefore, neither the Father nor the Son judges even the person who rejects the maximum light available in this world—the presence, words, and deeds of the incarnate Son of God.

I have been using 12:47 and 5:22 to draw out the implication of 3:16-17. Because the Father and the Son love the world, the reason the Son came into the world was not to condemn but to save the world, consequently neither the Father nor the Son condemns those who do not believe in the Son. Yet the coming of Christ does result in condemnation. "He who does not believe is condemned already" (3:18). Thus 3:17 (in light of 12:47 and 5:22) together with 3:18 presents us with a paradox. Neither the Father nor the Son condemns the one who refuses to believe, yet the one who refuses to believe is condemned already. How can this be?

I believe that the function of the next verse, 3:19, is to resolve this paradox by showing what the judgment in 3:18 consists in. *"And this is the judgment*, that the light has come into the world, and men loved darkness rather than the light, because their deeds were evil (3:19).[1] Leon Morris says: "... 'judgment' here is *krisis*, which denotes the process, not *krima*, which means the sentence. John is not saying, 'This is the sentence that God has decreed.' He is saying, 'This is the process. Here is how it works.'" The judgment in 3:18 does not involve personal condemnation by God. It consists simply in (a) the light of revelation shining through the person, words, and deeds of Jesus and (b) the refusal of some to embrace this light. In one sense it is the light itself which judges these people. The light of revelation in Jesus exposes the evil in their hearts, calls for repentance, and compels a response. If, in response, a person refuses to repent, refuses to disengage himself from this evil, he will naturally "prefer darkness to light," and will "not come to the light, lest his deeds should be exposed" (3:20). Indeed

---

[1] John's metaphor of light refers to moral and spiritual illumination. Anything which makes a person aware of good and evil, right and wrong, virtue and vice, functions as light. Such awareness confronts the person with choice. Conscience is one source of light. We are all aware of good to be pursued, right actions to be done, and virtue to be further cultivated. Paul says that "what the law requires is written on [the Gentile's] heart" (Rom. 2:15). Also, according to Paul "the things which have been made" function as light by making the "eternal power and deity" of the creator manifest (Rom. 1:19-20). Another source of light is the law of God revealed through Moses. Also against the backdrop of conscience and/or the law of Moses, the conspicuous virtue or vice of other persons functions as light. When confronted by the virtue of someone far better than we are, we attain a clearer grasp of what virtue is, our own relative lack of virtue is revealed, and we are summoned to strive for such character. The supreme instance of this is confrontation with perfect virtue, God incarnate. The natural tendency of light is to draw the person to truth and goodness. Speaking of the light which would emanate from the full manifestation of his love, his sacrifice on the cross, Jesus says, "and I, when I am lifted up, will draw all men to myself" (John 12:32). In summary, light refers to moral and spiritual illumination which reveals good and evil, and, by condemning evil and drawing the person to goodness, confronts the person with an inescapable choice. The vastness, order, beauty, and bounty of the created order, conscience, God's law revealed through Moses and witnessed to powerfully by the prophets, virtuous people, and especially the incarnate Lord—during the days of his flesh, and supremely in his revelation in the Eschatological ages—all manifest this light.

such persons will hate the light because it threatens to expose their deeds (John 3:20: 15:24). In another sense, these people judge themselves by their response to the light. By their rejection of the light they reveal the fundamental choice of their hearts and thereby condemn themselves. It is with them as it was with the Jews of whom Paul said, "you thrust it [the word of the gospel] from you, and judge yourselves unworthy of eternal life" (Acts 13:46). By preferring darkness to light, these people referred to in John 3:18 condemn themselves, judge themselves unworthy of eternal life[2]

So understood, 3:19 resolves the paradox created by the juxtaposition of 3:18 and 3:17. Neither the Father nor the Son condemns the person. The condemnation consists in the light of revelation exposing evil, calling for repentance, compelling a response and, in the person refusing to repent, refusing to come to the light. This understanding of how judgment takes place also does full justice to John 12:47 (in the light of 3:16-17 and 5:22), "I do not judge him; for I did not come to judge the world but to save the world."

Jesus' declaration in 12:47, "I do not judge him," is expressed in the present tense. It might be thought that although Jesus did not judge human persons in the days of his flesh he will judge them when he returns in glory. But note what Jesus goes on to say in the next verse: "He who rejects me and does not receive my sayings has a judge; the word that I have spoken will be his judge on the last day" (John 12:48).[3] Jesus says that the word which he has spoken will be the judge on the last day for those who resist him. Does this mean that Jesus himself will not judge them on the last day? I think it does. We have seen that Jesus' statement, "I do not judge him" (12:47), is in the present tense. In the first part of 12:48, Jesus says that the one who refuses to receive his sayings "has a judge." This statement is also in the present tense. At the same moment, the moment when Jesus spoke these words, both of the following things were true of those who were rejecting Jesus: (1) Jesus was not judging them, and (2) there was one who was judging them. Thus it is clear that it is this (as yet unidentified) one rather than Jesus which was judging them at that time.

In the second part of 12:48, Jesus does two things. First, he identities the one who was judging them ("the word I have spoken…."). Second, he affirms that this

---

[2] I do not say that this judgment is final. Perhaps they will later come to faith. But until they do, they have judged themselves unworthy of eternal life.

[3] The Greek phrase translated "has a judge," is a participle phrase. A more accurate translation of the Greek would be "has one who judges him." The participle is in the present tense. In Greek a participle in the present tense signifies that the action denoted by the participle takes place in the same time as the time indicated by the main verb in the sentence. The main verb is "has," which is in the present tense. Hence the action denoted by the participle (the action of judging) is represented as taking place at the time of the utterance. The thought expressed then is that the one who rejects Jesus has one who is even then judging him.

arrangement extends even to the last day ("...will judge them on the last day."). It follows that on the last day it is the word that Jesus spoke *rather than* Jesus, himself, which will judge them. Given John 5:22, "The Father judges no one, but has given all judgment to the Son," it follows than on the last day neither the Father nor the Son will personally judge those who reject Jesus and his sayings.[4] Thus we can rule out the view that "the word that I have spoken will be his judge on the last day" means that the word which Jesus spoke will provide the standard against which either the Father or the Son (or the Holy Spirit) will judge these people on the last day.

What then is meant by "the word that I have spoken will be his judge on the last day?" I believe 3:19 provides the answer to our question. In both 3:16-18 and 12:47-48 there is the same paradox—the affirmation that God's purpose in the light's coming into the world is not condemnation but salvation, followed by the affirmation that, nevertheless, those who do not receive the light are, or will be, judged. I have argued that the function of 3:19 is to resolve this paradox by showing how, in one sense, the light judges people by exposing their evil, calling for repentance, and compelling a response, yet in another sense, these people judge themselves by their response to the light.

Because we know what it means to say that the light judges people, we will understand what it means to say that the word Jesus has spoken will judge people, if that word functions as light.[5] That it does is indicated in the passage we are presently studying. In John 12:46, Jesus says, "I have come as a light into the world," and then immediately speaks of his sayings, "If any one hears my sayings...," indicating that his sayings communicate that light. Although the sayings communicate the light, they are not the light. Jesus says, "He who...does not receive my sayings has a judge; the word that I have spoken will be his judge on the last day" (emphasis added). The Greek word translated "sayings" in the first part of this verse is *rhemata*.[6] Jesus does not say that his *rhemata* will be the person's judge on the last day; he says, "the logos [word] I have

---

[4] Jesus says a second time in this same passage (John 5:27) that the Father "has given him authority to execute judgment." This second verse makes it clear that this holds not only in the present but also on the last day. In the very next verse Jesus goes on to say, "Do not marvel at this; for the hour is coming when all who are in the tombs will hear his voice and come forth, those who have done good, to the resurrection of life, and those who have done evil, to the resurrection of judgment."

[5] We have already seen reason to believe that the word is light. John 3:19 teaches that in the days of his incarnation the light of his presence, words, and deeds, was judging people. In John 12:48 we saw that the word which Jesus spoke was at that same time judging the same people. The implication then is that the word which Jesus had spoken was the light that was judging them.

[6] I am, of course, not suggesting that Jesus was speaking Greek when he uttered this saying. I am assuming that John's witness to this word from Jesus is a divinely inspired witness, accurately conveying the substance of what Jesus was saying.

spoken will be his judge on the last day." While *rhemata* is plural, *logos* is singular. The many sayings (*rhemata*) of Jesus express the same word (*logos*). The light which judges people now and which will also judge them on the last day is the *logos* (word) which Jesus expressed through his *rhemata* (sayings).

This word *logos* is the same Greek word which is translated "Word" in John 1:1. "In the beginning was the Word; and the Word was with God, and the Word was God." Jesus himself is the "Word of the Father, the revelation of the Father in human form (1:14). "No one has ever seen God; the only Son, who is in the bosom of the Father, he has made him known" (1:18). This verse is John's commentary on "And the Word [*logos*] became flesh and dwelt among us, full of grace and truth; we have beheld his glory, glory as of the only Son from the Father" (1:14).

What is the connection between the *logos* that Jesus spoke and the *logos* which Jesus is? Perhaps the most significant of Jesus' sayings in the Gospel of John are about himself, who he is in relation to his Father, who he is in relation to his disciples, what his will is, etc. To illustrate: "I am the bread of life" (6:35), "I am the light of the world" 8:12), "The Father is in me and I am in the Father" (10:38), "I am the resurrection and the life" (11:25), "He who sees me sees him who sent me" (12:45), "I am the way, the truth, and the life" (14:6), "I am the true vine" (15:1), "This is my commandment, that you love one another…" (15:12). The *logos* expressed in these *rhemata* is Jesus himself, the Word which was with God, which is God, and which has become flesh.

I conclude, therefore, that the word that Jesus has spoken refers primarily to himself who is the Word. The last day is the day "when Jesus Christ is revealed" (1 Peter 1:13). On that day there will be a full revelation of "the glory of God in the face of Christ" (2 Cor. 4:6). The full revelation of this Word will constitute the greatest possible light. If, when confronted with the light of the Word on the last day, a person, because his deeds are evil, hates the light, then that person will thereby make a *definitive decision against God*, and will be thereafter forever incapable of free repentance.

The following is a summary of the first and most crucial part of my interpretation of eternal judgment, based on John 3:16-21, 5:22, and 12:46-48. The Father and the Son love the world. Therefore, their will is not to judge the world but to save the world. Their loving will to save rather than to judge extends to the last day. Therefore, on the last day neither the Father nor the Son will condemn anyone. Nevertheless, some will stand condemned on the last day. The condemnation consists in the fact that on the last day the glory of God will be fully revealed in Jesus Christ and they definitively refuse this full light.[7]

But doesn't Jesus judge on the Last Day? Having reached the conclusion that both the Father and the Son refuse to judge anyone, either now or on the last day, we must face an obvious objection—that there are numerous passages where it is clearly said that the Son will judge persons on the last day. For example, we read in Matt 25:31-41:

> When the Son of man comes in his glory, and all the angels with him, then he will sit on his glorious throne. Before him will be gathered all the nations, and he will separate them one from another as a shepherd separates the sheep from the goats, and he will place the sheep as his right hand, but the goats at his left….. Then he will say to those at his left, "Depart from me, you cursed, into the eternal fire…." And they will go away into eternal fire… and they will go away into eternal punishment….

This and many other passages clearly portray the Son pronouncing eternal judgment on the last day. Yet the passages in John we have studied also clearly affirm that the Son (and the Father) will not judge anyone on the last day. If (as I am assuming in this study) scripture is self-consistent, then we must distinguish different senses of judging. In one sense Jesus will not judge on the last day; in another sense he will. Let us return to our passages in John and see if we can specify the sense in which neither the Father nor the Son will judge any one on the last day.

---

[7] I have relied heavily on John 3:16-21, 5:22, and 12:46-48 in establishing an interpretation of eternal judgment. I believe that the teaching on judgment I have drawn from John 3:16-21, 5:22, and 12:46-48 should exert a strong control in the interpretation of other passages on judgment, for three reasons. First, these passages contain the most explicit words in the New Testament concerning the precise question with which we are dealing: the question of whether or not God would eternally condemn a person still capable of being saved. There is the explicit statement, "I do not judge him," and the explicit explanation of why Jesus does not judge him, "For I did not come to judge (or condemn) the world but to save the world." And this foundation of Jesus' refusal to judge is stated not once, but twice (in ch. 3, where the desire to save and not to condemn is attributed to God; in ch. 12, where Jesus affirms it of himself). There is the clear inference (if not explicit statement) that Jesus' refusal to judge, and hence the attitude of heart in which the refusal is grounded, extends even to the last day. Finally there is the explicit word, "the Father judges no one, but has given all judgment to the Son" (5:22), which clearly implies that whatever we discover about Jesus and judgment can and must be extended to the Father also. Second, these passages not only provide us with a doctrine of judgment; they explicitly ground this doctrine of judgment in the very heart of the gospel—"For God so loved the world that he gave his only Son, that whoever believes in him should not perish…" (John 3:16). Third, these passages present us with the teaching of Jesus himself on judgment. (It is clear that John attributes the words in 12:46-48 to Jesus. It is unclear whether 3:16-21 is put forth as the words of Jesus or whether they are the words of John. But the crucial word, "I do not judge him," and the application of this to the last day, are clearly attributed to Jesus.)

I think we can specify this sense by considering *the reason* Jesus gives in John 12:47-48 for his refusal to judge any one on the last day. The reason is that he wills to save the world. Thus, neither the Father nor the Son will, on the last day, judge any one in any sense incompatible with their loving will to save, which extends even to the last day. Therefore, neither the Father nor the Son will ever judge anyone in any way that adversely affects that person's opportunity for salvation. Because both the Father and the Son have a loving will to save each person, even on the last day, it follows that (a) neither will reject anyone who repents and turns to God even on the last day, and (b) neither will refuse to extend the grace for repentance on the last day to any one who is capable (with that grace) of free repentance.

If anyone is eternally rejected by God on the last day, that can only be either because that person prior to that day had freely made himself incapable of free repentance or because on the day of final judgment that person freely and definitively refuses to repent. (It can, I believe, be argued that it is reasonable to believe that any one who persists in freely refusing to repent even in face of the full light, as will be the light that will shine on the last day, will thereby make him/herself incapable of free repentance at any later time.) God's eternally rejecting a person who is no longer capable of free repentance is not incompatible with God's enduring loving will to save all who are capable of salvation.[8]

The implication of this for salvific exclusivism is clear. Given the truth of the view of judgment which I have argued, even if the death and resurrection of Jesus and an explicit faith response to that saving act is a necessary condition of salvation, no one will fail to attain salvation for no fault of his/her own.

---

[8] We can now specify two senses of judgment and see that for God to pass final judgment in the second sense is perfectly compatible with his refusal to pass final judgment in the first sense. Sense 1: God (both the Father and the Son) will never pass final judgment against any one capable (with God's grace) of free repentance. Sense 2: God will pass final judgment against all who have by free refusal of great light made themselves incapable of free repentance. It is in sense 1 that Jesus, according to John 12:47-48, affirms he will judge no one on the last day. If it is plausible that it is only in sense 2 that Jesus is pictured as passing final judgment in Matt 25:31-46 (and other such passages), then the teaching about eternal judgment to be drawn from these passages is consistent with our interpretation of John 3:16-21, 5:22-27, 12:46-48. I believe that it can be shown that this is plausible (though space does not permit this here). In summary, John 3:16-21; 5:22; and 12:46-48 provide us with strong reason to believe that it is the teaching of the New Testament that God will not eternally reject any person still capable of free repentance.

C. S. Lewis and the Problem of Christian Behavior toward Others

Harry Lee Poe[*]

During the 1930's, a period Robert Graves referred to as *The Long Weekend*, most Britons preferred not to see the danger looming across the Channel in Germany. Winston Churchill droned on and on about it, but no one took Churchill seriously. The combination of his involvement in the Dardanelles disaster in World War I and his championship of the uncrowned King Edward in the pursuit of the woman he loved made Churchill an easy person to dismiss.

Beginning in the mid 1930's with his publication of *The Pilgrim's Regress*, however, C. S. Lewis registered growing concern about the posture of the growing Nazi menace and its implications for Christian behavior toward others. The allegorical narrative of *The Pilgrim's Regress* examined a range of philosophical options a person might take up in the course of life, and one of these was the ideological nihilism that Hitler's fascism embodied. He pictured this approach to life as "Savage," a Germanic barbarian who relishes the heroism of fighters as "an end in itself."[1] Written during the Spanish Civil War, after the horrors of the Russian Revolution, the rise of Mussolini in Italy, and Hitler's successful grab for power in Germany, *The Pilgrim's Regress* compares the similarities of the rival ideologies as sub-species of a common sub-human type that always threatens "to reappear in human children."[2] Lewis includes in this the Marxomanni, Mussolimini, Swastici, and Gangomanni.[3] The danger of this type was evident to Lewis who foresaw trouble of some kind.

In 1936, Lewis published *Out of the Silent Planet,* a science fiction tale of interplanetary travel to Mars that allowed Lewis to speculate on angelic powers and principalities, Platonic philosophy, and the de-humanizing drive of modern technology. The hero, Ransom, becomes involved in the events that will take him to Mars when he intervenes to rescue a boy whom the villain, Weston, characterizes as "incapable of serving humanity and only too likely to propagate idiocy. He was the sort of boy who in a

---

[*] Harry Lee Poe serves as Charles Colson Professor of Faith and Culture at Union University in Jackson, Tennessee. He has written several books and numerous articles on how the gospel relates to various areas of culture, including *Christianity in the Academy, The Gospel and Its Meaning*, and *Christian Witness in a Postmodern World*. He has written two books with Jimmy H. Davis on science and religion: *The Designer Universe* and *Science and Faith: An Evangelical Dialogue*. Poe also serves as program director for the triennial C. S. Lewis Summer Institute in Oxford and Cambridge.

[1] C. S. Lewis, *The Pilgrim's Regress* (Grand Rapids: Eerdmans, 1981), 100.

[2] Ibid.

[3] Ibid.

civilized community would be automatically handed over to a state laboratory for experimental purposes."[4] Just such a civilized community was emerging in Hitler's Reich with just this sort of rationalization. The second great rationalization for inhuman treatment of others comes when Weston and his accomplice, Devine, decide to kidnap Ransom in order to hand him over to aliens whom they believe want a human as a sacrifice to their gods. Though they say it's a pity, but they are willing to do it "in a great cause."[5]

While Weston and Devine pursue their noble cause of the extension of human power over the universe, Ransom flees into an unknown landscape where he anticipates the horrors of the aliens. In this setting, Lewis uses the science fiction genre to explore how people think about other people different from themselves. Ransom, the "pious man," imagines unspeakable honors associated with the aliens.[6] He imagines them in terms of everything vile and loathsome he has experienced on earth:

> No insect-like, vermiculate or crustacean Abominable, no twitching feelers, rasping wings, slimy coils, curling tentacles, no monstrous union of superhuman intelligence and insatiable cruelty seemed to him anything but likely on an alien world . . . . He saw in imagination various incompatible monstrosities – bulbous eyes, grinning jaws, horns, stings, mandibles. Loathing of insects, loathing of snakes, loathing of things that squashed and squelched, all played their horrible symphonies over his nerves.[7]

In order to treat a person in an inhuman way, it helps to think of them as a loathsome, sub-human creature deserving of extermination. (Darwin's theory encouraged this line of thought among modern thinking people who could justify colonialism on the grounds of racial superiority. It was obvious that the white-man, specifically the western European, was winning the battle of natural selection.) Even upon closer contact and the realization that his imagination had been wrong, Ransom exchanges the modern H.G. Wells fantasy for "an earlier, almost infantile, complex of fears" in which he now thought of them, since not insects, as "giants—ogres—ghosts—skeletons."[8]

As the story develops, it becomes apparent that the humans, rather than the Martians, are the monsters. Lewis paints a world in which not one, but three distinct intelligent species enjoy the same planet without competition, exploitation, or conflict. In this

---

[4] C. S. Lewis, *Out of the Silent Planet* (New York: Macmillan, 1977), 19.

[5] Ibid.

[6] Ibid., 35.

[7] Ibid., 35.

[8] Ibid., 47.

context, Ransom struggles to understand "which was the real monster."[9] Even Ransom, who says his prayers at night, cannot conceive a world in which the real monsters do not rule.

Though virtuous, Ransom holds prejudices that stand shoulder to shoulder with the villain Weston. When brought before the Oyarsa, the archangel who rules over Malacandra (Mars), Weston defends his actions as one who bears on his "shoulders the destiny of the human race":

> Your tribal life with its stone-age weapons and bee-hive huts, its primitive coracles and elementary social structure, has nothing to compare with our civilization – with our science, medicine and law, our armies, our architecture, our commerce, and our transport system which is rapidly annihilating space and time. Our right to supersede you is the right of the higher over the lower.[10]

The "right of the higher over the lower" represents an implication of *philosophical* Darwinism as opposed to evolutionary biology. Philosophical Darwinism represents ideology rather than science.

Weston is most eloquent, inspiring, and convincing as he argues for the right of Life, an allegorical personification of natural selection, to eradicate any form of life that stands in the way of the ascent of man:

> 'It is in her right,' said Weston, 'the right, or, if you will, the might of Life herself, that I am prepared without flinching to plant the flag of man on the soil of Malacandra: to march on, step by step, superseding, where necessary, the lower forms of life that we find, claiming planet after planet, system after system, till our posterity-whatever strange form and yet unguessed mentality they have assumed— dwell in the universe wherever the universe is habitable.'[11]

If the ends justify the means, then the more glorious the cause, the more horrendous the methods become to achieve it.

The Oyarsa observes that humans have learned to break all of the laws that all sentient beings know except "love of kindred," one of the lesser laws.[12] Love of kindred

---

[9] Ibid., 69.

[10] Ibid., 135.

[11] Ibid., 137.

[12] Ibid., 138. Lewis would later expand on this theme in *Mere Christianity* and term it the *Tao* in *The Abolition of Man* (New York: Macmillan, 1955), 28-29.

can soon become the basis for violating all of the higher laws. Lewis would return to this theme in his first *Broadcast Talks* when he remarked, "There are also occasions on which a mother's love for her own children or a man's love for his own country have to be suppressed or they will lead to unfairness towards other people's children or countries."[13] Lewis considered this partisanship to lie at the heart of the fall of Adam who accepted the fruit without argument. In his *A Preface to Paradise Lost* which began as a series of lectures in 1939, Lewis observed of Adam:

> He is at that moment when a man's only answer to all that would restrain him is: 'I don't care'; that moment when we resolve to treat some lower or partial value as an absolute – loyalty to a party or a family, faith to a lover, the customs of good fellowship, the honor of our profession, or the claims of science. . . . If conjugal love were the highest value in Adam's world, then of course his resolve would have been the correct one. But if there are things that have an even higher claim on a man, if the universe is imagined to be such that, when the pinch comes, a man ought to reject wife and mother and his own life also, then the case is altered, and then Adam can do no good to Eve (as, in fact, he does no good) by becoming her accomplice.[14]

By the time Lewis spoke these words, the war had begun.

The war was the ever present background for the radio broadcasts in the 1940's that would be published in separate slim volumes before Lewis combined them into a single volume called *Mere Christianity* in 1952. In considering the question of moral law and whether or not people can make value judgments about right and wrong, Lewis observed,

> If no set of moral ideas were truer or better than any other, there would be no sense in preferring civilized morality to savage morality, or Christian morality to Nazi morality. . . . If your moral ideas can be truer, and those of the Nazis less true, there must be something—some Real Morality—for them to be true about.[15]

When he was asked to write *The Problem of Pain* in 1940, the war was the reason the publisher wanted such a book. Lewis wrote,

> Certainly at all periods the pain and waste of human life was equally obvious. Our own religion begins among the Jews, a people squeezed between great warlike

---

[13] C. S. Lewis, *Mere Christianity* (San Francisco: HarperSanFrancisco, 2001), 11.

[14] C. S. Lewis, *A Preface to Paradise Lost* (New York: Oxford University Press, 1961), 127. It is interesting to note that both his scholarly treatment of Milton's *Paradise Lost* and his popular treatment of basic Christianity were spoken to audiences before they were published for readers.

[15] *Mere Christianity*, 13.

empires, continually defeated and led captive, familiar as Poland or Armenia with the tragic story of the conquered.[16]

In one sentence, Lewis succeeds in pulling together the long history of the partition and domination of Poland with the history of the Jews and the Armenians, a group held captive by the Ottoman Turks for centuries and then the victims of the first great genocide of the twentieth century. In calming the fears of his advisors over the ultimate solution for the problem of the Jews, Hitler would point out that everyone had forgotten about the Armenians. Lewis had not forgotten.

The references to the war in Lewis's works written during the war are too many to mention in a brief treatment of this sort, but they are frequent. Little reminders, such as the time of day at the beginning of *Perelandra*, "past black-out time," appear throughout this war time work.[17] The tale of *The Screwtape Letters* ends with a man killed in an air-raid. Screwtape ranted, "One moment it seemed to be all our world; the scream of bombs, the fall of houses, the stink and taste of high explosives on the lips and in the lungs, the feet burning with weariness, the heart cold with horrors, the brain reeling, the legs aching; next moment all this was gone, gone like a bad dream, never again to be of any account."[18] When life ends, all the horrors of life disappear. What does a Christian do when the horror is over?

Britain and her allies. He has also succeeded in tapping all of the emotion involved in hating the enemy of the group. At this point, Lewis introduces the unspeakable, the unthinkable: forgiveness. Lewis regards forgiveness as an absolute obligation for a Christian, and he is painfully aware of how unattractive it is to anyone who has been wronged in sufficient manner that forgiveness is an option. In introducing the obligation of forgiveness, Lewis remarked cordially,

I said in a previous chapter that chastity was the most unpopular of the Christian virtues. But I am not sure I was right. I believe there is one even more unpopular. It is laid down in the Christian rule, 'Thou shalt love thy neighbor as thyself.' Because in Christian morals 'thy neighbor' includes 'thy enemy,' and so we come up against this terrible duty of forgiving our enemies.

Every one says forgiveness is a lovely idea, until they have something to forgive, as we had during the war. And then, to mention the subject at all is to be greeted with howls of anger. It is not that people think this too high and difficult a virtue: it is that they think it hateful and contemptible. 'That sort of talk makes them sick,' they say.

---

[16] C. S. Lewis, *The Problem of Pain* (New York: Macmillan, 1971), 16.

[17] C. S. Lewis, *Perelandra* (New York: Macmillan, 1977), 14.

[18] C. S. Lewis, *The Screwtape Letters* (San Francisco: HarperSanFrancisco, 2001), 172.

And half of you already want to ask me, 'I wonder how you'd feel about forgiving the Gestapo if you were a Pole or Jew?'[19]

Lewis replied to the rhetorical question that it would be best to "start with something easier than the Gestapo."[20] Loving an enemy as oneself begins with the difficult task of loving oneself. We do not love an enemy because they are not nice, but we do not love ourselves because we are nice. We think ourselves nice because we love ourselves. Loving one's enemy does not mean "thinking them nice."[21] Lewis stressed that "Christianity does not want us to reduce by one atom the hatred we feel for cruelty and treachery."[22] He even fell back on the old proverb, "hate the sin but not the sinner."[23]

While Lewis believed that Christians have an obligation to love and forgive their enemies, he also believed they have the right and sometimes responsibility to punish and kill their enemies. Lewis was not a pacifist, as he elaborated in his essay "Why I am Not a Pacifist."[24] He did not believe that all killing constituted murder anymore than all sexual intercourse constituted adultery.[25] In *Perelandra*, Lewis described in vivid detail a hand to hand struggle that results in the killing of a man who had given himself over to demon possession.[26] With the simple resolution that "This can't go on," Ransom determined to kill the thing that Weston had become.[27] Because Christians believe in life after death, then killing and death are not the worst things, though they are dreadful. He reasoned,

> . . . what really matters is those little marks or twists on the central, inside part of the soul which are going to turn it, in the long run, into a heavenly or hellish creature. We may kill if necessary, but we must not hate and enjoy hating. We may punish if

---

[19] *Mere Christianity*, 115.

[20] Ibid., 116.

[21] Ibid., 117.

[22] Ibid.

[23] Ibid.

[24] See C. S. Lewis, "Why I Am Not a Pacifist," *The Weight of Glory*, ed. Walter Hooper (New York: Touchstone, 1996), 53-71.

[25] *Mere Christianity*, 119.

[26] *Perelandra*, 172.

[27] Ibid., 145.

necessary, but we must not enjoy it. In other words, something inside us, the feeling of resentment, the feeling that wants to get one's own back, must be simply killed.[28]

In time of war or peace, the Christian's greatest enemy that must be killed before it kills is the impulse to hate, resent, or seek revenge. Instead of these feelings, the Christian has an obligation to cultivate an attitude of good will for all selves.[29] With this idea Lewis returns to a major theme of *Out of the Silent Planet*.

Lewis argued that the impulse to murder, hatred, resentment, and revenge come from pride. Regarding pride as the greatest sin, Lewis observed that "it was through Pride that the devil became the devil."[30] Pride involves a form of competitiveness that takes no pleasure from anything except in "having more of it than the next man."[31] The pleasure comes in being "above the rest."[32] Lewis believed that pride "makes a political leader of a whole nation go on and on, demanding more and more."[33] The allusion to the posturing of Hitler and the Nazi war machine would not have been lost on Lewis's radio audience.

Lewis believed that the cultivation of charity comes through action. For a man of thought, it is interesting to note that Lewis said, "Do not waste time *bothering* whether you 'love' your neighbor; act as if you did," instead of "Do not waste time *thinking* whether you 'love' your neighbor."[34] Lewis believed that behavior changes attitudes and feelings:

> But whenever we do good to another self, just because it is a self, made (like us) by God, and desiring its own happiness as we desire ours, we shall have learned to love it a little more or, at least, to dislike it less.[35]

Treating people with charity will inevitably result in having charitable feelings toward them, but Lewis argued that the inverse was also true. Reflecting on the war, Lewis

---

[28] *Mere Christianity*, 119-120.

[29] Ibid., 120.

[30] Ibid., 122.

[31] Ibid.

[32] Ibid.

[33] Ibid., 123.

[34] Ibid., 131.

[35] Ibid.

speculated that "the Germans, perhaps, at first ill-treated the Jews because they hated them: afterwards they hated them much more because they had ill-treated them. The more cruel you are, the more you will hate; and the more you hate, the more cruel you will become – and so on in a vicious circle forever."[36]

Though Lewis had a profound sense of individual differences between people as well as the value of these differences, he also had a strong conviction that "the whole human race is, in a sense, one thing – one huge organism, like a tree. . ."[37] For this reason he rejected the idea of dismissing people by labeling them "as mere members of a group or items in a list. . . ."[38]

Conclusion

The war provided Lewis with a context for exploring the curse of the fall and its continuing impact on individual lives. In a sense, Lewis had an easier task with such an immense example of evil that no one could ignore. On the other hand, his real concern was to help people see that the evil of Hitler was not nearly the threat that the evil within their own hearts represented.

---

[36] Ibid., 131-132.

[37] Ibid., 185.

[38] Ibid.

Religious Toleration and Dangerous Fanaticism: The Natural Limits to Religious Liberty in a Liberal Democratic Society

Pamela Werrbach Proietti[*]

As we look out at our world in the third millennium of Christian history, our present circumstances bear uncanny resemblances to the situation that John Locke and his British predecessors had experienced in early modern seventeenth century England. We Americans are presently acutely aware of threats to public security and public peace from religiously inspired forms of violent intolerance and fanaticism. Prior to 9/11, Americans had enjoyed a domestic tranquility virtually unbroken since the time of our own civil war, because the wars we did fight in the twentieth century were always on foreign soils. (The violent role played by the Ku Klux Klan during the 1960s struggle over civil rights, and for almost a century before, stands as an exception to this general domestic tranquility.)

John Locke's political philosophy was composed and published in the shadows of violent civil wars in recent English history; these wars were inspired by the fanatical intolerance between Protestant and Roman Catholic Christians. Locke was convinced that the fanaticism and intolerance of at least some part of our religious leadership would continue to plague both religious and political communities for all times. Although Locke was not aware of the danger that radical Islam would pose to human liberty three centuries after his own death (Locke died in 1704), some of his ideas prove fruitful in understanding those forces in our contemporary world that are promoting intolerance and persecution of people on the basis of religious beliefs. (See pages 5-9, in John Locke, *A Letter Concerning Toleration*, originally pub. in 1689.)

This essay is about the possible forms that dangerous religiously-inspired fanaticism can take; the essay is also about the possible methods available to those decent human communities seeking to control these extremely dangerous and antisocial passions. We will focus on the ideas of John Locke, because Locke was one of the earliest political philosophers (along with Spinoza, his Dutch predecessor) to advocate a liberal democratic method for controlling those fanatical religious leaders who, if left to their own devices, can cause so much violent conflict and dissension within the political community. Locke drafted and published four major essays on the subject of religious toleration; his ideas about toleration would eventually provide the foundation for the

---

[*] Pamela Werrbach Proietti has studied at Dominican University, River Forest, Illinois, and Boston College, where she is ABD in political philosophy. She has taught at the University of Dallas and Saint John's College, Santa Fe, as well as the University of Memphis. Her earlier research took a reasoned and unusual because moderate approach to the controversy over the status of women in the traditional classics of philosophy. Much of her work has focused on John Locke and the British Enlightenment. More recently, she has begun studying the relation of the Enlightenment philosophers to the Scholastic tradition that preceded them.

American solution to this problem. Many of the central ideas in *The Federalist Papers* are grounded in Locke's political teaching; the brilliant solution of American Founder James Madison to the problem of religious-inspired intolerance comes directly from the arguments developed in Locke's four letters on religious toleration. Locke's solution to this enduring political problem has worked well for our nation for over two centuries.

Locke and our American Founders (Madison, Hamilton, Jefferson, et al) advocated a political society where individual liberty, along with the more traditional goals of public order and public justice, would be protected. (See both John Locke's *Two Treatises of Government* and *The Federalist Papers*, by Hamilton, Madison, and Jay.) The profound attachment within Western liberal democratic societies to the natural rights of the human person, and especially the natural right to individual political and religious liberties, is for the most part (if not entirely) harmonious with the traditional Judeo-Christian teaching about the dignity of the human person. This teaching can be seen in the divine promise given to Abraham, in the intimate conversations between God and Abraham, between Job and his God, between God and Moses, and between Christ and so many individual human souls. The Bible, both the Old and New Testaments, is filled with stories of personal encounters and conversations between God and individual human beings; these humans often argue with God; Job and Abraham both accuse God of either directly committing or tolerating injustice. Clearly a part of our human dignity is revealed in the use of our human reason to examine the world of Creation; this reason can even be rightly used to challenge God, for which noble questioning the God of the Old Testament finally praises Job. (See the conclusion of the Old Testament book of Job, where God finally speaks directly to Job, ultimately praising him for his commitment to truth.)

We should not be surprised that respect for the individual religious conscience, and also a respect for the natural liberty and dignity of the human person, first developed and then matured in the Jewish and Christian world. Both John Milton and John Locke, who lived in one of the most enduring bastions of political liberty, developed persuasive arguments against government censorship of the exchange of ideas. Locke vigorously advocated the expansion of the individual's sphere of religious liberty, while also seeking to allow the government to exercise strict control over the harmful social influences of religiously inspired fanaticism. Sadly, the war waged by Locke and so many other philosophers, i.e., a war in defense of individual human liberty and human dignity against the forces of tyranny and oppression, has not yet been decisively won. For those of us who live in the West today, some urgent questions have arisen: What form will this war on behalf of human dignity take in the new millennium? Are we facing a long-term culture war between the Judeo-Christian West and the radical elements within the Muslim world of the Middle East and Asia? Exactly how widespread and how dangerous are the present-day forms of fanatical and intolerant Islamism? Judging from the carefully crafted ambiguity of the public statements made by the North American Islamic leaders after September 11th, we must suspect that radical and intolerant Islamism is far more widespread and more powerful than we had previously known. After describing John Locke's plan for defeating the forces of religiously inspired fanaticism and intolerance in his own time, we will speculate about what suggestions Locke might make for our Western leaders today, as they grapple with the very clear and present danger of radical Islam inspired fanaticism.

Locke understood that religious beliefs are often embraced and maintained entirely by force of the passions. Reasoning usually fails to moderate religious zealotry. Locke mentions, without believing this path to be possible in practice, that religious toleration could easily become widespread if Christian clergy would preach from the pulpit the centrality of charity and toleration of others in the truly Christian life. (See John Locke, *A Letter concerning Toleration*, page 21.) Locke drops this idea fairly quickly, believing it to be an impossible dream; yet this dream has become a rather widespread reality in the American republic exactly three centuries after Locke's death (John Locke, *A Letter concerning Toleration*, pages 52-54). More churches preach toleration of one's neighbor in America today than many would have believed possible even a century ago. The churches still preaching fanatical and violent forms of intolerance today comprise a tiny minority of Christian churches in the United States. This remarkable situation is the result of the real solution to religious intolerance that Locke had devised and our Founders had implemented over two centuries ago; the real solution to violent intolerance lies in a separation of the religious and the civil-political spheres by means of limited and just political institutions. (We Americans can debate about a possible "civil union" between homosexual partners in the civil laws of our country, because we have previously separated the civil and religious aspects of marriage, following John Locke's proposed model for such a separation.)

There are two essential spheres of human concern, roughly corresponding to the two parts of the human being, i.e., the body and the soul; these two spheres of activity can be partially separated from one another. The interests of these two spheres of human life are rather different, with the body requiring preservation and bodily comfort and the soul searching to fulfill very different and spiritual needs. Two separate and different types of associations are needed to serve these two separate human spheres of concern, i.e., the civil society and the church association. Neither should improperly interfere with the other's proper sphere of action; each has a significant role to play in our human lives (John Locke, *A Letter concerning Toleration*, pages 9-28).

Locke regards the religious authorities as constantly ambitious for using the civil power to further the interests of their particular church against the interests of opposing churches; likewise, the civil magistrates might be tempted by their own political ambition to interfere improperly in the private religious affairs of citizens. The best means of preventing this abuse of power is to give those who govern both the power to control those religious leaders who threaten public peace and the power to promote religious diversity (with the goal of weakening all the existing churches, and thereby never giving any church the possibility of becoming a "majority church"). Church leaders must not be allowed to preach opinions contrary to human society and/or to the moral rules necessary to preserving society. Church leaders who refuse to teach the duty of tolerating all men in matters of religion can be suppressed by the magistrate, because these churches threaten both the rights of fellow citizens and stability of the government and laws (John

Locke, *A Letter concerning Toleration*, pages 45-48). Any church that professes highest allegiance to a foreign government, or to any foreign power, also threatens the security of the nation. (Locke was opposed to the Roman Catholic Church on this ground; Catholics owed their ultimate allegiance to the Pope in Italy, rather than to their government authorities and civil laws at home. See Locke, *A Letter concerning Toleration*, pages 46-47.) From these examples, one can see that Locke regards all religious leaders as potentially dangerous to public peace; he is even willing to be intolerant of any church that chooses to openly preach intolerance of other believers. Is Locke reminding us of an important political principle that we too often ignore in our contemporary "politically correct" stance of tolerating all ideas—even the truly dangerous ideas of those who seek to destroy our basic political and religious freedoms? It appears that John Locke, were he alive today, would not be a card-carrying member of the ACLU!

Locke points out that our government authorities are often responsible for deciding when certain religious beliefs or certain religious rituals threaten the public safety or welfare. He gives the example of a man who wishes to slaughter a calf in a religious ceremony; he should be allowed to do for religious purposes whatever is generally considered legal in secular life. He should also be allowed to kneel, to drink wine and to eat bread in his religious ceremonies. Another example used by Locke is a theoretical religious ritual of infant sacrifice; this ritual is by nature illegal for both the secular and religious spheres. The secular authorities need not and ought not to allow religious groups to break fundamental and necessary civil laws; persons are not allowed to trample on the rights of other persons simply because their religious beliefs dictate this irrational behavior (Locke, *A Letter concerning Toleration*, pages 30-34). This Lockean argument obviously applies to the Islamic religious laws about relations between men and women. Any religious laws (such as the laws claimed to be taught in the holiest book of Islam) which would deny to women their basic natural and legal rights would not be tolerated by any legitimate and just system of government and civil laws any more than a religious ritual of infanticide could be tolerated in a decent and decent society.

The most insoluble type of conflict between civil and religious authorities occurs whenever a law necessary to society is challenged by those who object because the particular law violates their religious convictions. Locke's solution appears to be very precise and workable at first glance; simply respect any action done in good conscience and then also expect the violator of a legitimate and necessary civil law to accept the punishment (Locke, *A Letter concerning Toleration,* pages 53-54). There is even the possibility that the conscientious objector is pursuing a socially useful path—as might be the case with most legal challenges to abortion laws in the United States. (Such public challenges to presently existing American laws remind their audience of the important natural law principle of respect for human life.) There is also a possibility that a religious fanatic might with a clear conscience attack the most natural and fundamental moral principles of all decent communities, for example, by attacking civilian populations using tactics of terror. The goal of such terrorist attacks is to break the will of the people under attack and to undermine the civil authorities and their ability to effectively govern. Although this goal seems never to be achieved in practice, at least never in the long run, religious fanatics operating both in the Middle East and within US borders seem determined to try these failed tactics once again.

What would Locke have to say about our present forms of violent religious fanaticism, about its causes and the possible solutions? What would he propose as a workable approach for dealing with the lawless and violent tactics of radical-Islam inspired terrorism?

Locke was examining various Christian-inspired versions of religious intolerance and violence; he does not directly address the problem of dealing with foreign enemies who are inspired by religious fanaticism originating in a foreign and primarily non-Biblical religion, the religion of Islam. However, he does describe one powerful tool for defeating the religious zealot that is applicable in our present situation: divide and conquer. Our Founders believed that Locke had found the best solution for controlling that natural human tendency toward religious conflict; they promoted both individual religious freedom of conscience and a broad diversity of competing religious sects. By encouraging many denominations of the Christian churches to plant their seeds in American soil, they could avoid the danger posed whenever a majority of citizens are gathered together in one large church. By not allowing government, either a national or a state government, to promote an Established Church, like the Church of England, they were protecting all citizens from potential abuses of power by a too-powerful clergy.

How can this domestic solution to religious strife and fanatical intolerance be applied to the contemporary dangers being posed by America's radical Islamic enemies? Perhaps President Bush has already proposed one important solution by trying to recognize and to support the more democratic and more tolerant elements within the faith of Islam; by allying ourselves with these competing expressions of Islam we are weakening the public relations possibilities for the radicals. Can such an alliance of American political and economic power, and even, in some cases, American military power, with moderate Islam be successful in defeating the forces of radical and violent Islamism? If we tried this approach in contemporary Iran, we might make astonishing progress in the battle for hearts and minds.

Do we also need to consider using some tougher measures against certain radical anti-American mosques, many of them located in New York City, Chicago, and other major American cities, which have become infamous since the events of September 11th? The previous assumption of our civil authorities seems to have been that we can safely allow these radical Moslems, who are preaching hatred and intolerance from the pulpit, to operate freely in our social and political systems. In late seventeenth century England, Locke had argued against such an absolute tolerance for both those preachers of religious intolerance and also those who had declared an intention of overthrowing our government, but we Americans have often concluded that protecting the freedom of violent fanatics to spread their messages of hatred and intolerance provides the best means of protecting our own individual freedoms; our federal courts eventually protected the free speech and association rights for the declared enemies of our free and open society in the 1950s and 1960s. Federal judges made these courageous decisions while dealing with radical American Communist Party agitators and radical racist groups such as the Ku Klux Klan. Attorney General Ashcroft has challenged some of these past assumptions about the proper balance between protecting our national security and protecting our natural rights and citizen liberties. Whatever we eventually decide to do about this fundamental public policy issue, this serious public debate will be a very good thing. We are once again debating the questions raised by Locke in the seventeenth century—questions concerning exactly how much tolerance a free society can safely allow to those who are truly the enemies of freedom. Contemporary political necessities are forcing our legislators and policy-makers to reexamine these fundamental political and moral questions that we had erroneously assumed had already been answered for all time and for all future generations of Americans.

A final message from Locke might be to reassess our foreign policy with the Arab-Islamic and the larger Islamic world before it is too late. We have often, using an inaccurate and short-sighted Cold War and neo-Machiavellian mentality, divided the world into spheres of temporary "allies" and "enemies." Many times the category of "ally" or "enemy" was determined by either the short-sighted and foolish goals of self-serving State Department bureaucrats or the truly mindless greed of narrowly selfish corporate interests. The American government, both Democratic and Republican administrations, had decided for many decades of the previous century that an extremely corrupt and autocratic Middle Eastern satrapy known as the House of Saud was a reliable regional ally for the United States. Powerful elements within the government of the United States did not even begin to reexamine that imprudent approach to foreign policy until September 11th, 2001. Clearly, we need to re-think our former definition of "political allies." Locke would tell us that Turkey is a reliable ally in that region; Turkey has a government that has chosen to embrace what Locke believed to be both "rational" and "natural" principles of republican government, including a separation of church and state, government by on-going consent to laws and popular electoral participation, and an increasing social commitment to protecting individual political and civil rights. Both Israel and Turkey are more reliable allies to the United States than are those prevalent tyrannical regimes, either secular or theocratic in their foundations, which respect neither political nor religious freedoms.

The war on terrorism may finally be decisively won when all forms of tyrannical government, including those tyrannies with theocratic foundations, have ceased to exist. This victory will not be possible without making some difficult reassessments of both our nation's foreign and domestic policies. The ideas of Locke would be helpful in our contemporary debates about these fundamental and recurring political problems.

Note: All of the above citations refer to volume six of *The Works of John Locke*, 1823 edition, reprinted by Scientia Verlag Aalen, Darmstadt, Germany, 1963.